THE GRIMOIRE

FASA CORPORATION 1990

TABLE OF CONTENTS

TABLE OF CONTENTS

TABLE OF CONTENTS

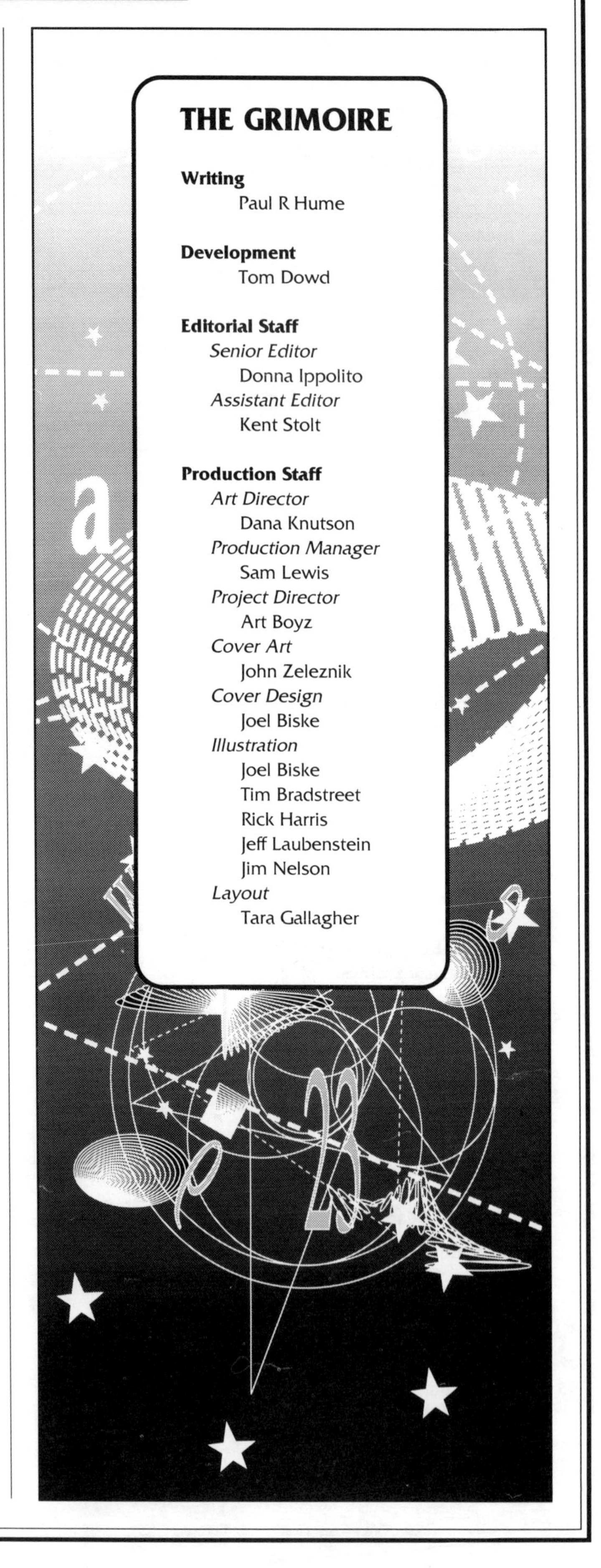

THE GRIMOIRE

Writing
Paul R Hume

Development
Tom Dowd

Editorial Staff
Senior Editor
Donna Ippolito
Assistant Editor
Kent Stolt

Production Staff
Art Director
Dana Knutson
Production Manager
Sam Lewis
Project Director
Art Boyz
Cover Art
John Zeleznik
Cover Design
Joel Biske
Illustration
Joel Biske
Tim Bradstreet
Rick Harris
Jeff Laubenstein
Jim Nelson
Layout
Tara Gallagher

CREDITS

ACKNOWLEDGEMENTS

My deeply heartfelt thanks:

To all the deckers running on the Matrix at Compuserve and GEnie, with special thanks to Janet, Nightie, Luc, IRQ7, Nomad, Jordan, Scorpia, Bryan, and the inimitable Mr. Stackpole. A tougher bunch of nitpickers would be hard to find.

To my players: Slim (Chris Lowe), Rose (Bob Willis), The Steel Mage (Thomas Rae), Briar Pain (Rex Muller), Snake (Carl Burke), Alan Ward (Mark Powers), and Fat Freddy (Rich Puchalsky), who have put up with me as the story of the Sixth World and its magic unfolded—sometimes in nasty directions.

To Bob Charrette, who started this (mumble) years ago when he asked if I'd ever played D&D. To Tom Dowd, for making me feel old on occasion.

To AC, who showed me where the magick lives.

—PRH

Published by
FASA Corporation
P.O. Box 6930
Chicago, IL 60680

"Magic will set the tone of history from now on; of that there is no doubt."
—NEWSLINE, Program 398 February 12, 2028

RIMOIRE: 2050 is a sourcebook of advanced and expanded forms of magic. In developing these new rules, contradictions to some rules in the basic **Shadowrun** rule book occurred. For all intents and purposes, the rules in this **Grimoire** supercede any previous rules. The individual gamemaster and his players are, however, always free to choose by which rules they will abide. If an earlier version of a rule or a completely different variation of a rule suits a particular group's style of play, they should adapt the rules system as they see fit.

Those familiar with the original **Shadowrun** magic system will want to pay close attention to certain sections in this book. The **Astral Space** combat system has been reworked to provide a better play balance. (Thanks to everyone who wrote us with their observations and suggestions.) Coupled with the new **Astral Quest** and **Metaplanes** rules, we think players will find astral space now truly is the exciting realm it was meant to be.

New additions and expansions to the magic system include the awaited **Enchanting** and **Spell Design** rules, as well as a new overview of Nature Spirits, Elemental Spirits, and the two new categories of **Watchers** and **Free Spirits**. There are also rules on **Adepts** (specialized, single-skill magicians), and **Initiates** (magicians of greater power and ability than those previously possible). Through Initiation, a magician is able not only to raise his Magic Attribute, but to gain the new abilities of **Metamagic**.

Rounding out **Grimoire: 2050** are revised **Spell Descriptions**, including clarifications of some of the older spells and some new designs.

"We're not people. We're magicians. People aren't willing to pay the price for the path we follow."
—'The Beachwalk Seminars,' Soror Het Heru, Santa Monica, CA, 1989

hat makes a magician?

Ask a mage: "Study. Practice. Will. Years of discipline to hone the inherent talent into power."

Ask a shaman: "When the Spirits speak, he must listen. Hear the power within and dance to its music with his totem. A dance he must practice all your life."

Or ask a Wiccan, or a voudoun *houngan*, or a Shinto miko, or...well, ask ten magicians what *makes* them magicians, and you'll get thirteen different answers.

This book is not about magical training or which techniques are valid and which are superstitious drek. That squawk's been going loud and long for centuries, and the Awakening has only made it harder to tell. Nowadays it's possible for some kid from the Barrens to use native talent and a half-dozen spells from a pirate grimoire to splatter someone with a Thaumaturgy doctorate from Texas A&M&M. So whose training was worth more?

But the late mage and the street-wiz who smoked him have this in common: both have made magic the most important thing in their lives, and they have devoted the major portion of their time and energy to that commitment. That's what makes a real magician. Anything else is just dabbling.

What this has to do with playing **Shadowrun** is that magicians are the only ones with major demands on their *Karma*. Everybody else saves it up, buys some skills, and tries to keep a few points in the karmic credstik to save their butts when a run turns ugly. But magicians are a different story, chummer. They're already burning Karma to learn new spells (**SR**, p.150). Using this book, they're gonna be spending still more to conjure more powerful Spirits, cast heavier spells, and penetrate the deeper secrets of magic through Initiation. Why do magicians get hit that way for big-time Karma? Because a real magician's life force and luck—his Karma, in other words—determine what he does.

MAKING MAGICIANS

For roleplaying, a player must keep several points in mind when developing a magician character.

First, a magician worth his salt will probably not excel in any other field. Unless the character has an incredible run of luck, magicking will eat his or her Karma and nuyen like candy. If a magician starts the slide down the magic slope toward burnout, he will end up devoting his life to keeping a step ahead of the loss through Initiation (a new option for magicians), or with a headful of magical knowledge that he cannot really use.

Second, magicians are the smallest minority of the population. One percent of the people in the world can use magic at all. Perhaps 90 percent of those are minor magicians, or never get the proper training, or go crazy trying to deal with what they are. There are maybe three to four million fully capable, trained, competent magicians in the Sixth World, though some studies suggest that the percentage is rising with each new generation. Though rarity makes the magician valuable, it also makes him feared. He or she is different with a capital D. A corporation, for example, will put up with drek from a wage mage that would get a mundane suit fired—or maybe even disappeared. Magicians are hard to find, and the corp takes what it can get. On the downside, the corporation watches its magicians like a hawk, playing them off against one another, because the company just can't trust mavericks.

Lots of folks will live their whole lives without ever seeing a magician close up, much less seeing one make magic. They get their ideas about magic from the trid shows and simsense chips, where magicians are either sex-idol adventure stars, comic relief, or sinister villains, all tossing off killer spells without raising a sweat. Ignorance makes people think magicians are super-powerful types who can fry an enemy in the wink of an eye.

Third, the magician lives in a world that mundanes simply cannot understand. He senses things that they do not. He lives by rules that would get someone else slapped into a padded cell, tranked to the eyeballs. Lonely place, the magician's world. It's no wonder that magicians tend to congregate in their own bars, their own groups, for business and for pleasure. When they can. If they can.

"Some people want to study it, some want to outlaw it, some drekheads even pretend it never existed."
—Monkeytribe: Survival Manual for Erect Bipeds, Mullins Chadwick, Putnam-Izumo, New York, 2041

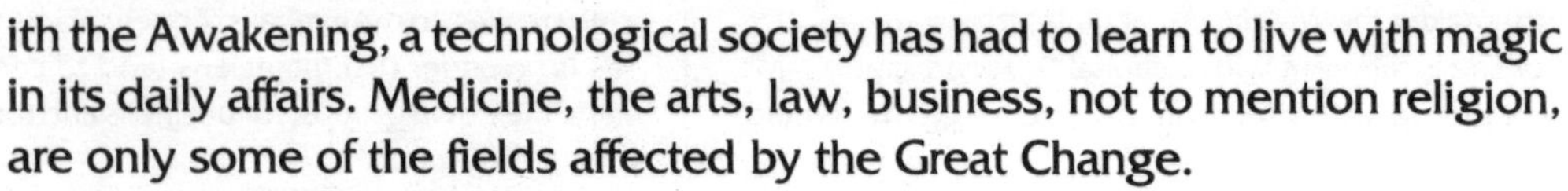

ith the Awakening, a technological society has had to learn to live with magic in its daily affairs. Medicine, the arts, law, business, not to mention religion, are only some of the fields affected by the Great Change.

Forty years into the Change, magic powers alone will not get a magician onto the talk show circuit, nor does a trial for felonious magical assault still get page-one headlines.

This chapter examines how magic has affected life in 2050.

THE MAGICAL CHILD

Magical ability usually manifests at or just before puberty, between the ages of ten and twelve years for most Humans and Metahumans, but falling as low as eight years for some of the Awakened races. Cases of younger children becoming magically active are rare. Some magical children first display their powers spontaneously under stress. An angry child may, for example, suddenly hurl a low power spell, or the "invisible friend" of another may suddenly become visible. Many young physical adepts have been discovered in the rough-and-tumble of childhood games or junior athletics.

A magical child's aura will show the telltale signs, but it is difficult to sense before the power becomes active. After that, the aura will show clearly as that of a magician, though some experts claim to assence the difference between trained, aware young magicians and those who are yet unaware of their potential power.

Children in the NAN tribes, in corporate communities, and in the most sophisticated cultures are watched closely for early signs of power. Those possessing it are treasured. They are trained in the uses of magic, either as apprentices to tribal shamans or in schools and universities with major programs in occult science. The motives for providing this training vary widely. The tribes, as a rule, respect the power and want to see it properly channeled. The corporations are chronically short of magicians, and look forward to seeing a good, loyal wage mage emerge at the end of the training.

Magical children in other environments have less predictable fates. Some may grow to adulthood never knowing they are capable. Others may be taught to believe that magic and other phenomena of the Awakening are evil, and will subconsciously block their talent. Such a psychic lock may make it impossible to train this magical potential in later life. Street kids, too, may never know that they have magical ability. Those who do somehow discover their gifts usually escape from the streets, most often snapped up by a corporate recruiter looking for talent. Others will seek training from a street magician, using their powers for good or ill on their home turf.

In extreme cases, backward communities have destroyed magical children for showing "unnatural powers." Such lynchings have become rarer as the hysteria that followed immediately after the Awakening has died down.

MAGIC AND RELIGION

The initial impact of the Awakening on most major religions was one of profound shock. Though some church leaders behaved at first as though the Apocalypse had come, most faiths eventually came to terms with the situation humanely and sanely.

Christianity, in particular, had to struggle with the resurgence of magic on Earth. For centuries, Christian churches had taught that magic was a forbidden study, a vain deceit of the devil. In 2024, however, Pope John XXV, the Roman Catholic pontiff, issued an historic encyclical, *In Imago Dei* ("In The Image of God"). In that document, the Pope set forth the following as official Church doctrine:

·That Metahumans are possessed of souls and capable of salvation. Discrimination against Metahumans is not Christian.

·That magical abilities are not, by nature, evil. Rather, like any other human ability, they may be used for good or evil ends.

·That Spirits were living manifestations of nature. Thus, Conjuring is not in itself evil.

Expanding somewhat on the last point, John XXV declared that Conjuring touches so many questions of faith and doctrine that Catholics may not practice it without specific permission of the Church. This permission is usually granted only to clergy.

Most Christian churches followed Rome's lead. Indeed, some sects, most notably Unitarianism, had already taken more liberal positions. Only the most rigidly fundamental sects still maintain their traditional abhorrence of magic, Spirits, and the Awakened.

The three main sects of Judaism recognize that magical phenomena can come from the Lord. Orthodox Judaism restricts magical work to healing and defense against hostile magic and Spirits, however. Certain esoteric, ultra-orthodox sects, with a tradition of cabalistic study and wonder-working *tzaddikim*, do not observe these restrictions. Conservative and Reform Judaism do not restrict their members' magical activities, though use of magic on the Sabbath is forbidden in all three sects. All persuasions, of course, consider it sinful to use magic for evil ends. Judaism upholds full equality for Metahumans.

In the Islamic world, the return of magic recalled the great days of Moorish magic in Renaissance Spain and North Africa, when Arab magicians and alchemists dominated the art. Today, the magical arts are accepted and studied widely by the children of Islam. Though some prejudice exists against Metahumans in Sunni-dominated areas, it is more social than religious.

The more conservative Shiite sect of Islam maintains that the Koran forbids dabbling in magical powers, and the use of magic remains a capital crime in Shiite-controlled areas. Metahumans are barely tolerated. Orks and Dwarfs are regarded as particularly accursed. Lynchings are common.

The great religions of the East: Hinduism, Buddhism, and Shintoism, are neutral on the subject of magical workings. Indeed, some of the more mystical sects number powerful magicians among their followers. The lack of acceptance of Metahumans in the Far East is more a social than a religious phenomenon; higher-caste Hindus are particularly prejudiced against Metahumans.

The last few years have seen new religions arise, some more magically oriented than others. In North America, the Church of the Whole Earth, Inc., began as a loose coalition of urban shamans, Wiccans, eco-activists, and others of like mind. The group embraces a liberal, pantheistic attitude, but tends toward worship of Mother Gaia, the Earth Goddess. A typical service shows an interesting blend of traditional American Protestant practices and typically shamanic celebration.

Another new "religion" that has been growing quickly is the Universal Brotherhood, active in the Americas and many parts of Europe. This sect, numbering several hundred-thousand members in North America, teaches members mental systems of self-help, backing this up with financial aid, employment, education, charitable work, and other similar benefits. The Brotherhood's mass revivals are noted for their positive effect on both faithful and visitors alike. Though the group has no overt magical connection, they encourage magically capable members to excel at their art.

MAGIC AND THE LAW

The very nature of magic made legislation to deal with it inevitable. So far, the United Canadian and American States (UCAS) and the Confederated American States (CAS) have passed laws concerning the results of magical acts. Bills to regulate the art itself have continually failed to pass or have been struck down by the courts. Several major points are now firmly established in common law.

A felony committed with magic is always considered a premeditated act. Killing someone by magic is considered first-degree murder if brought to trial, unless it is possible to prove self-defense or other mitigating circumstances.

Criminal acts committed by a Spirit are the responsibility of the magician who summoned the being.

Because both the UCAS and CAS retain major elements of the former U.S. Bill of Rights in their legal systems, magical methods such as Mind Probe cannot be used to produce evidence, as this violates the Fifth Amendment prohibition against self-incrimination. Reading an aura to determine magical connections, say, to a spell lock maintaining a criminal spell, however, has achieved the same status as fingerprinting or DNA-patterning.

Many large jurisdictions employ a Forensic Magician, whose position is analogous to a Coroner or Medical Examiner. When expert testimony on magical conditions and methods is presented as admissible evidence, it is always subject to scrutiny by a duly sworn forensic magician. This includes evidence only obtainable in Astral Space.

Spectral evidence, that is, evidence given by Spirits, is not admissible in a court of law.

In civil law, an ongoing debate rages over spell copyright. Under present statutes, the designer of a spell may copyright the spell formula and charge fees for its sale or be paid royalties for sales by others. In practice, this law is used to prosecute those who pirate formulas and distribute them in quantity. Though reverse-engineering a spell from technical data is also deemed a violation of copyright, it is almost impossible to prove because a spell itself is judged an expression of natural law, and thus is not subject to patent or copyright. The anti-piracy tool used by most spell developers, especially in the corporate sector, is secrecy. Spell data is simply not published. There is a thriving business of industrial espionage dealing in magical secrets.

The term "corporate law" has taken on a double meaning in 2050. Besides business law, it also refers to the laws that various corporations enforce within their jurisdictions. Ever since the extraterritoriality decisions of the early 21st century, corporations can opt to prosecute criminals under their own legal codes. Depending on the corporation and its legal code, a misdemeanor or simple tort in civil law may be a felony, or even a capital crime. As for magical crimes, acts committed by corporate magicians are generally not subject to legal investigation, while magic used by other magicians to the detriment of the corporation receives dire punishment. This assumes, of course, that the corporate security agents have not summarily sent an offending magician to a "higher" court.

MAGIC AND BUSINESS

Magic has direct application only at two extreme ends of the business spectrum. Magic is a mainstay of such relatively trivial industries as fashion and entertainment. These may represent large and rich markets, but the presence of magicians in a Rubinstein salon or working on special effects at Industrial Light & Magic™ is not likely to transform global economics. At the other end of the spectrum, the use of magic is part of the most delicate and expensive prototype experimentation carried out by high-technology research and development. This is most notable in biological research, but magical techniques also have applications in the physical sciences. The rituals involved require a delicate melding of magic and esoteric scientific theory that only a handful of theoretical occultists can comprehend. It should come as no surprise that these double-domes are prime candidates for extraction runs. A company can replace its CEO more easily than it can one of these talented fellows.

Magic's greatest impact in the business sphere has been in the area of corporate security. Just as the advent of Matrix technology began an escalating "arms race" between deckers and corp-data security specialists, the corporations had to procure the services of magicians before the nut-case eco-freaks and anti-establishment NAN sympathizers got organized enough to hurt them.

The fortunes of corporations and executives who used magic to claw their way to the top also pointed out the advantages of occult muscle to the powers-that-be. Aztechnology is a prime example of how far magical power and ruthless business practices can carry a corporation.

FUCHI
BUY
FUCHI
TODAY
NAS
RICK
HARRIS
'90

"Some folks can do more than I can, but no one is better than I am at what I do"
—Sorcerer Adept Philip Anger

o create a character who is a full-fledged magician, that character must take magic as his highest priority, per the basic **SR** rules, p. 53. That is a Priority Level of 4 if the character is Human, and 3 if Metahuman. There are also some characters who can do *some* magic, but only in a limited area. These are called *adepts*. Note that some full-fledged magicians tend to look down on adepts as "one-shots," "semimundos," or simply "semis" (i.e., semi-mundanes).

To become an adept, that character must have Magic as his *second* priority if he's Human, or *third* if Metahuman. Thus, a Human adept would assign Magic a Priority Level of 3, and a Metahuman adept would assign Magic a Priority Level of 2.

Like full magicians, adepts have a Magic Attribute and lose points from that attribute as they suffer Essence Loss or Deadly Wounds. With the exception of physical adepts (see below), adepts are subject to the Geasa rules (see **Geasa**, p. 28). All adepts can improve their Magic Attribute through Initiation.

MAGICAL ADEPTS

A magical adept can use *one* magical skill. Period. If he is a sorcerer adept, his magical work is limited to Sorcery, and he cannot use Conjuring or Enchanting to do magic. A typical magical adept is a sorcerer. There are conjuror adepts and enchanter adepts, too, but most adepts prefer the versatility and power of Sorcery. Whatever skill the adept picks, he follows the normal rules for using it.

Like other magicians, magical adepts have to choose between the shamanic and hermetic traditions. They follow the rules for that tradition in spell learning, and so on. Shamans get totem benefits and penalties, if applicable to the skill. Adepts can also use a power focus like any other magician, if it is useful to their skill.

The principal difference between a magical adept and a full magician is that the adept has no access to Astral Space. A magical adept cannot use

Astral Perception or Projection at all! This also means that he cannot use most forms of metamagic, as it requires the use of Astral Perception (see **Metamagic**, p. 22).

SHAMANIC ADEPTS

A different form of adept is the *shamanic adept*, who, as the name implies, must be a shaman. This adept can *only* cast spells or conjure Spirits for which he receives a totem advantage. For example, a shamanic adept of the Bear totem can only cast Health Spells and can only conjure Forest Spirits.

NOTE: Shamanic adepts do not receive totem modifiers for these activities. They are subject to all the usual requirements of their totem. It is impossible to be a shamanic adept in a totem like Coyote or Raven that receives no advantages, nor is it possible in a totem where all spells receive a modifier based on time or place, but not purpose.

Shamanic adepts have the full use of their Sorcery and Conjuring Skills in defensive magic and are capable of Astral Sensing and Astral Projection.

PHYSICAL ADEPTS

A *physical adept* dedicates his magic to improving his body and its abilities. Powers attributed to legendary martial artists, warriors of shamanic peoples, berserkers, and the like, suggest that such adepts existed to some extent before the Awakening. The first publicly documented physical adept in modern times was Francis Daniels, an engineering Ph.D and fourth *dan* ki-aikido black belt. Much of our understanding of the powers of the physical adept are due to Daniels' research, conducted prior to his death in the riots attending the collapse of the U.S. Government in the Washington D. C. metroplex in 2030.

When creating a character who is a physical adept, distribute his or her Magic Attribute to "buy" various improvements in the Physical Attributes, Reaction, Senses, and Skills. The adept can also "buy" various unique powers, similar to the effects of certain spells. For him, they are permanent abilities.

Physical adepts who are Initiates may gain additional Magic Points to spend. They can build up powers that cost more than 6 points. The points are only a gauge and not actually lost.

Focuses, even power focuses, do *not* give physical adepts any help at all. A physical adept cannot automatically use Astral Perception or Astral Projection, but he can "buy" Astral Perception as one of his powers.

POWERS OF PHYSICAL ADEPTS

Astral Perception
Cost: 2

The adept has the ability to enter the Astral Plane via Astral Perception, but he cannot use Astral Projection. He can use Sorcery Skill in Astral Combat, but he is not able to cast spells. If an Initiate, he can use metamagical powers that affect Astral Perception, such as Masking (see **Metamagic**, p. 22).

Automatic Successes
Cost: See below

Automatic Successes power is apparently what gave the great martial artists of the Orient their legendary combat abilities. When using this skill, the adept automatically gains the purchased number of successes. If using the skill in place of another, one Automatic Success is lost for each circle passed on the Skill Web. Successes apply equally whether the character is using the General Skill, Concentrations, or Specializations.

This skill is especially powerful in Melee Combat (**SR**, p.70). Whether or not the adept makes a Resisted Success Test, he gets the Automatic Successes for use in either counterattack or as additions to his Dodge Pool. For example, an adept with 4 Automatic Successes in Unarmed Combat is attacked in melee, he would have 4 "counterattack" successes even if he decides to avoid combat and rely instead on his Dodge Pool. These Automatic Successes operate exactly like successes generated through the normal die rolls.

The Automatic Successes also count for Damage Resistance Tests that can use the Defense Pool. An adept with 4 Automatic Successes in Unarmed Combat would have those as part of his Unarmed Defense Pool for use in resisting damage. The successes renew along with the rest of the pool. The adept allocates them against the opposition, as needed. He may make this allocation *after* his attackers have made their Success Test against him.

These Automatic Successes do not apply to ranged weapon skills of any kind!

AUTOMATIC SUCCESS COSTS

Skills	Magic Cost
Athletic	.5 per success
Combat	
Armed Combat	1 per success
Unarmed Combat	1 per success
Stealth	.5 per success

Killing Hands
Cost: See Below

Normal hand-to-hand damage does (Strength)M1 Stun Damage. The physical adept may use his magic to turn his Unarmed Combat attacks into deadly blows. When using Unarmed Combat, the adept with Killing Hands may choose to do either the normal Stun Damage or the improved Lethal Damage. The maximum Wound Category is Deadly (D).

The Killing Hands attack is effective against creatures with Immunity or magical defenses against normal weapons. Their defensive bonuses do not count against Killing Hands.

Note also that Killing Hands is a bare-handed strike and cannot be augmented by either weaponry or magic.

KILLING HAND COSTS

Wound Category	Cost Per Category
(Str)L1	.5
(Str)M1	1
(Str)S1	2
(Str)D1	4

Pain Resistance
Cost: .5 per point

Pain Resistance Points allow the adept to reduce the effects of damage when recording it on either Condition Monitor, but solely for the purpose of reducing any Initiative or Target Modifiers due to injury. A character will not suffer the full penalties for a wound that does not incapacitate him.

Note: Any injury that would immediately result in all 10 boxes being filled in *does* result in the character becoming unconscious or dying. The Rating covers both Physical and Mental Condition Monitors. That is, if the adept has a Pain Resistance Rating of 4, subtract 4 from the number of boxes filled in on either Monitor to see what penalty he actually receives.

Ariela Silverblade, a physical adept on a Tir Tairngire assassin squad, buys 4 points of Pain Resistance. In combat, she takes a Light Wound (fill in 1 box on the Physical Condition Monitor). Subtract 4 from 1. The result is less than 0, so she does not suffer the +1 Target Number/–1 Initiative penalty. Then Ariela takes a Serious Wound, filling in 5 more boxes, for a total of 6 boxes filled in on the Condition Monitor. 6 – 4 is 2. She gets the penalty for a Light Wound. The poor lady now gets zapped with a Sleep Spell, but it only does Moderate Stun Damage. Fill in 3 boxes on the Mental Monitor. 3 – 4 is less than 0, so the damage has no effect on her Target Numbers.

The Pain Resistance Rating also allows the character to resist pain from torture, magic, illness, and so on. The Rating can either be added to Target Numbers for affecting the adept with pain (interrogation by torture, for example) or subtracted from his Target Numbers to resist pain (as in a Body or Willpower Test against the symptoms of a painful disease). Again, Pain Resistance does not prevent or heal actual damage, but may prevent or reduce the damage's affect on the character's Skills or Initiative.

This Rating cannot be used to improve the chance of a Body or Willpower Resistance Test against damage.

Physical Attribute
Cost: see below

With Magic Points, the adept can raise a Physical Attribute but *not* a Mental Attribute.

If the adept wants to increase a Physical Attribute using Karma in the normal way (**SR**, p.150), the cost is based on the total Attribute, that is, including the magical improvements.

The cost depends on how much higher (or lower) than his Racial Maximum is the final Attribute Rating:

Less than or equal to Racial Maximum:	.5 per +1 Rating
Over Racial Maximum:	1 per +1 Rating

Harley is a physical adept, and has 6 Magic Points to expend. His initial Strength is 4. Being an Ork, he can raise that to 8 (the racial maximum on Strength for Orks), allocating .5 Magic Points per extra point of Strength. This costs him 2 points. Harley decides to pump it up to 10, that is, 2 points over the maximum, which costs another 2 points. That leaves Harley with 2 Magic Points to spend. Oh joy. Enough to jack up his reflexes, too. Harley is now a magically powered bundle of surprises for the first arrogant cyber-samurai who tries to play "Ring around the Orkie."

Physical Sensory Improvement
Cost: .25 per improvement

These improvements can include Low-Light or Thermographic Vision, High or Low Frequency Hearing, Enhanced Smell or Taste, and so on. Unless an improvement involves radio or similar technological phenomena, anything that can be improved by cyberware can be improved by this power. Unlike cyberware, there are no package deals.

Increased Reaction
Cost: See below

With Increased Reaction, the adept can increase his reflexes, with an effect similar to that of Wired Reflexes. For each level, he receives a +1 to his Reaction and a +1D6 to his Reaction per Level. The maximum level is 4.

INCREASED REACTION COST

Reaction Level	Cost Per Level
Level 1	1
Level 2	2
Level 3	4
Level 4	8

PHYSICAL ADEPTS AND MAGIC

A physical adept can lose Magic Points just like any other magician. Should it happen, the loss affects any improvements the character has purchased. An adept must give up a full point of improvements for every point of Magic he loses. If he gains additional Magic through Initiation, he can restore lost improvements or put the new Magic into different improvements.

Once Magic Points have been allocated to "buy" a power, the power cannot be changed, but it can be upgraded with the addition of more Magic at a later time. For example, if a player puts 2 Magic Points into Killing Hands at (Strength)S1, he could add another 2 points later to increase it to (Strength)D1.

Physical adepts are not subject to the **Geasa** rules (see p. 28) when they lose Magic. Their power is less vulnerable to the psychic shock of losing Magic Points, less delicate than the powers of a real spell-tosser.

"Initiation means a beginning. Every day in a magician's life is a new beginning."

—Wake Up Call: Living in the Awakened World, Mullins Chadwick, Putnam-Izumo, New York, 2047

nitiation works on many levels to make a magician better at what he does. It sharpens his sensitivity to magical energy and purifies his system, allowing him to handle more power. Magicians who tie their religion and their magic together say it brings them closer to their god or gods. Are they right? No one knows for sure.

As for the **Shadowrun** rules, Initiation has the following effects:

•It increases the Magic Attribute and can raise it above the normal maximum of 6.

•It lets the initiated magician, or *Initiate*, use metamagic (see **Metamagic**, p. 22).

Initiation costs Karma, because it takes time to study, meditate, carry out ritual, and so on. A magician can "take an Initiation" through solo work or as a member of a magical group. In a group, he pays less Karma because the other members of the group are helping him. The difficulty with groups, however, is that they are secretive and hard to find. They are selective about who can become a member, and members must live up to their rules. Some magicians find it worth spending the extra Karma not to hassle with groups.

GRADES OF INITIATION

Initiation is measured in *Grades*. Count grades starting with 0, not 1. When a character takes his first Initiation, he becomes a *Grade 0* Initiate. When he takes his second, he's a Grade 1 Initiate, and so on. This kind of grading is actually a hermetic system. Most shamanic traditions do not dwell on numbers or other linear measures of magical progress. In a game system, on the other hand, numbers help to keep track of any magician's progress.

BENEFITS OF INITIATION

When a magician makes it to Grade 0, he is officially an Initiate. He can use metamagic (see **Metamagic**, p. 22) and travel on the Metaplanes of Astral Space (see **Metaplanes**, p. 69). However, Grade 0 does not increase his Magic Attribute.

At each grade higher than 0, the Initiate adds 1 point to his Magic Attribute. Various magical operations will also gain advantages because he adds his grade to his other scores. Anywhere this bonus applies is specifically noted throughout these rules.

One universal bonus for shamans is that they add their Initiate Grade to their Totem Advantage dice. This applies in all cases of Totem advantage, whether Spellcasting or Conjuring.

Each time a magician takes an Initiation, he can try to get rid of a geas (See **Geasa**, p.28). He makes a Willpower Success Test with a Target Number of 6 plus the total number of Magic Points lost so far. One or more successes lets the Initiate eliminate one of his geasa (Initiate's choice). He can only get rid of geasa one at a time. To eliminate the next, he must wait until he takes his next grade.

KARMA AND INITIATION

The higher the grade, the more Karma it costs (surprise!). To determine the basic cost of an Initiation, add 6 to the grade the character is attempting. As always in **Shadowrun**, the better the character is, the harder it gets to improve.

As stated above, the Karma cost depends on whether the magician is solo or working in a group.

•If self-initiating, the Karma cost is 3 x basic cost.

•If the Initiate is part of a group, the Karma cost is 2 x basic cost.

Reduce the multiplier by .5 if the character must undergo an *Ordeal* as part of the Initiation (see below). That is, self-initiation with an Ordeal costs 2.5 x the basic cost, and group initiation with an Ordeal costs 1.5 x the basic cost. Always round down.

> Darkfoot is a shaman of the Owl totem. He is ready to step out into the wider magical realm of the Initiate. A loner, he decides not to seek Initiation through a group. Darkfoot must pay (6 + 0, his current grade) x 3, or 18 Karma Points to gain Initiation. If he undergoes an Ordeal, this is reduced to 15 Karma Points. Sometime later, Darkfoot, now a Grade 0 Initiate, wants to advance to Grade 1. The basic cost is now 6 + 1. Still working solo, Darkfoot must pay 7 x 3, or 21 Karma Points for his Initiation. If he accepts another Ordeal, he pays 7 x 2.5, or 17.
>
> If Darkfoot had been initiated as a member of a group, he would have paid 12 Karma Points for his Grade 0 Initiation, or 9 if he took an Ordeal. His Grade 1 Initiation would have cost 14 Karma Points, or 10 with an Ordeal.

ORDEALS

Initiation is supposed to involve an *Ordeal*. As the word suggests, an Ordeal is something unpleasant, or at least demanding. It might be a test, a series of tricky meditations, a magical task, and so on.

If nothing else, it is good roleplaying to submit to an Ordeal, because Initiates are supposed to be making a stronger commitment to magic than non-Initiates. As a gaming reward for this, an Ordeal reduces the multiplier on the Karma cost for an Initiation by .5. The higher Karma cost for Initiation without a specific Ordeal represents the time and effort the magician must invest in all the little Ordeals that tend to come his way when taking a grade. Don't try to fool the cosmos, chummer.

Each Ordeal should be different. It is not possible to repeat an Ordeal "for credit," with the exception of a *Deed* (see p. 21). The character may have to go through the same Ordeal for other reasons later on, but the Karma "discount" on Initiation only applies once for a particular Ordeal. For example, in joining a new magical group, a magician may have to repeat the *Oath* Ordeal (see p. 21). If he already took this Ordeal in another group, repeating it here will not get him the Karma discount.

The magician must choose the Ordeal when he is ready to take an Initiation and has paid the Karma for that Initiation. He can't "get the Ordeal out of the way" ahead of time, with the exception of a *Deed*. Having submitted to the Ordeal, the Initiate gets his new grade. Once he has specified the Ordeal he will perform, he cannot change it. If at first he don't succeed, he better try again, 'cause he ain't advancing any further until he does.

ORDEAL TYPES

Astral Quest

The Astral Quest is available only to Initiates because it involves projection to the Metaplanes of Astral Space (see **Metaplanes**, p. 69). A shaman must journey astrally to the metaplane of his totem. A mage has it rougher, for he must fulfill a Quest on each of the Elemental Metaplanes: Fire, Water, Air, and Earth. The Quest Rating is equal to twice the grade the magician is seeking, so this Ordeal is relatively easy at the lower levels of Initiation, becoming quite challenging at the higher ones.

If he fails the Quest, the magician must wait to repeat it, strengthening himself by ritual and meditation. He makes a Willpower Test with a Target Number equal to the grade he is attempting. Divide 10 days by the number of successes. If the player rolls no successes, he makes another test, but the base time increases by 10 (i.e., 20 days on the second try, 30 days on a third test, and so on). He continues this way until he makes a successful test and has a definite figure. The magician must give all his attention to the task for this many days, but he can do so in segments: a few days here, a few days there. During this period of preparation, he may not engage in other activities such as healing, studying, and so forth. Once this time has elapsed, he may attempt the Astral Quest again.

If a mage fails on one metaplane, he must repeat that Quest, but does not have to go back and redo any Quests that have already succeeded.

Asceticism

The magician gives up a point in one Physical Attribute. This *cannot* be gained back using Karma, as per the basic **Shadowrun** rules. The magician loses the point because of rigorous fasting, strenuous yoga-type exercises, ritual combat, or other physically dangerous practices. The magician cannot sacrifice a point from an Attribute that has a score of 1.

Deed

This is the *only* Ordeal that can be repeated "for credit." The magician goes out on some shadowrun with a goal that is appropriate to his magical group (if he has one), or his totem (if a shaman), or his moral code (if he has one of those). Success in the goal makes it a Deed.

The player running the magician and the gamemaster can agree on a Deed in advance. Alternatively, the gamemaster can let the run a magician has just finished fit the bill. The magician earns absolutely no Karma for that run, however. The gamemaster will probably not want to permit a run to serve as a Deed if the only Karma the magician has coming is the 1-point payoff for surviving, or if the run ends up a hosed-up mess.

The gamemaster has a lot of leeway, depending on his particular players and game situation. If the gamemaster approves the run as a Deed, the player-magician can turn down his Karma Award for the run, and bingo, the Ordeal is done. The magician can carry out a Deed before he is ready to take another grade. In other words, he can "save" the Deed and use it as the Ordeal for his next Initiation. A player can only save up a Deed until his character's *next* Initiation, however. Use it or lose it. The gamemaster is, as always, the final arbiter.

Deeds should be appropriate to the magician's goals and ethics or those of any group he has joined. Some runs that might count for a Deed are:

- The magician has overcome some kind of magical evil or threat to life.
- The magician has helped defend someone from wrongful persecution or death.
- The magician has experienced powerful magic, been in the presence of great Spirits, gone on an Astral Quest for some great end, or in some other way widened his experience of magic.
- If the magician has lived up to his magical and/or ethical codes, been true to his totem or the strictures of a group, or simply behaved in a manner that the gamemaster believes is appropriate.

Familiar

The magician must conjure up an Ally (p. 81), which costs at least as much additional Karma as the Initiation itself. There is an advantage to this Ordeal. To conjure an Ally usually costs a Magic Point and one point of Karma. The Ally conjured for this Ordeal does not cost a Magic Point. However, if this Ally is banished, goes "free," or is destroyed any time in the future, the magician must check to see if he loses Magic Points, just as though he had taken a Deadly Wound (**SR**, p.146). This Ally will be more loyal than the usual run of Spirits and is less likely to go "free" on its creator. This aspect of the Ally, however, is for the gamemaster to explore.

Geas

The magician takes on a geas of his choice. The magician accepts this geas for *life*. It *cannot* be cancelled out in a later Initiation. See **Geasa**, p. 28.

Meditation

The magician spends a month or longer in daily meditation, trying to bring his physical being under the control of his mind. He must pass three Unresisted Attribute Tests:

- A Charisma Test with a Target Number equal to his *Strength.*
- An Intelligence Test with a Target Number equal to his *Quickness.*
- A Willpower Test with a Target Number equal to his *Body.*

Unless *all three* tests are successful, the magician must spend another month working at the meditation. No other activity (studying, healing, learning, training, or, of course, shadowrunning) is permitted during this time. Tests are at +2 to the target numbers if the character's lifestyle is less than Low (**SR**, p. 148). Living in the wild during this period incurs no penalty if the magician has some form of Wilderness or Survival Skill of 3 or more; otherwise, the +2 penalty applies. The idea is that the magician must be able to concentrate on the meditation process without too many distractions from his environment.

Oath

The Oath Ordeal is available only to members of magical groups. The magician swears an oath to obey the group's rules and strictures. If he is ever expelled or resigns from the group, he may lose a point of Magic. Some groups require this Ordeal of all new members. Even if a magician swears several such oaths in his career, only the first one "counts" as an Ordeal for Initiation purposes. If, however, the magician loses his membership in a group to which he has sworn an oath, he checks to see if he loses a point of Magic as though he had taken a Deadly Wound (**SR**, p.146), even if this not his first oath. A magical oath is not taken lightly, and the penalties for breaking one can be severe.

Thesis

The magician creates a master formula that contains all he is as a magician and everything he knows at that point in his life. Hermetic theses are usually written texts. Shamanic theses are usually artworks, expressing the spiritual insights of the maker. The thesis loses its effectiveness if it is only stored electronically. It must exist physically.

The thesis is created in the same way as a spell formula (see **Spell Formulas**, p. 54). The author should guard the thesis carefully. As long as it exists, anyone who obtains a copy can use it as a material link to target the author via Ritual Sorcery (**SR**, p. 83). For this reason, Initiates are reluctant to make more than one copy. If all the copies are destroyed, however, the Initiate immediately loses 1 point of Magic. So magicians get nervous if only one copy is in existence. Nice little dilemma, don'cha think?

Some magical groups that try to control their members require this Ordeal. The thesis is usually for the second Initiation someone takes with them, as these same groups tend to require an oath at the first Initiation. They also require that members file a copy of their theses with the group, as it acts as a link for Ritual Sorcery. Frag with the group, and who knows what might come popping outta Astral Space some dark night.

Meta– That which comes after and above, sometimes referring to 'following,' 'deriving from,' or 'greater than.'

—Webster's International, Fifth Edition, 2048

ome magic only an Initiate can do. This is magic that controls magic itself, or metamagic. Initiates can use the five basic abilities of metamagic.

Centering is a ritual technique that helps the Initiate control the way his body channels magical energy. It can reduce Drain, overcome penalties for wounds or fatigue when using magic, and overcome some environmental penalties that affect magic and magicians.

Quickening allows a magician to make a sustained spell permanent in its effect without the use of a spell lock.

Dispelling cancels out magical effects without having to "kill" them in Astral Combat.

Shielding allows an Initiate to use a more powerful form of spell defense to counter hostile magic.

Masking lets the Initiate disguise his aura in Astral Space and to pierce such disguises by others.

CENTERING

Centering can reduce the Drain of magic or act as a countermeasure to various penalties affecting magical target numbers. It operates by using a non-magical skill as a focus for the magician's concentration.

For centuries, magicians of many countries and traditions have studied such skills as singing, dancing, playing musical instruments, speaking ancient languages, and so on. Since the Awakening, Initiates in various traditions have discovered the reason behind the practice. The mental and physical discipline involved in the skill help to focus the will of the magician, enhancing his ability to handle magic without suffering harm. They *center* him; put him in harmony with the center of his being, the well from which all magic springs.

CENTERING SKILLS

The magician has to use a *Centering Skill*. This is a special skill, usually something artistic or intellectual, that is essentially dedicated to magical purposes.

The following list describes general types of skill. The actual Centering Skill would be something like the Special Skill of Classical Greek or the Special Skill of Guitar. Centering Skills are a form of the catch-all category known as Special Skills (**SR**, p. 61).

Dancing

The magician dances as he weaves his spell. Native American dances are typical of those used for magic.

Singing

The magician sings as he does his magic. This can range from chant to novahot rock, and fall anywhere in between. Magical traditions tell of bards who can make magic with their songs. The priests and magicians of Native American tribes such as the Navaho are often notable singers.

Playing Musical Instruments

The magician plays an instrument to center himself. According to legend, magicians have used drums, harps, pipes, horns, even violins. In the Sixth World, magicians also use electric guitars, maxaphones, ultra-synths, even synth-link rigs if they decide to get the cyber for it. The use of drumming is well-documented in the shamanic traditions as an example of the use of a musical instrument. Oriental magicians are said to favor the music of bamboo flutes as a centering technique.

Ancient or Arcane Languages

The magician may utter his spells in an ancient language or one that has magical potency. Hermetic magic in the West has used Latin, Greek, and Hebrew for centuries. Many traditions use the ancient language of their country of origin for magical purposes. Magicians in the northern European countries often chant the ancient runes, the letters in which the epic *eddas* of their ancestors were written, as a centering technique.

Meditation

The magician composes his mind in meditation to center himself. This may be a form of moving meditation, like the ancient Chinese *tai chi*, or one performed at rest, such as yoga or Japanese zazen sitting.

CHOOSING CENTERING SKILLS

Players will no doubt want to make up new Centering Skills, and that is fine. Though the Awakening made magicians understand and value the old traditions of their art, it also set off a wave of experimentation to find new and better ways of magic. For purposes of game balance, however, it is probably best if the Centering Skills are *not* ones of great use in non-magical areas. Take, for example, centering by shooting a gun. A case could be made for it, based on the zen qualities of marksmanship involved in such a skill as archery. The same certainly goes for Armed and Unarmed Combat Skills. This would, however, give the magician the advantage of being able to physically beat up on his foes while readying himself to cast a devastating spell, and to get bonuses for doing it. Why wouldn't a player want to take zen-flamethrower skill for centering and become a magician? Watch out, street samurai, here I come!

It is less problematic if a magician's Centering Skill also helps him to make a living or to gain some fame, as in the case of a rocker/magician who uses his musical talents to center. In fact, some Sixth World bands probably contain just such members. Of course, the magician needs his instrument for centering, and that can be hard on Stealth, especially if he likes to play it with the amp running meltdown-hot.

Shamans traditionally use performing arts like dancing, singing, or playing an instrument. Mages are usually more comfortable with less emotional skills such as chanting or the use of mystical languages. Both traditions may employ some form of meditation skill to center. But don't get locked into stereotypes. A mage can dance up a storm (as it were) to center himself, and a shaman can roll out Latin or Hebrew tongue-twisters, if that is what he chooses as a Centering Skill.

A magician is not limited to only one Centering Skill, either. He can study many, but can get the benefit of only one at any one time. For example, a magician might study singing and dancing as Centering Skills. He can even sing and dance when casting a spell, but he would only use one Skill Rating, presumably the higher one, when making die rolls in the Centering Tests described below.

Note, too, that a Centering Skill can NEVER be chip-based. The magician has to know it himself and have learned it the hard way.

CENTERING TESTS

Centering Tests can be made any time a character uses a Magic Skill. A magician can center when casting a spell, conjuring a Spirit, enchanting a focus, and so on.

The magician must be *able* to use his Centering Skill. That is, he must be able to perform the skill freely and (if need be) loudly. A magician cannot use dance to center if he is tied up or has a broken leg. He cannot use singing or spoken words if he is gagged. Note that use of an appropriate Centering Skill can also count as fulfilling a geas. If a magician has the Incantation geas, and tries to center by singing, chanting, or speaking his spells in an ancient language, he fulfills the geas at the same time.

The player makes the Centering Test before making any other tests to do the magic. A magician can choose to use centering to reduce Drain or to reduce penalties affecting his magic.

His grade will act as a bonus, making the Centering Test easier to pass than it would otherwise be. Note that the Grade Bonus applies *only* to the Centering Test, not to the other tests needed to cast his spell and to Resist Drain.

CENTERING VS. DRAIN

Centering against Drain lets the magician make an advance attempt to reduce the Drain of using magic. The player makes an Unresisted Test against the Drain Code for doing the magic, using the Centering Skill for the number of dice. Any successes from this test apply as automatic successes for resisting Drain when the time comes to check for that.

Any modifiers that apply to the actual Drain Resistance Test apply equally to this Centering Test. In addition, reduce the Target Number for the test by the magician's grade. Remember that the lowest possible Target Number in **Shadowrun** is 2.

On a roll of all 1s, the operation is aborted, and the normal Drain Resistance Test is made at once. Any successes from earlier Centering Tests do count, however.

A Grade 2 Initiate uses singing as his Centering Skill while summoning a Force 5 Nature Spirit. He has a Singing Skill of 4. As the Initiate's Charisma is 3, the Drain for the summoning is 5S1. To make the Centering Test, the magician rolls 4 dice (Singing Skill) against a Drain of 5S1, reducing the Target Number by the magician's grade.

He scores 2 successes, which can now apply as automatic successes when resisting Drain after actually casting the spell. These will automatically reduce the Drain to Light. He must still make a Charisma Resistance Test against the full drain of 5S1, but a single success there will knock the Drain down to nothing.

CENTERING VS. PENALTIES

Centering can also act as a countermeasure to penalties affecting the magician's Success Test for his magic.

The Target Number for this Centering Test is the same as the number needed for Magic success, with all the penalties in effect. However, subtract the magician's grade from the Target Number.

Every Centering Test success reduces the penalties against the actual success test by −1. Note that this can only reduce penalties against the Target Number. It cannot reduce the actual Target Number itself. Casting a Mana Spell at a character with a Willpower Rating 5 still has a Target Number of 5, no matter how many Centering Successes he scores.

Beaumains, a Grade 4 Initiate, is tossing a Power Bolt at an enemy. The target has a Body Attribute of 4, is in Partial Cover (+2), and the light is poor (+2). Beaumains is also Lightly Fatigued, which adds +1 to the Target Number. Beaumains faces a Target Number of 9. While his street samurai muscle keeps the target pinned down with rifle fire, the mage centers in, wailing out the chords on his Kashawaya Pow-R-Key synthesizer. He has a Special Skill Rating of 5 in Rock Keyboards. Rolling 5 dice (his Keyboards Skill) against a Target Number 5 (the actual Target Number of 9 minus his grade, which is 4), he scores 3 successes. He must now make the Success Test for the spell, with a Target Number of 6, to see if he fries the unfortunate goon.

CENTERING AND SPELLCASTING

When using Centering to improve his spellcasting, the magician *must* use Astral Perception (**SR**, p. 89) during the whole Centering period because Centering requires a close watch on the energy patterns of his spell in Astral Space. This means that the magician is vulnerable to astral attack while he is Centering. If he is attacked, the combat is carried on simultaneously with the Centering Test. (See **Astral Combat**, p.65, for details.) The magician can make both his Centering and Astral Combat Tests at normal values. There is no extra penalty for distractions. Wounds received in Astral Combat do, of course, affect all tests, depending on the damage done, though the Centering Test may overcome these.

To use Centering, the magician declares the spell he is casting in the normal way (**SR**, p. 80), then he declares that he will make a Centering Test. After he makes the test, be it successful or not, he casts the spell.

QUICKENING

Quickening is metamagic that can make any sustained spell permanent, *without* need for a spell lock! The spell is given a permanent "circuit" into Astral Space that keeps it running until it is broken, either in Astral Combat or by an Initiate using Dispelling ability, described below.

To Quicken a spell, the magician must sustain the spell for a certain period and must pay Karma. In addition, he must use Astral Perception to "keep the spell in sight" the whole time he is sustaining it. Because he is feeding Karma directly to the spell, he must carefully monitor the astral energies that compose the spell's structure.

The magician must declare that he will try to Quicken the spell at the time he casts it. After that, if the spell is cast, whether the magician does, indeed, make it permanent or not, he must make two Drain Resistance Tests. Once, as always, when he casts the spell. He makes the second test when the spell becomes permanent or should he decide to break off trying to make it permanent.

The base time to sustain the spell is a number of actions equal to the total number of dice used in the Success Test for casting spell. This includes dice from totem advantages, Elemental aid, focuses, the Magic Pool, or any other bonus. Make a Sorcery Skill Test and add a number of dice equal to the magician's grade. No other dice may be allocated to this test from any source. The Target Number for the test is the same as that for casting the spell. It can be hard to calculate for some Area Spells, where the Target Number varies according to the scores of the targets. In this case, the spell must be anchored on a central target and that subject's Target Number used.

To determine how many actions the magician must spend sustaining the spell, divide the base time by the number of successes. The minimum time is one action after the spell was cast. If the test fails, the magician must sustain it for *twice* the base time.

The magician can decide to drop the Quickening attempt if the time required seems too long, but he must make a second Drain Resistance Test, even though he is not making the spell permanent.

At the end of the last action required to sustain the spell, the magician pays Karma equal to the spell's actual Force (not the total number of dice rolled). The spell is now self-sustaining.

In the action when the spell becomes permanent, that is, when the magician pays the Karma, he, too, must make a second Drain Resistance Test. If the magician made an Unresisted Centering Test against Drain when first casting the spell, any successes from that test also reduce the Drain for this second test. A new Centering Test is *not* allowed!

Rikki Ratboy, in a nastier than usual mood after being pitched out of The Armadillo, hunkered down on the roof across the street from the samurai hangout. He began to mutter, and soon the red-eyed, long-whiskered mask of Gray Brother materialized around his scrawny features as the words of power hissed and squealed from his lips. He grunted triumphantly as a grayish-green cloud swirled into existence in the middle of the bar, visible to his astral sight if not to the wired-up drekheads boozing it up down there.

As the Stink Spell spread its indescribable foulness through the room, the clientele exited en masse via doors, windows, and a rather thinly plastered section of wall. Rikki grinned, but kept his concentration centered on the Astral Plane, delicately manipulating the swirling cloud of mana. After a few seconds, as sweat beaded his forehead, he spoke the locking spell and felt some of his life force leave him. Weary, but giggling at his revenge, the little Rat shaman scuttled into his native shadows, leaving a perpetual stink bomb swirling in the Armadillo. Nobody frags with little Rikki, chummer. Nobody.

Rikki is a Grade 3 Initiate and has Sorcery Skill 7. He cast a Force 1 Stink Spell, augmenting it with 5 dice from his Magic Pool. That's 6 dice, total. After he casts the spell (and Resists Drain against 2S1), he rolls to see how long he must sustain the spell to make it permanent. Because this is an Area Spell, Ricky centers it on some poor slob sitting at one of the tables. Amazingly, that makes his target a 6! (Maybe not such a poor slob after all! Better watch it, Ricky.)

He rolls 10 dice: Sorcery Skill Rating 7 plus his 3 Grades. He scores 2 successes. He must sustain the spell for 6/2 actions, that is for 3 actions. At the end of that time, he pays 1 Karma Point (for a Force 1 Spell), and the spell becomes permanent. He makes a Drain Resistance Test again at this point.

BREAKING QUICKENED SPELLS

Whether attacking Quickened spells in Astral Combat or trying to break them by the much safer metamagical ability of Dispelling, the amount of Karma paid to quicken the spell is used as the its Force. If it was easy to cast, it will be easy to break (once a magician arrives on the scene, that is).

DISPELLING

The only way non-Initiate magicians can break a spell, whether sustained or quickened, is by engaging the spell in Astral Combat, which can be dangerous.

Dispelling allows an Initiate to break a spell with, one hopes, less risk. The magician must assense the spell to try and dispel it. He can only break a spell that has a Force less than or equal to his grade, however. Lastly, Dispelling is an exclusive process: the magician cannot maintain a spell, provide spell defense, and so on when he is attempting to dispel. If these conditions are met, he can try the Dispelling operation.

He must make an Unresisted Sorcery Success Test with a Target Number equal to the Spell Force. No modifiers to this target are allowed. If the test succeeds, the spell is broken.

Whether or not the test succeeds, the Dispelling magician must now Resist Drain, as though he had just cast the spell himself. If the Spell Force is greater than his Magic Attribute, this is Physical Damage. Otherwise, it is normal Mental Drain.

He may attempt Centering to try to reduce the Drain for Dispelling.

Dispelling cannot "cancel" a permanent spell effect such as magical healing. Nor does it have any effect on Spirits or focuses. However, it *can* break spells held by a spell lock, spells being sustained by a magician, or Quickened spells that have been made permanent.

SHIELDING

Shielding is the initiated version of spell defense (**SR**, p. 81). Besides increasing the number of dice a character rolls to resist a spell, it enhances his Resisting Attribute as well, thus increasing the Target Number the attacking magician needs to succeed. A magician may not utilize Shielding and normal spell defense simultaneously.

For example, a magician allocates 4 dice to Shielding, then uses those dice to protect someone with Body 4 from a Physical Spell. Not only does the character being shielded roll 8 dice to resist the spell, but the attacking magician's Target Number would be 8, instead of 4.

Shielding dice can be added to the defense of a target fewer times than for normal spell defense. The maximum number of shields the magician can provide is equal to his grade plus 1. The Shielding, however, will last until the magician's next action.

MASKING

Masking hides the true nature of the magician's aura, allowing him to appear as a mundane when assensed. Initiates, however, may be able to penetrate this disguise. Initiates may also be able to penetrate the aura masks of other creatures able to hide their true nature on the etheric plane, such as certain Free Spirits.

When an Initiate assenses a Masked aura, the gamemaster should make a secret test. The exact test conditions vary, depending on the true nature of the thing being assensed.

The basic format of the test is an Unresisted Magic Test, with a Target Number equal to the Magic Attribute, Force, or Essence of the target, as appropriate.

A number of successes equal to the subject's grade minus the viewer's grade is needed to succeed. If the subject's grade is less than or equal to the viewer's, then one success is all it takes.

For example, a Grade 2 Initiate with a Magic Attribute 7 is assensing the aura of a Grade 4 Initiate with a Magic 6. The viewer rolls 7 dice, with a Target Number 6, and needs 2 successes (subject grade 4 – viewer grade 2 = 2) to determine that the subject's aura is Masked.

If the magician succeeds at the test and the subject is a Human Initiate, the gamemaster informs the character that he sees a true aura within a disguised one. The results of success may differ for other creatures who have Masking as an inherent power.

For ease of play, gamemasters may wish to apply the following guidelines.

Assume that an Initiate's aura is always masked unless he deliberately shows his "true colors."

Assume that an Initiate must deliberately try to assense a masked aura if he is studying a crowd. If there are only one or two Initiates present, the gamemaster can make a secret roll to see if they "notice" one another.

An astrally perceiving or projecting Initiate cannot mask his aura completely. An astral body that looks like a mundane with no meat body attached is pretty odd. Not unheard of, but odd. The Initiate can, however, choose to make his astral body look like a normal magician's instead of an Initiate's.

If the test fails, the character may try only once more. The Initiate declares that he will assense the aura again. If this test fails, too, the magician simply cannot pierce the Masking. The only way he can perceive the truth is if the subject drops the Masking or if some other Initiate discovers the truth and points it out to him. This second attempt is subject to the normal +2 additional attempt penalty.

There is *no* difference between a masked aura and the aura of a mundane, unless the Masking Test is successful. That means the gamemaster must be careful how he phrases answers to players' questions. "Looks normal" is always a safe reply, whether the subject of the assensing is a mundane or a masked Initiate.

"Everyone thinks magic is a free joyride."
—Wake Up Call: Living in the Awakened World, Mullins Chadwick, Putnam-Izumo, New York, 2047

eltic legends are full of references to something called a *geas*, or plural, *geasa*. (That's one geas, two geasa, O.K.?) The word means "bond" in old Gaelic. "Geases" is a mundane rube-word. A geas was a taboo, something that either had to be done or else scrupulously avoided. As with a lot of the old traditions, the Awakening has taught the reality behind geasa.

When a magician loses a point of his Magic Attribute, he loses some of his connection to the power. His self-image, the confidence that he *must* have to make magic, is damaged.

So he makes up for it by inventing little rituals to help keep his head straight. If he doesn't, his magic starts to slide. The little rituals become bonds—they tie up his actions—and then they are known by the old name: geasa.

GETTING A GEAS

Whenever a magician loses 2 full points of Magic (**SR**, p. 78, p. 146), he must choose a geas. To use this rule, magicians must keep a separate tally of their total Magic Attributes losses during their lifetimes. When a magician loses that second (or fourth, or sixth) point, he picks his new geas. Until he does so, he cannot use magic at all; his power is frozen by the psychological trauma of his loss.

Once he has decided on a geas, it will be difficult to ever get rid of it. Only when he becomes an Initiate is it possible for a magician to attempt to shed a geas. (see **Grades of Initiation**, p. 18).

WAY OF THE BURNOUT

Even if the gamemaster decides to adopt the Geasa rule, magicians can choose not to follow it. The magician can reject his geasa. He can decide that he is not going to live up to his geasa anymore. But once he chooses this option, there is no no going back. He can never change his mind.

Once the magician makes this choice, his geasa drop away. He can ignore them without any penalty to his magic. But…

•He can never become an Initiate (see **Initiation**, p.18). If he is already an Initiate, he loses his grades. He drops to Grade 0 and can never climb higher. If he is a member of a magical group, they may expel him. Treat this as though he had broken a number of strictures equal to his lost grades as described in **Magical Groups**, the next chapter.

•His Magic Attribute goes down immediately. It becomes 6 minus his total losses in Magic Attribute. If this makes him a mundane on the spot, so be it. The only time this really matters is if the magician was a high-grade Initiate who'd been replacing lost Magic Points.

This is the path of the Burned-Out Mage Archetype (**SR** p. 33). No longer able to handle the demands of maintaining the magical lifestyle, he begins his slide to the bottom of the magical food chain, finally rejecting magic completely and becoming a mundane.

A geas is a ritual the magician must carry out to use his magic or a limitation he accepts on using it. The geas has no power in itself; it is like a normal fetish that way.

When a magician breaks a geas, he can still try to get the magic working, but he is at a penalty: add +2 to his Target Number for *all* magical tests (targeting, drain resistance, defense, and so on). If he has broken more than one of his geasa, add +2 for every one broken.

The one good thing about geasa is that the magician need not bother with them when using Astral Projection. That is, his tests for Astral Combat, assensing items, and other similar actions are not subject to the Geasa Rule. However, if he is making any other magical test and just happens to be astrally active at the time, those tests get the penalty.

As will become clearer in the next chapter on magical groups, breaking a geas is not an infraction. The magician does not have to make up for breaking it. A geas is simply a condition the character puts on using his magic. If he uses magic without fulfilling that condition, he gets hit with a penalty for breaking the geas, but the effect is largely psychological. Once the character begins to fulfill the condition, the penalty vanishes.

STANDARD GEASA

Condition Geas

In this geas, the magician specifies a personal condition to make magic. He must, for example, be using Astral Perception, or be unwounded, or sitting in lotus position, or drunk, or whatever. When he is not in this condition, the geas is broken.

Domain Geas

The magician specifies a domain or environment in which his magic works freely. Most urban magic types will choose City, natch. In any other domain, the geas is broken.

Fasting Geas

If the magician eats or drinks anything, this geas is broken for the next 24 hours.

Gesture Geas

The magician has to gesture visibly and freely to make magic. If he is tied up, handcuffed, paralyzed, or otherwise not free to move his hands and arms, he breaks this geas.

Incantation Geas

The magician has to speak in a loud voice to make the magic happen. If he is gagged, has lost his voice, is silenced by a spell, or cannot otherwise speak clearly and audibly, he breaks this geas.

Sacrifice Geas

The magician must kill a sentient being to use his magic. If he has not performed a sacrifice in the last 24 hours, this geas is broken. The killing must be with his bare hands or a personal weapon (knife, sword, spurs, club, and so on). That is, the magician must be in physical contact with the victim. Killing by spell or ranged weapon does not count.

This geas is only applicable to non-player character magicians. Player characters may *not*, under any circumstance, be under this geas. Many magical scholars believe that blood magic is incredibly dangerous and can only lead to grave, dark consequences.

Shaman's Geas

Only magic that earns a totem advantage fulfills this geas. Doing any other kind of magic breaks it. Only a fully capable shaman can take this geas. It is not available to shamanic adepts (see **Adepts**, p.14) or to non-shamans.

Talisman Geas

The magician must use a talisman, or personal fetish. This can be anything, including a focus. If the magician is not holding or wearing the talisman, he breaks this geas. If the talisman is lost, taken away, or destroyed, the magician must retrieve it or get another similar to the original. If the magician picks a non-magical item as his talisman, he must replace it with the same kind of item. It is not enough to say "a crystal." It must be at least as specific as "a quartz crystal set in a silver medallion, hung on a golden chain." It is recommended that at least three distinct characteristics be specified about any non-magical talisman.

If the magician chooses a focus as his talisman, he can replace it with any focus of the same type and rating. If he declares that his +3 Power Focus is also his talisman, he must keep in mind that if anything happens to it, he's hosed until he gets and bonds another +3 Power Focus. Note that if he permanently uses up rating points from a focus, it is not the same talisman anymore because its rating went down.

Time Geas

The magician specifies that his magic works freely only by day or by night. If he tries to use magic at another time, the geas is broken. The magician might also choose a single season of the year during which his magic may be used freely. The rest of the year, the geas is broken.

Rikki Ratboy gets shot up bad on a run, and almost doesn't make it. Though his pals do patch up the bullet hole, Rikki still loses a point of Magic. Later, in a moment of weakness, he gets a datajack put into his head. Shazam! Our Rikki is down 2 points of Magic and has to pick a geas. He chooses Gesture. Rikki joins a lodge of Rat shamans, and in the new few years becomes a Grade 3 Initiate, picking up 3 points of Magic. He loses 2 after they experiment on him during a brief hitch in an Omega-class max-security prison. He also picked up some experimental cyberware, so maybe it works out even. Anyway, Rikki has to pick a second geas. Being a street boy, he chooses Domain. He can only work magic right in a city.

On his first run after getting out of the Hotel with Barred Windows, Rikki ends up in a nasty firefight in a heavily wooded park (Forest Domain) and gets a .40 magnum slug in his broken right arm. Besides the arm, he has broken both geasa: he's out of his Domain and he sure can't gesture freely. All his Magic Tests will be at +4. If he can get out of this fraggin' park into the streets, or a building, or something, he will be at +2. He's living up to his Domain geas, but he's still out of luck on the Gesture geas until he gets that arm patched up enough to wave around.

CREATING NEW GEASA

Some bright wiz-boy may decide he wants to make up his own geas. That's sub-zero by us, but here are the guidelines for how it oughtta work.

The geas must be something that affects all the character's magic, not just Sorcery.

If it is some special action to perform, one performance lasts only 24 hours, as in Sacrifice. It is recommended that such a geas involve some other person as well, rather than being an action the magician can go off and do by himself.

Avoiding some act can be a geas, too, and the geas is broken for 24 hours after the character performs the act. The action to avoid must be something common, as in Fasting. It must also be a true necessity of the character's life.

If it is a condition that must (or must not) exist in order to do magic, for example, the presence or absence of sunlight, moonlight, a season, a physical state, and so on, that condition must be consistent with the type of magic performed.

ACE MAGIC SUPPLY
BEST PRICES!
LARGE SELECTION
OPEN 24 HRS
Rick Harris '90
HOTEL
NACHO MAMA
OPEN 24 HRS
STREET PIZZA

"Orks like me, Elves like you. In the lodge, we share bonds of more than blood. We are one."

—Harry Mason, Past Hierophant of MOOSE (Metahuman Order of Occultists, Sorcerers, and Enchanters)

rders, covens, lodges, temples, and circles are just some of the names magical groups may take. People tend to be social critters, even oddballs like magicians. A drinking society that caters to magicians and their shoptalk is not necessarily a magical group, however. Neither is a trade association or even a school faculty or wage mage research team. What makes a group magical is the same as for an individual magician: a magical group has made the advancement of their art their main commitment. It is why they formed the group and why they stay together.

In order to be effective, to be an initiating group, a magical group must have developed an *Astral Contact*. This is a psychic link to the energy of Astral Space, the stuff that gives magic its juice. It gives the group its power the way a genetic link to Astral Space gives power to the magician. Members of an Astral Contact Group get the Karma discount on their Initiations.

Only an Astral Contact group is a true, magical group. Anything else is just a gathering of magicians. Forming such a group is described later in this section.

STRICTURES

Groups usually have *strictures*. Similar to geasa, these are group rules that are tied to the group's magic. If a member breaks a stricture, it may interfere with the group's Astral Contact unless they expel the member responsible. Setting up an Astral Contact takes time (and lots of Karma), so magical groups don't care much for people who mess with the rules.

Some strictures apply to what individual members must or cannot do. If a member violates such a stricture during the game, make a note of it. When the member applies for his next Initiation, this violation may be so serious that the group expels him.

It does not matter whether or not someone witnesses the magician breaking a stricture. The act alone sets up "bad vibes" in his aura that are visible to fellow group members when he wants to take his next Initiation with the group. The question is not whether he gets away with breaking the stricture, but whether the effect of the violation is grave enough to disrupt the group's Astral Contact. There is no way for a magician petitioning for Initiation to conceal that he has broken a stricture.

To determine whether the Initiate's offense is serious, make an Unresisted Magic Test. The Target Number is *twice* the grade the magician is trying to attain and he needs a number of successes *greater* than the number of strictures he has broken.

If the magician passes the test, his slips have not been severe enough to be dangerous. Wipe out the tally of broken rules; the Initiation will give him a clean slate. If he has the Karma to spare, the magician can use Instant Karma to buy the successes he needs.

If he fails the test, the group must either expel the offender or lose their Astral Contact. Many groups won't think twice, and out he goes. Other groups, however, will be inclined to examine whether the member "does the wrong thing for the right reason." Some kind of hearing or trial is in order. The groups may decide to let the erring member remain in the group if he can accomplish some appropriate Quest or Deed. This is an opportunity for some good plot complications or new roleplaying ideas.

If the group loses its Astral Contact, they must restore it before Initiate members can benefit from group membership in reducing the Karma Cost of Initiation. See **Founding a Group**, p. 36.

Rikki Ratboy is an Initiate in a group of Rat shamans, with the strictures of Secrecy and Exclusive Ritual. On his last couple of runs, Rikki threatened one chummer with a curse by the group, and so broke the secrecy rule. He also helped a mage in the team use Ritual Sorcery twice. That is three violations (Rikki always did have this problem with rules). When Rikki is ready to take his next Initiation with the group, his fellow shamans check out his aura and see that he's broken a stricture. Rikki has a Magic Attribute 7 and wants Initiation into Grade 3, so he rolls 7 dice, with a Target Number of 6 (double the grade). He needs 3 successes to wipe out his three violations. He blows it.

Rikki points out to his fellows that he'd have been killed if his curse threat hadn't made the other guy back off. As for the ritual work, it was part of a run that netted him 500,000 nuyen and he's wondering if his fellows wouldn't like to add a 20 percent cut of the cheese to the group bank account. The group sees merit in this argument, but they don't have the time or Karma to spend rebuilding their Astral Contact right now. Despite Rikki's persuasive efforts to buy himself out of trouble, he's out of the Lodge.

A group stricture is a taboo that can only be broken by the group as a whole. Strictures about membership, for example, can only be broken if the group decides to take someone as a member who does not fit the rule. If a group violates one of these strictures or decides to change the strictures that govern them, they lose their Astral Contact, for the group is no longer the same and must forge a new Astral Contact. Some groups break up over such an issue. Some members are unwilling to go through the trouble of "fine-tuning" themselves to Astral Space again.

INDIVIDUAL STRICTURES

These strictures govern the actions of individual members of a group. Most groups usually have three or four such strictures.

Attendance

Magical associations schedule regular meetings for group rituals, at which attendance is mandatory. Most groups with an Attendance stricture schedule such meetings every one to three months, often on dates corresponding with a phase of the moon, the beginning of a season, or some other significant regular interval.

Being out of touch is no excuse for breaking this stricture. It is the member's responsibility to inform the group where they can leave word of the schedules.

Belief

All members must adhere to a specific moral or philosophical belief. Any activity that violates the belief breaks the stricture. Many variations are possible with this stricture, but gamers will probably want to stick with the kinds of moral or religious beliefs familiar to them.

The gamemaster is the final judge of whether a specific action, or lack of action, violates a belief. In the real world, whole libraries have been written in argument over doctrine or dogma.

Exclusive Membership

Members of one magical group may not be members of any other magical group. If a member joins another group, that is, undergoes an Initiation in that group, he breaks this stricture. This can get a little complicated. If a member of an exclusive group joins another exclusive group, he has committed a violation against both.

Exclusive Ritual

Members of the group may not perform Ritual Magic with magicians who are not members of the group. Each time they do, it counts as a violation of the stricture.

Fraternity

Members of the group are expected to do whatever possible to assist other members on request. Refusing to provide assistance that is within the member's ability is a violation.

Karma

Members must spend much free time working on group-related matters. Reduce all Karma Awards to a member of this group by 1. A member can decide not to give up the Karma Point when he gets an award, but this counts as a violation of the Karma stricture.

Obedience

The Obedience stricture requires members to accept commands and demands on non-magical matters. In other words, the group has a say in the private lives of its members. Most such groups have rank systems, with members expected to follow orders from those of higher rank. Rank is usually a function of grade or at least the number of grades taken as an Initiate of that group. Failure to obey a superior in the order violates this stricture.

Secrecy

The group never admits its existence in public. Members never admit to membership. Rumors abound, of course, so magicians looking to join a group may find a connection to a secret group as easily as any other. A secret group may also decide to approach an individual and reveal its existence for some reason. Public exposure of the group is limited, however. If a member tells a non-member that he is part of the group, this breaks this stricture. It is also a violation for a character to tell a non-member about the group even if he does not admit to being a member.

GROUP STRICTURES

These are strictures that only the group, acting as a whole, can break. If the group makes an exception to one of its group strictures, it automatically loses its Astral Contact. It is entirely possible that a magical group will have no group strictures at all.

Limited Membership

The group can only admit individuals of a particular gender, race, religion, and so on. Note that this counts as one stricture even if it includes several limitations. For example, a Dianic coven would be limited to women who practice Wicca (i.e., witchcraft) as a religion.

Link

All members must give the group a material link (**SR**, p. 83). This can be a small cell sample (a few drops of blood will do) or a thesis (see **Initiation**, p. 18). Some groups return this link to a member who leaves the group, while others keep the link as a threat of Ritual Sorcery targeted at members who step out of line. This depends on the philosophy of the group.

Oath

All members must, in their first Initiation with the group, accept the Oath Ordeal (p. 21). If the Initiate has never undergone this Ordeal, it counts for the reduced Karma cost on that Initiation. If he has sworn an oath earlier, then it does not count as an Ordeal, but still binds the Initiate, as specified in the rules.

CUSTOMS

Besides strictures, most magical groups have general rules and customs. Breaking too many of these can also get a member booted out of the group. Unlike violating a stricture, it is not magically visible. Breaking a stricture leaves traces in the offender's aura that are perceived when he comes up for his next Initiation. It does not matter if someone else previously observed him violating the stricture. Violating a custom, on the other hand, has no effect if done in private.

Customs can be sensible or dogmatic, bigoted or enlightened. Groups with a particular political, religious, or social agenda are likely to have customs relating to those agendas. A group of shamans with an Earth Mother religious bent are likely to have customs strongly supportive of conservation or they may even practice eco-terrorism. A group of magicians backed by a local chapter of the Humanis Policlub will probably have some nasty customs relating to Metahumans. A group composed of top corporate wage mages will emphasize loyalty to the corp. Adherence to a group symbology might also be a custom. ("If ya wanna be in the fraggin' group, ya gotta wear the ears!")

Adding customs gives a group some color, and provides concrete details for roleplaying. Customs can also prevent a group from turning into a random set of numbers that players juggle just to get cheap Initiations.

GROUP RESOURCES

Besides Initiations, groups usually have other resources available to members. Resources are rated the same way as Lifestyles (**SR**, p.148) and are supported by member dues. Members can always chip in to buy specific group resources, too. Sometimes, even magicians have to pass the hat.

If the group has a patron, it is he who usually picks up the tab for the resources, making dues either low or non-existent, though members usually owe the patron magical services in return for his support.

Members usually pay their fair share of the cost of maintaining the resources, though at a kind of group discount. Dues are generally equal to the member's share of the cost of maintaining that Lifestyle. Thus, if a group with ten members decides to maintain an Upper Resource Lifestyle, dues would be 10 percent of 10,000 nuyen per month, or 1,000 nuyen per month.

Some groups might, alas, exploit their members, charging, say, Luxury dues but providing only Middle Resources or less. The balance goes into the leadership's pockets. On the other hand, a wealthy patron might provide elegant resources at no charge to members. At least, not in money.

STREET RESOURCES

The group has no material resources at all. Dues are cheap, though. It costs nothing to have a share in nothing. Whenever the group needs to pay for something, members must chip in.

SQUATTER RESOURCES

The group probably has a cheap headquarters set up somewhere, probably in some abandoned area in the Barrens. This would be at least a private place for ritual work. BYOG (Bring Your Own Gear). Not much else.

LOW RESOURCES

The group owns or rents headquarters space and can afford some simple working tools. They have some hermetic libraries or perhaps a permanent Medicine Lodge (roll 1D3 + 3 Rating), depending on the traditions of the members.

MIDDLE RESOURCES

The group has rented a nice space and possesses a decent set of working tools (1D6 + 6 Rating for Libraries and Lodges). Ritual materials are available from the group at a 10 percent discount.

UPPER RESOURCES

The group has a major headquarters somewhere, and either has several lesser offices and temple space elsewhere or can provide living accommodations for members at a Middle Level (but no car, entertainment budget, and so on). It has an excellent library and other facilities (2D6 + 6 Rating) and provides ritual materials to members at 25 percent discount.

LUXURY RESOURCES

The group has magnificent headquarters, possibly even a spacious estate, with a residence, a ritual building, herb gardens, and so on. It also has several other sites for magical use by members or else can provide living accommodations (still at Middle Level but with some perks such as vehicles). The group possesses superb library and lab facilities, equivalent to those of a major corporation or university, with no effective Rating limit. Members can obtain ritual materials at 50 percent discount.

PATRONS

A patron may be either an individual or organization that provides material backing in return for the group's magical assistance. Some patrons are more demanding than others.

Many corporations support magical groups among their top wage mages, and provide them with Luxury Resources. In return, the corp demands and gets the full-time services of the membership. Strictures and customs of such groups are based on loyalty to the all-powerful corp.

Most governments support one or more magical groups. In some cases, this is in return for the good that the magicians do for their people, as is the case of NAN states supporting shamanic lodges. Rumors also exist of government-backed groups involved in intelligence and other operations.

It is reputed that the High Prince of Tir Tairngire supports a group composed solely of physical adepts trained as assassins. Tir Tairngire's Paladins, the powerful secret police of the High Prince, are known to sponsor a magical group that provides magicians for covert operations.

The UCAS government is rumored to support at least one group of mages who are all FBI agents. It's a safe bet that the CIA is not without its house magicians, either.

Several policlubs are reputed to maintain magical groups. Even clubs that oppose the use of magic may secretly do so, presumably on the theory of "fighting fire with fire."

It is safe to assume that a major corp or government can provide any level of resources it desires. A wealthy individual or lesser corp might have to watch the nuyen. An individual supporting a group has to pay the "guest" charge for the resource level he is providing: 10 percent of the regular price per member, per p. 148 of **Shadowrun**.

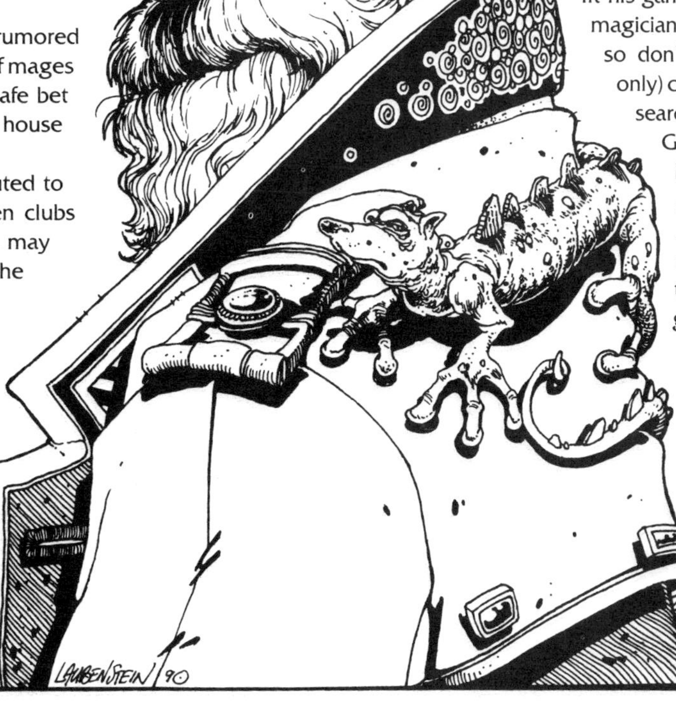

FINDING A GROUP

Like the old recipe for rabbit stew, first you gotta catch a rabbit. To join a group, the character must find one. Unless a magician comes into contact with a group while playing the game, he's gonna have to spend time following leads, visiting contacts, and doing other legwork to find a group. All he can do is hope that eventually one magical group will let him join. Of course, these same rules apply when someone is looking for a magical group for other reasons.

It takes a base time of 60 days to find a magical group. The magician should make an Unresisted Success Test using either Etiquette (Magical) or Magical Theory, whichever is higher. The Target Number is 12 minus his Magic Attribute. Reduce the Target Number by 1 for every one of the magician's contacts who is also a magician, talismonger, or fixer who deals often with magicians.

To find out how long it takes to locate a group, divide 60 days by the number of successes. If there are no successes, the character wastes 60 days. He might find a group that would not accept him as a member for all the nuyen in the Geneva computer banks. The time needed to search can be broken up into shorter segments. Ideally, the gamemaster makes a secret roll to determine how much time the character has. The magician might spend 10 days doing legwork, then go on a run, spend another 5 days, work on a spell, do another 10 days searching, and so on.

A non-magician can try to find a group the same way. He needs the same skills, but has no Magic Attribute to reduce the Target Number.

The gamemaster, meanwhile, can either randomly roll up a group (see **Building a Group** p. 37) or design one specifically to fit his game. It should be possible for the magician to join the group that he finds, so don't build a Dianic (i.e., women only) coven restricted to shamans if the searching character is a male mage. Give the poor spell-tosser a break by letting the magician find a group he likes and qualifies for. As the gamemaster develops more groups for his game world, there will be a wider menu of groups from which magicians can choose.

All this dice-rolling and legwork assumes that a magician is looking for a group at random. If he knows the name of a group, or at least one member personally, he can probably find it just by asking around. At worst, cut the base time for the search down to 30 days if the character knows what he is looking for. And if he is a *simpatico* kind of guy, the group may even look *him* up and invite him to join.

JOINING A GROUP

To join a group costs the new member 3 Karma Points and the first month's dues, so the character must have that on hand. Another member or members can put up the Karma, however. The Karma represents time spent preparing for membership, learning group rituals, and other preliminaries. Another member can also lend or put up the dues money, particularly if the group is eager to have the character join.

If the character has the Karma and the cash, the group will test him to determine whether his "vibes" blend well enough with the group's existing structure not to disturb its Astral Contact. He makes an Unresisted Success Test using his best score in a Magical Skill or his Magic Attribute, with a Target Number equal to the group's current membership. If the applicant is already an Initiate, reduce the Target Number by his grade. One success and he's in. If the test fails, the group cannot accept the applicant just now. He can try again in 1D6 months, reducing the Target Number by half on the second application. If he fails the test again, the group just cannot admit the magician.

Of course, if the character has the Karma to spare, he can use Instant Karma to buy the needed success.

FOUNDING A GROUP

It is possible that several player-character magicians may decide they do not want to join another group and follow somebody else's rules. Instead they want to declare themselves a group and, by the way, get Initiated on the cheap.

Nice try, chummers.

Remember that only an Astral Contact group is a true magical group, and that does not come easy. Without Astral Contact, members do not get the benefit of group Initiations.

So, what does it take to found a real magical group? For starters, it takes two or more members, each paying the 3 Karma Points to join. Then, once a month, the group tests to establish an Astral Contact. The number of dice rolled is equal to the number of members in the group. Members can "buy" another die for a test for 3 Karma Points. If the test fails, the extra die purchased does not carry over. Next month, an extra die will cost another 3 Karma Points. Members can pool their Karma to buy these dice. The Target Number for the Astral Contact Test is 12, with the following modifiers:

Group admits both shamans and mages	+2
Per stricture the group adopts	−1
Any member previously initiated in an Astral Contact group	−2
Per month of dedicated work by all members	−1

Dedicated work, as usual, means the members do *nothing else* all month except the assorted rituals and meditations needed to attempt to establish contact. No other training, healing, or shadowrunning.

Neddy, a mage, and Sings-To-Clouds, a shaman, decide to start a magical group. Each pays 3 Karma Points to join, and they decide to adopt the strictures of Secrecy and Oath. Previous to this, Neddy was an Initiate of a hermetic order until an unfortunate misunderstanding took place. When the first month's Astral Contact Test comes along, they roll 2 dice (two members). The Base Target Number 12 is modified as follows:

+2 for admitting both shamans and mages.

−2 for the two strictures taken.

−2 for Neddy's previous Initiation in Contact group.

The modified Target Number is 10. The dice come up 5 and 3. No contact this month.

The two magicians confer and decide to spend the next month hunkered down and working on their rituals in Neddy's hideout. When test time rolls around, each spends another 3 Karma Points for an extra die, so that 4 dice are rolled in all. The Target Number goes down to 9, because they have spent one month of exclusive work on the contact. The dice come up 8, 7, 4, 4. Drek!

This time, the magicians go their separate ways for a month, with Neddy pulling a run with Serena, another mage. He and Serena worked so well together that Neddy persuades Sings-To-Clouds that Serena should join their new group. She agrees, but is short on Karma. Neddy sighs and puts up 3 Karma Points for her. With three group members, the test requires 3 dice rolled this month, but the Target Number is still 9. This time they get lucky, rolling 9, 3, 5. The group has made an Astral Contact and can now initiate members at the reduced cost for groups.

BUILDING A GROUP

Though players may found their own group, a gamemaster will probably have to create one or more groups, too.

Magical groups do not just emerge. They usually have specific goals. The gamemaster will probably want to create one or two well-thought-out groups rather than a dozen randomly created ones.

The gamemaster can use the tables below to randomly generate groups, but he will benefit most by using the tables only to fill in minor details or when he needs to whip up a group in a hurry.

When creating a group, it is usually because the gamemaster wants to help the characters, threaten the characters, or because a character wants to join a group. In each case, he must ask himself why the group would want to help, harm, or associate with the player characters.

Helpful groups may share some goal that the runners are supporting (whether they know it or not). For example, if the run is directed against a corporate plan to "maximize a natural resource" (i.e., strip-mine and pollute the hell out of an area), then a shamanic group dedicated to preserving Mother Earth would wish to help the runners, even if the team's employer were a rival corporation trying to block the plan for its own reasons and the runners are only doing it for the nuyen.

Hostile groups are usually that way because the runners are interfering with some plan or interest of theirs or their patron. Such groups don't have to be "evil." For example, a group of corporate mages would try to defend their employers' interests against the scum-bucket street slime who are ripping them off. Or the runners might be pawns in some nasty corp plot, up against a magical group opposing the real reason for the run (which, of course, the players don't even suspect).

If the gamemaster is creating a group for a player magician to join, the ideal situation is for both gamemaster and player to build the group together. The player can outline what he's looking for in a magical group, with the gamemaster reserving the right to add strictures, invent customs that might not be exactly to the player's liking, and so on. It is primarily a cooperative venture, but the gamemaster is free to add anything that might lead to interesting subplots or dramatic tension.

GROUP PURPOSE

A group will have some reason for existing quite apart from its relationship to the player characters. Few, if any, magical groups come into being with the avowed purpose of "making life difficult for shadowrunners."

There are several general purposes that might motivate magical groups.

An **initiatory group** has the pursuit of magical knowledge and its development of the individual members as its primary purpose. Such a group may also have a social, political, or religious agenda, but its main reason for being is to promote the magical arts and share the experiences and resources of members. Initiatory groups range from open organizations that welcome genuine seekers of knowledge to narrow-minded secret organizations that tolerate no challenges to their model of reality and are contemptuous of outsiders. Magical knowledge and grade of Initiation usually determine formal or informal ranking within the group.

A **dedicated group**, on the other hand, usually has a specific religious or moral bias, linking its magic closely to its spiritual code. This type group will tend to use magic to refine its pursuit of this belief and to teach or demonstrate that belief to the rest of the world. Dedicated groups can range from organizations devoted to helping and protecting humanity with magic to fanatic organizations that want to use magic to force their views on others. Magical ability is usually the main factor in formal or informal rank within the group, but "correct" behavior can count for more than grade or skill.

A **conspiratorial group** is dedicated to a specific goal, usually involving power and wealth, ruthlessly using its magic and other resources to obtain it. For them, magic is a tool and a weapon. Such a group is usually secret and tends to seek control over its members, using strictures like Oath, Link, and Obedience to get it. Skill and grade are minor considerations in ranking. Politics and dedication to "the cause" count most. Conspiratorial groups can range from zealous freedom fighters trying to save "the masses" from tyranny (whether the masses want salvation or not) to masked plotters who meet in secret as they plot to enslave the world.

These three classes are, of course, gross oversimplifications. Some groups might combine all these qualities, but defining the basic nature of the group will be vital to deciding what strictures and customs make sense.

MEMBERSHIP SIZE

Most groups have a dozen or so members. Many are smaller, and a few may be much larger. Choose the size or roll 2D6 and consult the Membership Table. Larger groups, with a hundred or more members, might exist, but there would be no more than two or three such groups on Earth. You can't get that many magicians to agree on much of anything, much less on magical practice.

MEMBERSHIP TABLE

Die Roll	Membership
2 – 3	2 – 4 (1D3 + 1)
4 – 5	2 – 7 (1D6 + 1)
6 – 8	8 – 13 (1D6 + 7)
9 – 11	12 – 22 (2D6 + 10)
12	10 – 60 (2D6 x 5)

MEMBERSHIP LIMITATIONS

Most groups tend to have a limited membership stricture. Just as social groups tend to prefer like-minded members, magical groups value this trait even more. The most common restriction regards magical tradition, with most groups limited to either mages or shamans. Groups can mix traditions, but the psychological tensions it generates make establishing the Astral Contact even more difficult.

Be that as it may, decide on the limitations appropriate to the group being created or roll 2D6 and consult the **Membership Restrictions Table**. This table offers general ideas that the gamemaster may modify or use as a starting point for his own preferences.

MEMBERSHIP RESTRICTIONS TABLE

Die Roll	Restrictions
2	No restrictions
3 – 4	Biological Limitation: A member must be of specific gender or race.
5 – 6	Religious/Moral Limitation: A member must subscribe to a specific religion or moral code. This would include members of political activist groups.
7 – 8	Tradition: Group is limited to a single tradition (hermetic or shamanic only).
9 – 10	Social Limitation: Members must maintain a specific lifestyle, be it from specific culture, work for a given corp, and so on.
11 – 12	Two limitations: Roll 1D6 + 3 and consult table twice.

MEMBERSHIP STRICTURES

Having determined the group's basic purpose and fleshed it out with membership restrictions, several strictures will seem obvious. To randomly decide on strictures or to get an idea of which strictures are typical for certain groups, see the **Strictures Table**, which shows the chance on 1D6 that a given type of group will have a given stricture. For a completely random selection, roll 1D6 for each stricture to see if it applies to the group. The gamemaster may roll for strictures in the order he feels most appropriate for the group.

STRICTURES TABLE

Stricture	Initiatory Group	Dedicated Group	Conspirital Group
Attendance Exclusive	1 – 2	1 – 4	1 – 3
Membership Exclusive	1 – 2	1 – 5	1 – 4
Ritual	1 – 3	1 – 5	1 – 5
Fraternity	1 – 4	1 – 4	1 – 5
Karma	1 – 5	1 – 4	1 – 4
Link	1	1 – 2	1 – 5
Oath	1 – 2	1 – 5	Always
Obedience	1	1 – 4	1 – 5
Belief	1	Always	1 – 5
Secrecy	1 – 2	1 – 3	1 – 5

RESOURCES, DUES, AND PATRONS

Resources, Dues, and Patrons will be dictated by how a group fits into the campaign. If the gamemaster prefers to randomly select a group's resources, roll 2D6 and consult the **Resources Table**. To see if a group has a patron, roll 1D6 and consult the **Chance of Patron** column.

RESOURCES TABLE

Die Roll	Group Resources	Chance of Patron (Roll 1D6)
2	Street	None
3 – 4	Squatter	None
5 – 6	Low	1
7 – 8	Middle	1
9 – 11	High	1 – 2
12	Luxury	1 – 4

Monthly dues will be equal to the cost of maintaining this lifestyle (see **SR**, p. 148), divided by the number of members.

PRE-GENERATED MAGICAL GROUPS

The following descriptions may be useful to gamemasters who would like to work with a more developed idea before generating magical groups of their own, as examples of magical groups, or for use in a pinch.

SISTERHOOD OF ARIADNE

The Sisterhood is a dedicated group, its membership limited to women who are Wiccans. Wicca is another name, some say the true name, of the religion more commonly known as Witchcraft. Despite the propaganda of various governments and churches through the centuries, witchcraft has NO connection to devil worship or evil magic. Wicca (as practiced by the Sisterhood, anyway) is a religion oriented toward the worship of the Earth, or Nature. The Sisterhood is also somewhat militant, believing that patriarchy (male rule of society) is responsible for most of the planet's ills. They believe that matriarchy, rule by women, is a more natural and harmonious state. This puts them in the "Dianic," or strongly matriarchal, subset of Witches.

In addition, the Sisterhood opposes ecological pollution and exploitation of the Earth, and will use magic if gentler means fail.

Name: Sisterhood of Ariadne
Type: Dedicated (Religion: Wicca)
Members: 13
Limitations: Women only. Wiccans only.
Strictures:

Attendance: Monthly esbats (full moon rituals).

Fraternity (in this case, read Sorority).

Religious Obligation: Wicca. Protect the Earth. Uphold rights of women. No harmful magic except to protect self or the Earth.

Secrecy.

Resources/Dues: Middle. Dues are presently about 450 nuyen per month. The coven has leased a small house in a more rural section of town, with enough privacy to do some ritual work outdoors. The group buys magical supplies in bulk for the membership. The house also has a decent library of hermetic books (Sorcery 8, Conjuring 4), and the coven owns a portable Medicine Lodge with a Rating 5.

Customs: Strongly feminist politics. Membership limited to 13, a tradition in Wicca. Male visitors are absolutely forbidden at rituals. Many members are also active in promoting Metahuman rights, and there are three Orks, a Troll, and an Elf in the coven. Though open to both magical traditions, the group tends toward shamanism, and only two members are mages. The group is loosely affiliated with eco-activist policlubs, including those such as Greenwar, suspected of terrorist activities. Members often provide magical assistance on runs against corps attempting to pollute or exploit resources.

HERMETIC ORDER OF THE AURIC AURORA

Established in Seattle in the early 1990s, this Order is devoted to magical research and the development of its members. Though dedicated to the scholarly study of magic, the Order also uses its resources to oppose the use of magic to oppress or harm. Rumor has it that mages from the Order helped the team of runners who broke up the "wiz-kid" gang trying to enforce a magical protection racket on a Redmond neighborhood at the fringe of the Barrens.
Name: Hermetic Order of the Auric Aurora
Type: Initiatory
Members: 25
Limitations: Mages only
Strictures: Fraternity. Karma. Oath. Secrecy.
Resources/Dues: Middle. Dues currently 200 nuyen per month. Hermetic libraries in Sorcery, Conjuring, and Enchanting, all at Rating 9. Enchanting shop on premises. The Order operates out of its leader's home, a sizable storefront near Pacific University. The basement serves as ritual space for the Order. The ground floor is a small lore store, known to the cognoscenti as a place to find excellent buys. Living quarters are upstairs. Members receive a 25 percent discount at the store.
Customs: Personal freedom is highly valued. However, the Order prefers a quiet, scholarly approach to magic, and frowns on violent shadowrunning. Healing and magical assistance to the needy are the principle pursuits of the members, along with study and initiation. Though the Order has no formal stricture mandating an ethical code, the group maintains a high standard of ethics.

MITSUHAMA RESEARCH UNIT 12

Funded heavily by MCT and composed of wage mages loyal to the company, Research Unit 12 is a typical corporate group. It is part of MCT's internal security operation and serves as a "SWAT team" when magic is used against the corporation.

Research Unit 12 also carries out spot checks of site security, using mental control and Mind Probe Spells to "validate" employee attitudes, and maintain astral observation on important and/or suspect members of R&D teams.
Name: MCT Research Unit 12
Type: Dedicated/Conspiratorial (Protect and promote MCT interests)
Members: 6
Limitations: Mages only. MCT employees only.
Strictures: Exclusive membership. Exclusive ritual. Link. Oath. Obedience (to corporate superiors as well as to superiors within Research Unit 12).
Resources/Dues: Luxury. No dues.
Patron: Mitsuhama Computer Technology.
Customs: Members are expected to be loyal to MCT, though they cultivate a cynical attitude toward the more sentimental aspects of corp culture: group social activities, singing the company hymn, and so on. Success is the only measure of status. Failure is not acceptable. Unit 12 will use any means necessary to achieve a desired result. Members are expected to offer lavish "gifts" to their superiors when they come up for Initiation. The going rate is cash or goods worth 1,000 nuyen times the superior's grade.

BEAR DOCTOR SOCIETY

The Bear Doctor Society is a typical tribal group of shamans, devoted to the healing magic at which the Bear totem excels. This particular group is located in the Salish, but similar organizations flourish all over NAN territory.
Name: Bear Doctor Society
Type: Initiatory
Members: 8
Limitations: Bear totem shamans only. Salish tribe members only.
Strictures: Fraternity. Oath. Moral Obligation (see **Customs**).
Resources/Dues: High. Members pay half normal dues; community pays the balance. Current dues are 625 nuyen per month. The society maintains a Bear Medicine Lodge 8, as well as a 20-bed hospital with living quarters for members. This is in the Salish territory, of course.
Patron: The Salish tribe.
Customs: Most members are trained biotechs or otherwise skilled in the life sciences. The society keeps up with modern medical practice as well as magical and traditional tribal healing methods. Salish patients receive treatment free of charge, as do any patients who cannot pay. The society is devoted to protecting life and forbids needless killing. The requirements of the Bear totem are also viewed as moral obligations.

THE MOONLIGHT THORNS

A group composed of physical adepts, the Moonlight Thorns are the private bodyguards of a high Tir Tairngire nobleman. They are also rumored to be his elite assassins.
Name: The Moonlight Thorns
Type: Conspiratorial
Members: 5
Limitations: Elves only. Physical adepts only.
Strictures: Exclusive membership. Link. Oath. Obedience (to lord as well as group superiors). Secrecy.
Resources/Dues: Luxury. No dues. Members are luxuriously housed in their patron's estate, where they maintain a well-stocked dojo and armory. The group maintains safe houses as needed on missions.
Patron: Tir Tairngire nobleman.
Customs: Members are fanatically loyal to their patron, and members have sacrificed their lives to save his. According to rumors about the Thorns as assassins, they will not return alive from an unsuccessful mission: they either kill their target or die trying.

ENCHANTING

"The eye of the master melts the metal."
—11th-century alchemical maxim

nchanting is a general magical skill, similar to Sorcery and Conjuring, and fits into their branch of the Skill Web.

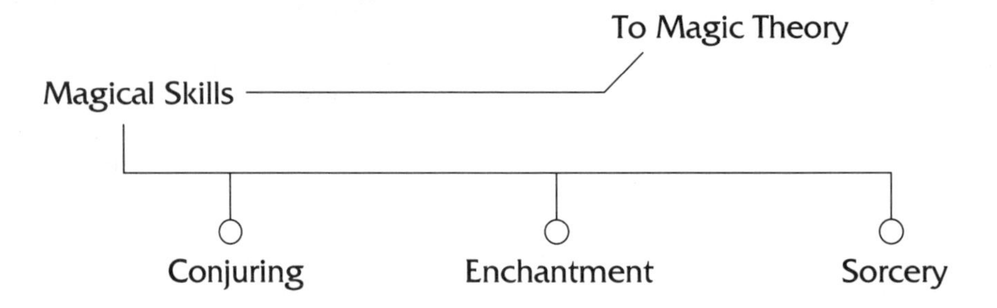

Enchanting governs the manufacture of magical ritual materials and fetishes (Talismongering), refining special magical materials (Alchemy), and making magical focuses (Artificing). Anyone, even a mundane, can use Talismongering Skill, but only a fully capable magician or an enchanter (i.e., an Enchanting Adept) can handle Alchemy and Artificing.

Enchanting is also useful for analyzing focuses and for reducing the cost of bonding them.

Talismongering, Alchemy, and Artificing are the three areas of concentration possible under Enchanting.

Talismongering is the manufacture of fetishes for a specific Spell Purpose (Combat, Health, and so on). It includes raw-material collection and analysis of magical items and materials.

Alchemy is the Arcanum of Herbs, the Arcanum of Minerals, and the Arcanum of Metals.

Artificing concerns a specific type of focus, and reduces bonding cost.

ENCHANTING AND DRAIN

Unlike other forms of magic, Enchanting causes no Drain. The magician brings the magical energy into manifestation very gradually, and "grounds" it safely into the item being enchanted. The wear-and-tear on the magician is thus reduced below the danger point.

Enchanting takes a good deal of Karma, however, as well as time and money. These requirements keep the flow of magical materials and items well under the demand in the marketplace. There are no assembly lines of burned-out mages grinding out magical goodies. Magic is an art, not a technology.

ENCHANTING GEAR

Enchanting requires special equipment, which comes under the heading of "working gear" (**SR**, p.124). Enchanting gear comes in kit or shop forms. There is no "facility" equivalent in enchanting, as all tasks are on a "craftsman" level and do not use factory-type resources. Of course, a magician might need a facility of the appropriate type to build a complex object from scratch before he starts enchanting it.

An enchanting kit is needed for Talismongering and to gather raw materials for enchanting. It can also be used to refine herbal or mineral materials. It costs 10,000 nuyen, and the gear will fit inside a large backpack or suitcase. Think of it as a good, portable chemistry kit with some, er, unusual extra supplies.

An enchanting shop is needed for Artificing or Alchemy, for analyzing materials or items, and for refining metal ores. It costs 100,000 nuyen. The equipment will fit into a mid-sized van, but to use it requires room to spread out (about 50 square meters). This is especially true if working with metals or doing Alchemy, which involve running furnaces and forges. *Not* recommended inside a van! This also means a shop for working in these materials needs fuel for the furnace, forge, and so on: electrical current, natural gas, fuel oil, or a plentiful supply of wood or coal. A shop can, of course, do anything a kit can do (except fit inside a backpack).

For gathering raw materials, or doing some talismongering, the gear is all that is needed. If the character plans to get into Alchemy or Artificing, there are other requirements. A shaman must carry out these operations in a Medicine Lodge. A mage needs a hermetic library for Enchanting Skill.

TALISMONGERING

Talismongering is concerned with the elements of enchanting that do not produce anything inherently magical. Rather, it is concerned with locating raw materials and preparing fetishes and ritual materials.

A character need not be magically active to do this. Many genuine talismongers are mundanes whose goods are plenty effective. Talismongering involves knowledge of plant lore, a little mineralogy, and the centuries-old formulas to make charms, powders, incenses, lucky pieces, and similar junk. That is, it seemed like junk until the Awakening came along.

Talismongering can take some of the strain off the credstik if a character has been burning up the old fetishes a lot lately. Indeed, a magician may often find it essential to gather his own raw materials when making a focus absolutely from scratch, which is very powerful magic.

ENCHANTING MATERIALS

The three general classes of material used in Enchanting are Herbal, Mineral, and Metal.

Herbal materials are plants, roots, flowers, bark, wood, even molds and fungus.

Mineral materials are crystals, precious and semi-precious stones, and rocks in general.

Metal materials are separate from minerals and include ores of iron, gold, copper, tin, aluminum, and the other metals.

GATHERING MATERIALS

Whether it is a walk in the woods or an expedition into the howling wilderness, Enchanting Skill can be used to gather raw materials for making fetishes and focuses. This makes for some good adventure ideas, too. The formula for certain magical items can turn out to require rare goodies found only in some out-of-the-way corner of the Earth. Even if that is not the case, magicians get special benefits when making focuses from never-used raw materials. Often, the only way to be sure that materials are virgin is to gather them personally.

The magician may have to travel to a remote location to find the right resources. This is a gamemaster decision, though he can work it out in cooperation with the player. Because of the resource rush (or resource rape, as some call it) that peaked in the early 21st century, it can take a real trek to find a source of ores or minerals that is not so polluted that all the magic is either gone or poisonously twisted.

Ironically, the demand for crystals and similar "New Age" goods in the 80s and 90s contributed to the poisoning of sources for magically useful materials. Entrepreneurs would zip into a park or other natural preserve at night, dynamite a hillside, scoop up the shattered quartz deposits, and sell the bones of Mother Earth to the hip disciples of the New Age as "power stones." Of course, not a scrap of magical energy was left in the minerals after such operations.

Most of the decent spots for materials-gathering are in NAN territory, and the citizens of NAN are not fond of outsiders, whether magicians or corporate strip miners, sneaking in to tear the life from Mother Earth. That makes tribal connections a real bonus for any would-be enchanter.

THE GATHERING TEST

Gathering one "unit" of raw materials takes a base period of 10 days. Make an Unresisted Enchanting Test with a Target Number 4. Divide the base time by the number of successes to determine the actual time spent. If no successes are rolled, the character spends 10 days finding nothing.

"Sheesh! Ten days to pick some fragging flowers?" he asks. Nope. Ten days (or a fraction thereof) to find a large enough amount of material of the right type, stage of growth, and quality to use in magic. This is not merely scooping up armfuls of shrubbery. The magician must examine every leaf before he decides it is right for magical use.

If the character has a special skill or concentration related to the material he is gathering, he makes another test using that skill, and adds the successes to those scored for Enchanting. For example, if he is seeking metal ores and has skill in Metallurgy, Geology, Mining, or other similar science, the player makes Unresisted Success Tests using Enchanting and that skill, both with a Target Number 4. He combines the successes from both tests to reduce the time it takes to gather a unit of raw material.

A shaman searching for materials in a domain suitable to his totem (even if his version of the totem "lives" in another domain) adds his Totem Advantage dice to the test. Thus, a Raccoon shaman gets this advantage unless she is in the mountains. Coyote gets the bonus anywhere on land, and so on.

Clever magicians may wonder if they can enlist the aid of Spirits. Indeed, they can. An Elemental of the appropriate type (almost always Earth) or a Nature Spirit can assist in finding materials. Add a number of dice equal to the Spirit's Force Rating to the Success Test.

A unit of metal or mineral ore weighs about 10 kilograms. A unit of plant material weighs about 5 kilograms.

The character must carry out certain ritual procedures when gathering raw materials, and these require an enchanting kit. The gamemaster may also require such useful items as picks, shovels, and pails. The use of heavy mining gear, powered tools, and anything that pollutes the environment (including explosives) will destroy the magical energy of the materials gathered.

Commercially mined or produced materials can be used to make a focus, but the enchanted object does not get the bonus for virgin materials.

REFINING MATERIALS

It requires only an enchanting kit to refine herbal materials. Refining metals takes an enchanting shop. For minerals, it depends on the purpose for which they will be used. Minerals meant for fetishes can be refined with a kit. Minerals meant for focuses require a shop.

The base time for refining materials is 10 days, and the character can process a maximum number of units of raw material equal to his Intelligence Attribute.

He makes an Unresisted Enchanting Test, with a Target Number 4. Divide the base time by the number of successes rolled to determine how long it really took. As with gathering materials, a relevant mundane skill can speed things up. If no successes are rolled, something has gummed up the works and nothing was refined. Try again. If the Rule of Ones raises its head, the raw materials have been spoiled and are of no magical value.

Success means that the raw materials are now refined. One unit of refined material is produced for each unit of raw material at the start. A unit of refined material weighs half as much as the original raw material: 2.5 kilograms for herbals and 5 kilograms for metals or minerals, per the table on p. 109.

Refined materials are used to make fetishes, virgin focuses, or as raw material for Alchemy.

MAKING FETISHES

Having obtained refined materials, whether prepared personally or purchased from a trusted dealer, the character can use Enchanting to make fetishes.

One unit of refined materials can make a number of expendable fetishes equal to a character's Intelligence or make one reusable fetish. To see how long it takes, the player makes an Unresisted Enchanting Test with a Target Number 4 and divides the number of successes into 24 hours. What? No successes? Well, chummer, the magician just blew 24 hours. Try again. A roll of all 1s leaves him with ruined materials—trashed, useless, kaput.

MAKING RITUAL MATERIALS

Refined materials are suitable for making the special ritual materials needed in Ritual Sorcery, Conjuring, building Medicine Lodges, and so on. These are almost always herbal or mineral compounds, which can be made with an enchanting kit.

Use the same ratings and tests for Making Ritual Materials as for Making Fetishes.

ANALYZING MAGICAL ITEMS

A character with Enchanting Skill can analyze any magical material or item. He need not be magically active to do this, but being able to assense the item does help.

No matter what the subject of the analysis, analyzing magical items requires an enchanting shop.

The base time to analyze an item is 24 hours. Make an Unresisted Enchanting Test with the appropriate Target Number from the **Magical Analysis Table** below. If the character can assense the material, reduce the Target Number by 1. Because the Target Number reveals the basic nature of the item under study, the gamemaster may want to keep the Target Number secret.

Divide the number of successes into 24 hours to see how long the analysis will take. As usual, if the character scores no successes, he is not able to determine the nature of the material or item at the end of 24 hours but can try again. On a roll of all 1s, the character has succeeded only in destroying the item he was studying.

Successful analysis tells the character what the material is and its rating (if it has one). It can even tell the difference between refined materials gathered with the correct procedures and mundane material with no magical qualities.

Of course, magicians can usually get this information simply by assensing the material (see **Astral Space**, p. 60). The cumbersome analysis technique is generally used by mundanes or adepts who cannot assense.

MAGICAL ANALYSIS TABLE

Magical Analysis	Target Number
Item Not Magical	3
Refined Raw Material	3
Ritual Material or Fetish	4
Alchemical Radical	5
Focus	Rating

ALCHEMY

A character can use Enchanting Skill to further process refined materials to make alchemical materials called *radicals*. When making a focus, the use of alchemical radicals makes it easier for the character to enchant the focus and may help reduce the Karma cost.

According to rumor, at least six or seven corps are carrying out feverish research to reproduce other legendary products of alchemy, but none has announced any success so far. Alchemical materials have only proven useful in the work of Enchanting. The old tales about magical potions, transmutation, and other such processes may turn out to be nothing more than that.

ARCANA

Alchemy deals with Enchanting raw materials to make radicals. As mentioned earlier, the three classes of Enchanting materials are herbals, minerals, and metals. Each class is an *arcanum* in Alchemy (plural = *arcana*). Unless someone specializes, the arcana do not matter much on the alchemical side of things, but the concept becomes important if a magician is using radicals when he actually enchants a focus.

MAKING RADICALS

Alchemy requires an enchanting shop. The process of trying to produce radicals from mundane materials takes 28 days (one lunar month), and this time may not be reduced. The Target Number for the Success Test is equal to the number of units of refined materials being processed. Remember that a target number can never be less than 2, even if processing involves only a single unit of material.

The alchemist must spend the entire time babysitting the cranky stages of the alchemical process, or *circulation*, as it is called. If he is away from the shop for any extended period, he must make an Unresisted Enchanting Test with a Target Number equal to the number of *hours* he left the circulation unattended. If the test fails, the process aborts and the character must start over. He can have another alchemist take care of business for him, but the second alchemist's Enchanting Skill must be at least as high as the first one's.

The procedures are very demanding and leave no time for study, other magical work, and so on. At the end of 28 days, the alchemist makes the Success Test. If he passes, he has produced a number of units of radicals equal to the original number of units he started with, multiplied by his successes.

A unit of radical material weighs one-hundredth as much as the raw material: 50 grams for herbals and 100 grams for metals or minerals, per the table on p. 109.

Peter Puffer sets up a circulation to produce radical iron for use in making a mageblade. He loads 3 units of refined iron ore into his alchemical furnace and begins his long task. After four weeks of catnaps, quick, skimpy meals, and cajoling the cranky equipment through the delicate steps of the circulation, he cracks the sealed vessel containing the material. Puffer has Enchanting Skill 5, so he rolls 5 dice. His Target Number is 3 because he started with 3 units of materials. He rolls 1, 3, 3, 4, 5: four successes. Puffer beams as he pours the molten mass from the philosophical vessel into a cooling bath. The 3 original units times 4 successes has yielded 12 units of radical iron.

ORICHALCUM

According to legend, it was the priest-kings of ancient Atlantis who first discovered orichalcum. Whether or not that is true, this orange-gold alloy is utterly absurd from any chemical or metallurgical point of view and only Alchemy can create it. This requires a special circulation, carried out as follows.

Combine one unit each of the radicals of copper, gold, silver, and mercury, the "raw materials" needed for the alchemical circulation. The circulation proceeds normally until the time for the final Success Test. The Target Number is 10, less the alchemist's Magic Attribute. The number of successes determines how many units are created. The alchemist can reduce the target number even more by spending Karma: 1 point reduces the Target Number by –1. He can also use Instant Karma to buy additional successes, as usual.

If the test succeeds, the alchemist produces a unit of orichalcum for every success. If the test fails, the circulation must continue for another 28 days. If the die rolls are all 1s, the process has been botched and the raw materials destroyed.

Orichalcum is of tremendous value in making focuses and has many uses. A unit of orichalcum weighs only 10 grams.

FOCUSES

Many magical items, or *focuses,* known to magicians of the Sixth World are described in **Shadowrun**, p. 79. This **Grimoire** adds some new ones and also twists on some of the originals.

FETISH FOCUS

The fetish focus is a new item. An expendable fetish that has been enchanted, a fetish focus can be used by anyone to enhance the casting of a spell. Once. The spell need not require a fetish, but if it does, the use of the fetish focus fulfills that requirement.

A fetish focus is similar to a spell purpose focus in that there are combat fetish focuses, manipulation fetish focuses, and so on.

Unlike other focuses, these items are popular because making one is a relatively quick and fairly inexpensive process and because they can be used by any magician without bonding.

The fetish focus has a rating, which may be used in one of two ways. First, the rating may be used as a number of extra dice to enhance the Success Test for casting the spell. Second, the rating can be used to resist Drain for casting the spell. In this case, the rating counts as automatic successes in Resisting Drain.

Unlike the dice provided by more flexible focuses, the fetish focus rating may not be split, with some dice allocated to casting a spell and some dice allocated to Resisting Drain. The character must decide which of the two functions the focus will serve at the time he creates it. When using the fetish focus, he applies the entire rating to fulfill its function.

SPELL LOCK

The spell lock remains as described in the basic game, with the following clarifications.

Like all focuses, a spell lock must be bonded. This can occur either prior to use or at the time that the lock is actually used. The bonding cost of a spell lock is always 1 Karma Point. No special procedure or game mechanic exists for this; the magician simply wills a spell lock bonded, spends the Karma Point, and he has a spell lock. The Karma spent must belong to the casting magician.

The spell lock will "lock" any sustained spell onto its target. The spell becomes permanent, and only Astral Combat or Dispelling can break it. Spell locks cannot be used to lock instant spells and they are not necessary to hold truly permanent spells.

Remember that the effective Force of a spell held by a spell lock is always 1 point. This is its rating for resisting Dispelling or for defending itself in Astral Combat. It is easy to overcome a spell lock. It does not matter if it is locking a spell with a Force of 1 or 100: the spell lock itself has a Rating of 1, which is what a magician must try to overcome if he wishes to break a locked spell.

The spellcaster must "attune" the lock to the spell as he casts it. If the spell succeeds, the spell lock is bound to that casting and cannot be used to lock any other spell. If the spell fails to overcome the target's resistance, however, the magician can use the lock again, either for a second try or for some other spell entirely. A magician may *not* cast a successful spell, then decide that its effects are too puny and try to cast a stronger version before using the lock. Neither can a magician decide to lock a spell after it succeeds. He must make the decision to use the lock before making his success test, and abide by the consequences of that decision.

The spell must be sustained until the spell lock can be attached to the target. If the spell is dropped before this, the spell lock is destroyed. The caster need not physically place the spell, however. As long as the magician has both the spell lock and the target visible, he may attune the spell to target as he casts it.

If using the spell lock to lock a spell cast by ritual sorcery, the caster can use the "astral spotting" method to pinpoint the target if it is not in his own life-of-sight. Both target and spell lock must be in sight of the spotting magician or elemental (**SR**, p. 83), however. It is entirely possible for magical terrorists to obtain a spell lock and get it into the hands of an intended victim. Then, spotting the spellcaster astrally, they slam their nasty magic into him, and it immediately becomes permanent.

This is just one more reason why firms specializing in astral security rarely lack for customers.

SPELL PURPOSE FOCUS

The spell purpose focus is described in the basic game. It provides extra dice for any test needed to cast a spell of the same purpose, to resist its Drain, or defend against attacking spells with that purpose. Rating points may be permanently sacrificed to buy automatic successes in any of these tests.

SPECIFIC SPELL FOCUS

Specific spell focuses are described in the basic game. They provide extra dice for casting a specific spell. These dice may apply to the Success Test to cast the spell and to resist Drain from that spell, but may not be used for any other purpose. Rating points may be sacrificed to buy automatic successes in any of these tests.

SPIRIT FOCUS

As described in the basic game, a Spirit focus is specific to the type of Spirit. A Fire Elemental focus, for example, is useless for conjuring other Elementals, a Forest Spirit focus will not impress a Storm Spirit, and so on.

Watcher focuses can be created as well.

The Spirit Focus Rating may add extra dice to any tests needed for conjuring, controlling, or banishing a spirit of the correct type. Rating points may be permanently sacrificed to buy automatic successes for any of these tests.

The magician may use the Spirit Focus Rating only once in a summoning, whether it be a speedy summoning that lets a shaman call a Nature Spirit or the lengthy ritual by which a mage summons Elementals. The dice from the focus may, however, be split between the Success Test and the Drain Resistance Tests for these rituals.

When engaged in a banishing contest with a Spirit, the Rating is renewed on each of the magician's actions. The same applies to a control contest with another magician.

The benefits of a Spirit focus are of *no* use in banishing or binding a Free Spirit. A magician who knows the Spirit's true name (see p. 92) could build a Spirit focus specifically for use against that Spirit, however. Though a normal Spirit focus, it would be limited to enhancing tests directed against that individual Spirit.

POWER FOCUS

The power focus is the most useful all-around focus in **Shadowrun**. Its rating directly augments the user's Magic Pool, and it is refreshed each time the Magic Pool is. A Power Focus rating can apply to any magical test in Sorcery or Conjuring, or in Astral Space. Rating points may be sacrificed to buy automatic successes in any of these tests.

Note, however, that the use of a power focus (or of any focus) does not help Enchanting whatsoever.

WEAPON FOCUS

A weapon focus is different from the Magical Weapons described in the basic game. A weapon focus adds its rating to the user's Armed Combat Skill in a fight (assuming that he is magically active, i.e., has an active Magical Attribute of at least 1 and has bonded the weapon). Adepts, including physical adepts, can also use these weapons.

Though rumors of enchanted missiles abound and the military-industrial complex is funding massive research, no one has yet found a way to enchant any kind of missile, much less firearms or bullets. A weapon focus only functions when in the hands of its owner.

A weapon focus does increased damage in Astral Combat, and Awakened creatures that have defenses against normal weapons and damage do *not* have that defense against damage from a weapon focus. It is curious that orichalcum by itself has no marked effect on such paraspecies. The mystic metal is effective only when bound into a weapon focus.

When used against a being with a Vulnerability, a weapon focus raises the Wound Category to the level the being would suffer from the substance to which it is vulnerable to (**SR,** p. 178).

If used against creatures that regenerate, a weapon focus may slay the creature. If the wound is Deadly or takes the creature down because of previous damage, the creature must make an Unresisted Essence Test, with a Target Number equal to the Focus Rating multiplied by 2. If the being fails the test, it does not regenerate. If it succeeds, it makes its normal test for regeneration.

All weapon focuses require orichalcum as part of their manufacture. The number of units of orichalcum is equal to the weapon's Reach +1. These units are in addition to any orichalcum used to enhance other means of enchanting the weapon.

The magical weapons described in the basic rules are, in fact, "stacked" focuses, combining the functions of weapon focuses and power focuses.

ARTIFICING

Artificing is used to actually make all the magical focuses that magicians use (**SR**, p. 79). Artificing requires an enchanting shop and the item to be enchanted or the materials from which it will be made. First, however, the character must design the focus formula.

DESIGNING A FORMULA

Before a magician can make a focus, he must have the *formula*. A focus formula is similar to a spell formula (see p. 54) and requires Magical Theory Skill to design it. Focus formulas are specific as to type, rating, and form. If a character designs a formula for a +2 Power Focus, it will *not* help him make a +3 Power Focus. Further, each formula is unique and cannot be upgraded. Someone might have the formula for a +4 Combat Spell Focus, but has not a clue about how to design one for a +5 Combat Spell Focus (or +3, for that matter). Nor would the formula for making a wand be any help in making a focus in the shape of a cloak.

Characters can either try to buy an existing formula or design their own. The base time to design a focus formula depends on the type of focus, per the Focus Design Table.

FOCUS DESIGN TABLE

Type	Base Time
Fetish Focus	10 days
Spell Lock	10 days
Specific Spell Focus	10 days*
Spell Purpose Focus	30 days
Spirit Focus	30 days
Power Focus	60 days
Weapon Focus	60 days

* (also requires the spell formula, see p.54)

Make an Unresisted Magical Theory Test with the Rating of the focus (or 2, whichever is higher) as the Target Number. Divide the base time for the job by the number of successes. If no successes are rolled, then the formula is incomplete. The magician must spend the base time puzzling out where he went wrong, and then he can try again. He can make the attempt in one stretch or piecemeal, as it suits him.

Once the formula is finished, anyone with Enchanting Skill can use it to make that specific type of focus. The designer must specify the *material basis* of the focus (see below) at this time, which becomes part of the formula as well. Thus, the final formula might be: "+3 Combat Spell Focus (Wooden Staff)." The form is part of the formula as well as the function.

However, the formula does allow some variations. The same formula can serve to make focuses using mundane materials, virgin materials, alchemical materials, and so on.

Like spell formulas, focus formulas are too complex to be memorized. Hermetic and shamanic formulas exist. Translating a formula from one tradition to the other is equivalent to designing one from scratch, but with a –2 to the target number (–4 if translating a formula the character has designed personally).

EXOTIC MATERIALS

The Exotic Materials rule is an optional one. When a focus formula is finished, roll 1D6. If the die result is less than or equal to the Focus Rating, the formula calls for an exotic material. If the rating is 6 or higher, the focus *automatically* requires one, and possibly more, types of exotic material. Subtract 6 from the rating, and roll again. Continue in this way until the rating is reduced to 0 or less.

For example, a magician decides to make a focus with a rating of 14. Because 14 is higher than 6, that is one exotic material requirement. That 8 is *still* higher than 6, which brings the total to two exotic requirements. Roll 1D6. On a 1 or a 2, yet a third exotic material would be required.

Exotic materials can be built into the focus or used up in the process of enchanting it. The main thing is having the goods to do the job.

If the required exotic material usually enhances the enchanting process, the materials that satisfy this requirement do *not* have that effect (e.g., alchemical materials). The exotic requirement is in addition to anything the magician voluntarily decides to put into the focus.

Just how exotic can the materials be? Roll 2D6 and consult the following table of possibilities. Gamemasters are encouraged to use their imaginations to come up with others.

When the focus designer hears what he must come up with, he may decide he doesn't care for the requirements. No problem, chummer. He can go back and design the formula all over again. Then see if the next batch of requirements is easier to live with.

Exotic Materials (Roll 2D6)

Die Result	Material
2	Some body part from a freshly killed Dragon
3	10 units of herbs from a remote corner of another continent
4	Focus must include one unit of a metal alchemical radical
5	1D6 x 10,000¥ worth of fine gems
6	One liter of blood from an Awakened critter
7	No exotic material required
8	Focus must include one unit of an herbal alchemical radical
9	1D6 x 10,000¥ worth of precious metals
10	A lock of hair (or feathers or scales) from an Awakened critter
11	10 units of minerals from a remote corner of another continent
12	Some bodily fluid from a live Dragon ("You want me to do WHAT in this cup!")

THE MATERIAL BASIS

The item the character intends to enchant is the *material basis* of the focus, also called a *telesma*. The right material basis can make both the job of enchanting and the Karma cost easier.

Just about anything can serve as the telesma: a wooden wand, a jewelled charm, a weapon, a car.

It is also possible to buy something "off the shelf" and enchant it. This would constitute a *mundane telesma,* that is, the material basis is an ordinary item with no intrinsic magical affinity. Enchanting a mundane telesma provides neither benefits either to any Success Tests nor reductions of the Karma it costs to make them.

A character can also build the material basis from a *handmade telesma,* which is easier to enchant.

Someone could also go out and gather the necessary raw materials and make a telesma from scratch. This is a *virgin telesma* and is magically attuned to the maker because of the preparations he has undertaken. Not only are these easier to enchant, but they cost less Karma to make. Virgin telesma are usually confined to items made with handicraft skills. The amount of labor involved in making a virgin automobile is almost inconceivable. Refining or synthesizing the plastics, getting a sufficient amount of virgin metal, building an engine from the handmade parts. Not particularly cost effective, is it?

It is usually possible to make or buy and then enchant a single telesma at a time. A fetish focus is a special case, however. If the telesma for fetish focuses are properly prepared, a character can process them in batches equal to his Intelligence Attribute. All costs in time, tests, materials, and so on treat this batch as a single focus. That is, a magician with an Intelligence Attribute 4 can make four identical fetish focuses at one time. If the formula for these were for a +3 focus, all tests, Karma costs, and so on, would be as though for the creation of a single +3 focus.

ALCHEMICAL MATERIALS

Adding alchemical materials to the telesma makes it easier to enchant and will reduce the Karma cost as well.

As already discussed, the three arcana of Alchemy are the arcanum of herbals, the arcanum of minerals, and the arcanum of metals. Characters can use alchemical radicals from one of these arcana in the ritual of enchantment. They either become a part of the focus or are used up during the ritual, but it does not matter which.

Qualifying for this bonus requires using a number of units of a radical from that arcanum in the ritual. For example, to get a "one arcanum" bonus when making a +3 focus would require using three units of radicals from the same arcanum.

The bonus can come from using one arcanum, two arcana, or all three. See the section on **Bonding Focuses**, p. 48.

Orichalcum can also be used in the ritual. Every unit of the mystic metal used gives a bonus to the Target Number for making the focus and a potential reduction in its Karma cost.

Whether the materials are built into the focus or simply consumed during the ritual, they are bound to that focus and cannot be retrieved for any other purpose. Consider them expended.

THE ENCHANTING TEST

Once the magician buys or makes the telesma, he can proceed to the enchantment itself. The rituals of Enchanting take time, and as with Alchemy, nothing else can distract the enchanter. He is constantly busy projecting astral energy through the telesma, making the correct observances of the sun and moon, casting horoscopes, chanting, dancing, and so on.

A mage needs an Enchanting library whose rating at least equals his skill. A shaman must perform enchantments in a Medicine Lodge, whose rating is at least equal to his skill. If the Library or Lodge has a lower rating, then use that score for the Success Test instead of the magician's Skill Rating.

The base time to enchant something is 30 days. Make an Unresisted Enchanting Test. The Target Number depends on the type of focus being made. Find the appropriate Base Target Number on the Enchantment Table, adding any modifiers that apply.

ENCHANTMENT TABLE

Item	Target Number
Spell Lock	*
Fetish Focus	3
Specific Spell Focus	4
Spell Purpose Focus	6
Spirit Focus	6
Power Focus	8
Weapon Focus	6
Modifiers	
Rating of Focus	+Rating
Handmade Telesma	–1
Virgin Telesma	–2
Alchemical Materials:	
One Arcanum	–1
Two Arcana	–2
Three Arcana	–4
Orichalcum (per unit)	–1

*A spell lock always has a rating of 1. The Target Number for Enchanting a spell lock is always 5.

Make an Unresisted Enchanting Test. Divide the base time (30 days) by the number of successes. If there are no successes, too bad. Keep the ritual going for a full 30 days and try again. The character has to keep the ritual going without a break until he succeeds or until the whole enchantment fails and the materials are wasted. On a result of all 1s, the process aborts and the materials are lost.

FIRST BONDING

Having fulfilled the ritual, the magician must pay Karma to complete the enchantment. If he lacks the necessary Karma, the process is useless; the enchantment aborts and the focus is useless. The materials are wasted.

This Karma also bonds the focus, either to the maker or to any other person the maker chooses. If he is making the focus on commission for someone else, that person must be present for this "First Bonding." The person being bonded to the focus may pay some or all of the Karma involved, with the maker paying the rest.

Karma costs for the first bonding are equal to a base amount multiplied by the rating of the item. The use of virgin telesma, alchemical radicals, and orichalcum in the focus or enchanting ritual can reduce the base. If orichalcum is used to reduce Karma costs, the units added to the enchanting process are *in addition* to any used to enhance the Enchanting Target Number. The minimum base cost for the First Bonding is 1.

FIRST BONDING COST:
(multiply Base Karma times
Focus Rating for actual Karma cost)

Focus Type	Base Karma Cost
Spell Lock	3*
Fetish Focus	2
Specific Spell Focus	3
Spell Purpose Focus	5
Spirit Focus	4
Power Focus	7
Weapon Focus	8

* Spell Locks always have a Rating of 1.

Modifiers	
Virgin Telesma	–2
Alchemical Materials:	
One Arcanum	–1
Two Arcana	–2
Three Arcana	–4
Orichalcum (per extra unit)	–1

STACKING ENCHANTMENTS

It is possible, but difficult, to make a focus that has multiple, or "stacked," purposes. A focus might be a +2 Power/+3 Combat Spell Focus, for example.

The Target Number for the formula design is the sum of the ratings. In the above example, it would be 5. The resulting formula would be good only for building a similarly stacked focus. Someone could not use it to design only a +2 Power Focus or a +3 Combat Spell Focus.

If that rule is in use, the tests for Exotic Materials would also be based on the total Rating of the focus.

Similarly, any benefits for alchemical materials would require amounts of material equal to the total Rating.

The enchanter does get something of a "group discount" on the Target Number for Enchanting the item. The Target Number for the ritual is equal to the *highest* applicable score, plus *half* the Base Target Number for any other functions the item has, plus the *average* ratings involved.

For example, Enchanting a Power Focus has a Base Target Number of 8, while Enchanting a Combat Spell Focus has a Base Target Number of 6. The higher score is 8, so the Base Target Number for the enchantment is 8 (highest Target Number) + 3 (half of lower Target Numbers), or 11.

The ratings are +2 and +3. The average is 2.5, which rounds down to 2, as do all fractions in **Shadowrun**. The final Target Number for the Enchanting Test works out to 13. Hope this chummer has some bonuses coming.

The Karma cost for the first bonding is equal to the higher base cost, multiplied by the total Ratings for the focus. In our example, the Power Focus Base Cost is 5 and the Spell Purpose Cost is only 3, so the base Karma cost to make or bond the item would by 25: 5 times the total Ratings of +5.

When bonding a stacked focus normally, the Karma for all functions must be paid separately. The focus is not bonded until the focus is completely bonded, however. In bonding the focus from our example, for example, the Karma cost for bonding power focuses is 5 x Rating, and the cost for Spell Purpose Focuses is 3 x Rating.

Therefore, a new owner of the +2 Power/+3 Combat Spell Focus would have to pay 10 Karma Points to bond the Power "part" of the focus, and 9 Karma Points to bond the Combat Spell function. That's 19 Karma points in all, and the character cannot use either power of the focus until he pays the whole amount.

BONDING FOCUSES

Whether it was paid for or, ah, liberated, a focus will not work for a magician until it is bonded. This takes Karma. For powerful items, it takes *lots* of Karma.

A magician can attempt to use Enchanting Skill to bond a focus for less Karma than usual. He can use the skill on his own behalf or for another character. If for someone else, however, the Target Number for the test is at +2. This technique requires the use of an enchanting shop.

Make an Unresisted Enchanting Test with a Target Number equal to the Focus Rating. For stacked focuses, this test must be made separately for each function of the focus.

Reduce the bonding cost for the focus by –1 for every success scored. The minimum cost is equal to the Rating of the focus.

For example, a +4 weapon focus normally takes 24 Karma Points to bond. A magician with Enchanting 5 rolls 5 dice, with a Target Number of 4 (the Focus Rating). If he scores 3 successes, the cost to bond the item is reduced by 3, to 21.

This test can only be made once for a given focus and a given owner. It is not possible to knock off a few points here and a few more there when trying to bond an item.

Karma can be invested for bonding "a little at a time." For example, a character obtains a +4 Weapon Focus requiring 24 Karma Points to bond. Seeking out a friendly enchanter, he gets the cost reduced to 21. Now that is a lot of Karma. If the character only has 8 points to spare at the moment, he can invest some or all of it in the focus. Say he puts in all 8. After a few runs, he has accumulated 12 more Karma Points. He puts 6 in the weapon focus (which is now up to 14) and uses the rest for other purposes. A bit later, he picks up 7 more points and puts them into the focus. That takes him up to 21 points of Karma, and the weapon is now bonded to him.

If some other magician gets his hands on the focus and bonds it, any Karma the first magician invested in the process is lost.

The following **Bonding Table** updates the one published on p. 151 of the **Shadowrun** rules.

MAGICAL ITEM BONDING TABLE
(Base Costs for First Bonding –2)

Item	Karma Cost
Fetish	None
Fetish Focus	None
Specific Spell Focus	1 x Rating
Spell Purpose Focus	3 x Rating
Spirit Focus	2 x Rating
Power Focus	5 x Rating
Weapon Focus	6 x Rating
Spell Lock	1

UNIQUE ENCHANTMENTS

Enchanting opens up some interesting possibilities for adventures. As described earlier, the search for materials can send the player characters off to the boondocks looking for rare herbs and minerals. They might even end up somewhere on the wrong end of a ticked-off Dragon. (Is there a right end of a ticked-off Dragon?).

Besides these lighthearted exercises in the law of supply and demand, the gamemaster can also use the concept of *unique enchantment* in his adventures.

A unique enchantment is something made with Enchanting Skill. It can be a focus, a specific alchemical radical, or even a fetish made with particular raw materials. It need not *do* anything in a direct magical sense, but should be necessary to fulfill some requirement of the adventure.

The discussion of Spirit Focuses mentioned that they that are designed to conjure a specific Free Spirit. Similar devices might be traps (that hold a Free Spirit like a genie in a bottle) or a shrine or statue where the Spirit can survive loss of mana (and, incidentally, leave traces of its astral signature). A Spirit might even commission the building of this last toy, and encode its true name into the formula it gives the enchanter hired to build it.

A magician might be required to prepare quantities of some alchemical material to overcome some ancient magic too powerful for normal methods to touch.

A Dragon might insist on being paid off in an oddball focus, built to the specifications of an ancient formula, in return for some service the runners need. The only problem is that the formula is a temple guarded by hordes of monsters.

What is interesting about a unique enchantment is that even if it has cosmic powers in the adventure designed to include it, that does not mean the shadowrunners have cosmic power forever after. It was *unique!* It may have turned that Toxic Spirit into guacamole, but the runners still don't have a super-powerful "Turn Spirit To Guacamole" focus. It only works when the planets are in this particular alignment, see. But no problem! They'll be back in that pattern in another 127 years.

Making unique enchantments or analyzing uniques that the characters happen to find can add a little extra to magically oriented adventures.

SPELLS AND SPELL DESIGN

"The difficult we do today. The impossible is over in R&D."

—Unofficial motto of EBM², Division of Thaumaturgy

Spells. The tools and weapons and toys of sorcery. Magicians spend a lot of time and effort on their spells because spells are what give them power in the Sixth World. For starters, here are some explanations of spells, and clarifications and additions to the spellcasting rules from the basic game.

HOW SPELLS WORK

Spells are cast when a magician uses his inherent genetic ability to contact Astral Space. He opens a channel between the physical and etheric planes, configuring it according to his knowledge of Sorcery and the formula of the spell he is casting. The result is a spell construct on the etheric plane.

This construct is "programmed" by the spell formula. It moves at blinding speed from its caster to its target. Its basic energy is the Force the magician allocates to the spellcasting process. He can "add on" extra dice from focuses, Spirits, and so on after the basic construct forms, but these do not increase its life force. These dice will take effect if the spell reaches its target, but do not make it any stronger until that time.

All of this takes place virtually instantaneously when the magician casts his spell.

When a spell reaches its target, it creates the desired effect by transferring astral energy into the physical plane. Because this connects the aura of the casting magician directly to the aura of his target, line-of-sight targeting is the rule for spells. Area Spells set up a web of energy that connects the caster and all his targets into a single astral network and affects all viable targets within its area of effect. The effects of this energy transfer depend on the spell's design: it may create or destroy, heal or harm.

Spellcasting is a matter of intention and mental control. For example, some brash young sorcerors have attempted to aim an Area Spell through a pinhole to limit the effect to a single target. And then they wondered why the spell misfired under such circumstances. Might as well ask a painter wearing tinted lenses why the color values in a painting are false. How can a magician capture the universe-embracing exaltation of spirit that is the key to magic when he is playing such mind-games with himself?

It has been said that the emotional energy needed to cast a spell must be as strong as that needed to perform the action physically. Casting a Death Spell requires killing fury. An Illusion requires the laughing creativity of Coyote himself. A magician using Manipulation must have the same monomania as an artist working on a masterpiece.

One definition of magic is the ability to go mad in a very specific way for a limited time. On a psychological level, a spell is an induced neurosis or even a psychosis, created for a split-second to channel psychic energy in a particular way. Confusing this delicate process with calculating, rational thought may leave the magician unable to do much else.

SPELL FORCE

Some confusion exists over just what constitutes the Force of a spell. A magician learns a spell with a maximum Force. He can cast the spell with a Force ranging from 1 up to this maximum. This figure, and *only* this figure, is the actual Force of the spell.

Additional dice allocated to enhance the caster's Success Test do *not count* toward increasing the Force of the spell.

Only the actual Force Rating is used to determine whether Drain is doing Lethal or Stun Damage. Only the actual Force Rating is used to Resist Drain.

On the downside, the actual Force Rating is the one the spell uses for Astral Combat or to resist Dispelling.

Does this mean a magician with Sorcery 6, a +3 Power Focus, and a +2 totem advantage for the spell can cast it with Force 1, and then roll 11 dice to smack the target? Yes. And then he only needs a Target Number of 2 to resist Drain? Yes, again. (Remember, 2 is the lowest possible Target Number in **Shadowrun.**)

In this case, however, the magician has used up all his pool and focus dice offensively. If someone tosses a spell at him before his next action, he has nothing to augment his defense.

But gee, doesn't that mean a team with a magician will clean up against enemies who don't have magical support? That is exactly what it means. Welcome to the Sixth World, where magic is power.

COMBAT SPELLS

Combat Spells pump damaging energy directly into the aura(s) of the target(s). The magician's extra successes (if any) from the Resisted Spellcasting Test use the staging of the spell to increase the spell's damage. All Combat Spells get an initial damage rating of Lethal for the first success rolled by the caster. Extra successes increase the damage one Wound Category for each block of successes equal to the Spell's Staging Number.

AREA SPELLS

Area Combat Spells apply equally against all targets in the area of effect that the magician can see. It might help players to think of this as a sphere-shaped field of damage, rather than an explosion radiating from a central point.

The physical ratings of cover have no effect in resisting Combat Spells. All that counts is whether a target has visual

cover, relative to the spellcaster. This holds true for both Physical and Mana Spells. The reference to physical cover under the Powerball/Manaball Spell on p. 92 of the **Shadowrun** rules was confusing in this regard. It meant that Physical Cover Ratings had no effect on reducing damage for *either* spell.

When a magician is casting a Combat Spell that can affect targets inside a magical barrier, all targets within the barrier are protected by it as long as the magician remains outside (**SR,** p. 81). If the magician is *inside* the barrier, it does not help others who are also inside with him, but protects targets outside from his spells.

Physical Spells can, theoretically, blast everything in the area, almost like an explosion. The gamemaster need not worry much about this, except for special effects ("The guy in front falls screaming and the windshield of the car behind him blows out.") or to restrain exuberant magicians from casting Powerballs in elevators ("Floor? What floor?").

DETECTION SPELLS

RANGE

Range for Detection Spells, either hypersense or area effect, is rather limited. Note that this clarification of the basic rules allows for extending the range of Detection Spells by increasing the Drain Code of a spell. This must be designed into the spell formula itself. For example, a character who has Detect Enemies (**SR**, p. 93) and a personally designed Detect Enemies (Range x 100) version, knows two different spells. Detect Enemies has its published Drain of S1. Detect Enemies (Range x 100) has a Drain Code of D2.

Ranges are always calculated using the subject as the center of the area. Note that some spells in the basic rules imply that they are limited to the magician who cast them. This is an error. Unless the spell description specifically states that the spell can only be cast on the magician himself, published Detection Spells can be cast on anyone. They can be sustained as long as the subject is within the caster's line of sight.

It is possible to design personalized versions of Detection Spells that have lower Drain Codes.

TARGET NUMBERS

When making the Success Test for a general Detection Spell, note the actual results rolled. Say, for example, that a magician rolls 12, 8, 6, 4, 3 when casting Detect Enemies. He has four successes against targets he can see (Target Number 4), three successes against an invisible enemy or one lurking in hidden ambush (Target Number 6), and one success against an enemy stalking him in Astral Space.

MANIPULATION SPELLS

DAMAGING MANIPULATIONS

Some confusion has arisen over Manipulation Spells that do damage, as presented in the basic rules. We recommend the following revisions.

Damaging Manipulations create materials and/or energy that do damage. All such spells are Physical. They differ from Combat Spells in several ways.

In this spell, the magician is creating a physical effect that does damage rather than pumping astral energy directly into the target. The effect is aimed and uses the same modifiers as Fire Combat. The Base Target Number for the Sorcery Test is 4. A magician can aim an Area Effect Spell at a point in space rather than at a specific target.

Any extra successes the magician rolls go toward *increasing* the Damage Code of the spell, just as in Fire Combat. If the damage rises above Deadly, additional successes count toward reducing the armor protecting targets, still using the same rules as Fire Combat.

See the **Appendix** of this **Grimoire** for clarification of an error in the basic **Shadowrun** rules concerning Spell Resistance Tests (p. 107).

Having determined the Wound Category from the test, the target resists the spell's damage normally. The Force of the spell is the power level of the damage. Impact armor protects against the attack (counting as automatic successes for the target's Resistance Test using his Body Attribute). He may use dice from his Dodge Pool. Hard cover *does* add its protective effects (**SR**, p. 68).

In the case of Area Spells, all characters within the area of effect must resist the damage, similar to the way they would resist grenades. The magician need not *see* targets to affect them. The damage of a Manipulation Spell is real physical damage and affects anyone it can reach!

Damaging Manipulations always involve **Elemental Effects**. This is the medium that does damage, and it will have side effects.

The materials and energy created by the spell are still "magical." For example, a spell will not leave its own shrapnel lying around or puddles of acid eating away at everything that walks through them.

Blast Volt is a Damaging Manipulation Spell with a Staging Number 1. It is an Area Spell, with a Force of 4. The caster tosses it into an open doorway. Partial Cover adds +2. No other modifiers apply, so the Target Number is 6. The caster rolls 5 successes. That is 1 success to-hit, and 4 extra successes. This increases the damage to D1, and this damage will ignore 1 point of armor. With the Spell Force at 4, all targets within the spell's range must resist 4D1 damage.

Two goons were waiting inside the doorway to ambush the magician. Both are wearing Armor Vests (Impact Armor 1) and have 4 Body Attributes of 4. Goon 1 is not in cover relative to the target point of the spell. He rolls 4 dice, Target Number 4, and makes 2 successes. His armor counts for a third success, but the spell ignores 1 point of his armor. He nets two successes, knocking the damage down to Moderate. Goon 2 is crouched behind a light door of Thin Construction Plastic. This adds 2 to his Armor Rating (**SR**, p. 68). He makes his Resistance Test, scoring 3 successes. Add 1 success for his armor and 2 for the door. His total is 6 successes, reduced to 5 by the spell's extra damage. He still gets off without a scratch. Just to make it interesting, though, the gamemaster decides to see how the door does. It is simple plastic, with an object resistance of 5 (**SR**, p. 81). The gamemaster rolls 5 dice and scores 3 successes, plus the door's own 2 points of "armor". Despite the spell's armor-penetrating qualities, the door is undamaged.

ELEMENTAL EFFECTS

Damaging Manipulations and Combat Spells with physical side effects have "Elemental Effects," that is, they use the elements of nature to do damage. They are not connected to Elemental Spirits, though some cases are similar to the effects of Spirits. This section suggests various types of Elemental Effects, but the gamemaster may certainly explore additional possibilities.

Elemental Effects do primary damage, determined by the Staging of the spell. The primary damage may also react to armor and defenses in different ways. Primary damage may include side effects that always occur.

Elemental Effects also do secondary damage, i.e., special effects that the spell has on the environment.

Consider any spell using Elemental Effects to have "Drastic Effects," increasing both the Drain Code and Staging Number. Elemental Effects are only possible with Physical Spells, as they can damage living things and objects equally well. Thus, most spells doing Elemental Effects have high Drain.

When dealing with secondary effects during play, the gamemaster will have to be selective and make some judgement calls. For example, if a magician casts Fireball, the spell might start fires, cook off ammo, ignite fuel tanks, and set fire to armor and clothing all over the blast zone. An Acid Elemental Effect could melt surrounding material into smoking sludge.

It is not necessary or desirable to roll for every possible target in such cases. First, determine which living targets are killed by the primary damage of the spell. Feel free to embellish their demise with descriptive details. Innocent bystanders (living or not) may suffer equally. For example, if a magician tosses an Ice Bomb into the midst of a charging pack of bikers, roll to see which bikes skid out of control, but no dice roll is needed to send any passing motorists into a hurtling 360-degree turn.

If anyone is still left standing and in some way still vulnerable to the side effects of the attack, roll 2D6 to determine secondary effects for any non-living targets of the gamemaster's choosing.

The die result must be greater than, or equal to, the target's Object Resistance Rating (**SR**, p. 81). Increase the Object Resistance Rating by +4 against Combat Spells, as their Elemental Effects are less pronounced. Against Damaging Manipulations, the target uses Base Resistance if the spell is doing Deadly Damage, and gets +2 to its resistance against Severe Damage, and +4 against Moderate Damage. A Damaging Manipulation that does Light Damage cannot inflict special effects.

A magician casts Acid Bomb (formerly called Toxic Wave) at three shadowrunners. The damage turns out to be 5S2. First, the gamemaster determines whether the shadowrunners survived the primary damage. If so, he checks for secondary effects.

The gamemaster decides to see if the deadly splashes of toxic glop damaged their armor. The spell is doing Severe Damage, and the armor is high-tech plastic. The armor usually resists magic with a Rating of 7, but this increases to 9 because the spell is not at full potency. The gamemaster rolls 2D6 for each runner. If he scores 9 or more on one of these rolls, the affected shadowrunner's armor is damaged. The gamemaster notes that one of the runner's motorcycles is also in the area affected by the spell. He rolls 2D6 to try and flatten its tires. These are simple plastic tires with a Base Rating of 5, plus 2 because the Spell Damage is only Severe. If the gamemaster rerolls 7 or more on 2D6, the runners will hear hissing, plopping noises as the wheels of their cycles deflate into the gloop.

ACID

Primary Damage: Acid is resisted by Impact Armor, not Ballistic Armor. Anyone in full-body armor treated to resist toxic materials (e.g., a firefighter's suit) takes no damage. Acid creates a cloud of thick, choking fumes that add +4 to all Target Numbers for all those in the affected area for the rest of the turn. The affected area is also considered treacherous ground for the rest of the turn.

Secondary Effects: Anything hit by the Acid Effect can be melted into sludge, or at least badly pitted and burned. Vehicle tires flatten. Armor can be reduced by –1 to both Ballistic and Impact values, and this is permanent damage. If the Acid attack was Deadly, firearms can be corroded into junk.

BLAST

Primary Damage: Blast affects Impact Armor, not Ballistic Armor. Blast Damage increases its Wound Category against manifested Earth Elementals by one level, as it strikes them with the impact of rushing air. A spell doing Severe Damage would normally be Deadly to an Earth Elemental.

Secondary Effects: These are the usual effects of broken glass, shattered plaster, and so on. Unreinforced walls and structures can be badly damaged.

FIRE

Primary Damage: Fire is resisted using Impact Armor. Fire increases its Wound Level by +1 against Water Elementals.

Secondary Effect: Fire can, of course, ignite flammable materials. Highly flammable materials (gasoline, dry wood, paper, explosives, and ammunition) get –1 to their Resistance on the roll to determine Special Effects. If clothing ignites, the wearer starts taking damage at the end of every turn until the flames are extinguished. The damage is 6M2 at the end of the first turn he is on fire. Increase the Power and Staging of the damage by +1 per turn thereafter.

Treat exploding ammunition, grenades, and such as a weapon hit, with *armor doing nothing to reduce the damage.* The Dodge Pool may be used to help resist the damage as the singed adventurer tries to hurl the exploding material away from him.

Vehicle fuel may explode, but the vehicle gets +2 to its resistance on the Special Effects Test, unless its fuel is exposed to the open air.

ICE

Primary Damage: Add +2 to Impact Armor (representing warmth of clothing) to resist effects. Anyone in heated armor or clothes takes no damage. Ice increases its Wound Category against manifested Fire or Water Elementals by +1. The area affected by Ice is treacherous ground until the end of the turn.

Secondary Effects: Any affected moving vehicles must immediately make a test to determine whether they have crashed. They may also stall. Liquids may freeze solid. Plants wither and die instantly.

LIGHTNING

Primary Damage: Heat and impact are the effects of lightning. Impact Armor resists it, and a character in insulated armor or clothing is unaffected. The same might also apply to any character who is not grounded (say, a levitating magician).

Lightning increases its Wound Category by +1 against manifested Air Elementals, ionizing their form and dispersing its energies.

Secondary Effects: Lightning can short out any electrical or electronic equipment with –1 to the equipment's resistance against the special effects. It can destroy metal firearms and touch off their ammo. Vehicle engines may short out, and the fuel be ignited. Against this latter danger, however, vehicles get +2 when resisting the Special Effects Damage unless their fuel is exposed to the open air.

WATER

Primary Damage: Water causes smashing, crushing impact. It does Stun Damage, which Impact Armor can resist, but at –2 to its rating. All those affected must make a Successful Strength Test with a Target Number equal to the caster's Sorcery Skill or else be knocked down. Water does Lethal Damage to Fire Elementals, however, and increases their Wound Category by +1. Exposed electrical wiring is shorted out on contact. Affected areas are treated as treacherous ground for the rest of the turn.

Secondary Effects: Water may short out any electrical or electronic gear such as laser sights, smartgun adapters, and vehicle engines, but not cyberware.

SPELL FORMULAS

Learning a spell from the *spell formula* is described on p. 150 of the **Shadowrun** rules. However, no detail was provided about the spell formula itself. This section fills in the gap.

A spell formula is the symbolic theory of a spell. To learn a spell, a magician must either have a teacher or a copy of the spell formula.

The magical design contained in a spell formula is always the same for a particular spell, but its representation will differ according to the magical tradition. A shamanic formula, for example, might be a medicine item like a painting or carving, a set of runes, or a specially created medicine bag. A hermetic formula would be a written text or perhaps a complex diagram with many arcane equations and symbols. The formulas say the same things about the magical energy for the spell, but they say it in different ways.

INSPIRATION

Before a magician can design a formula, he must have some inspiration. He has to know what he wants the spell to do and have some idea of how it works.

A magician can reverse-engineer the formula for a spell that already exists, that is, any spell published in a **Shadowrun** product. It is assumed that such publicly known spells are documented in *The Manual of Practical Thaumaturgy* or some other magical "tech manual." These reference works do not publish the formulas, but instead give practical descriptions of the energies involved and their effects. A magician with such a description as a guide can deduce enough to get an inspiration about a spell's formula. Designing a formula this way is a copyright violation in many jurisdictions, for the law requires that formulas for copyrighted spells be ordered from the publisher or learned from teachers licensed by them. Most street magicians don't care drek about this, of course.

A magician can get the inspiration to design an unpublished spell if he astrally observes another magician casting it. To do this, the observing magician must be astrally perceiving or projecting and he must concentrate all his attention into observing the spell. He cannot move, fight, do magic, provide spell defense, or any other activity. If he fulfills these conditions, he can figure out the formula from what he has assensed.

If a magician designs a brand new spell, he can design its spell formula without needing any other inspiration. This applies when the player running a magician comes up with a new spell that he wants to add to the game world. Indeed, in this case, the magician *must* design the formula as part of the inventing process.

THE DESIGN

Designing a spell formula uses Magical Theory Skill. Anyone with Magical Theory can do it, even a mundane. Theoretical occultists, experts with high ratings in Magical Theory but no Magic Attribute, are rare, but they do exist, much as pure theoreticians exist in the physical sciences.

A shaman must do the design work in a Medicine Lodge whose rating is at least equal to his Magical Theory Skill. A mage or non-magician needs a Magical Theory Library with a rating at least equal his skill. If the Lodge or Library Rating is lower than the character's skill, he uses *its* rating instead of his skill rating. In this case, the craftsman is only as good as his tools.

Speaking of tools, the following might help the magician designing a spell:

•Mages can get aid from an Elemental as a service (add its dice to the Skill Rating).

•A Library or Medicine Lodge with a rating *higher* than a character's Magical Theory Skill raises the Effective Skill. He gets 1 extra die for every *2* points above the minimum. That is, a shaman with Magical Theory 5 working in a Medicine Lodge rated at 7 would have an Effective Skill of 6.

•Shamans can add their totem advantage to the dice for any test dealing with spells covered by their totem.

The test to do the design uses the effective skill rating in Magical Theory. The Target Number is 10 *minus* the magician's Magic Attribute.

Make a Resistance Test for resisting the Drain of the spell. For example, someone with a Magic Attribute of 5 is designing a spell with a Drain Code of M3. He makes the Resistance Test against 5M3 using dice equal to his Magical Theory Skill.

If the "drain" is reduced to nothing, then the design is ready in one day. If the "drain" is not reduced, roll 1D6 for every box that Drain would fill in on a condition monitor: 1D6 if the result is L; 3D6 if the result is M; 5D6 for an S; and 10D6 for a D. The time to complete the design is the dice roll result in days.

Having determined how long the design will take, the character can do it in chunks: a few days here, a week there, until the design is complete.

The completed formula is in the character's own magical tradition. A mage will produce a hermetic formula, a shaman comes up with a shamanic type. Translating a formula a character already possesses from one tradition to another gives –2 to the Target Numbers for the Resistance Test. That is, the Target Number is 8 minus the Magic Attribute. If translating a formula of a character's own design, he gets an additional –2, so the Target Number becomes 6 minus his Magic Attribute. Remember that the lowest Target Number possible in **Shadowrun** is a 2.

USING THE FORMULA

Once a character has a spell formula, he can use it to learn the spell himself, sell it to individual customers, publish it, or sell it to a publisher for profit or as "public domain" magic.

A spell formula is so complicated that even its designer is unable to memorize it. To obtain the spell formula for some operation requires a hardcopy or access to it via electronic media. Mages have an advantage here, because shamanic formulas do not lend themselves to computer storage. A shaman must usually have the actual formula-object in his possession, though the gamemaster can rule that a digitized image of the object or a hologram fulfills this requirement for strictly visual formulas.

See the **Magical Prices** section, p. 108, for more information on the costs of spell formulas.

INVENTING NEW SPELLS

Rules in this section will help gamers who want to design a spell not covered in any **Shadowrun** book. Whether it is a player who has a neat idea his magician wants to try or a gamemaster who needs that special something for a non-player wizard to toss at the player characters, here is how to do it.

Remember that designing a spell cannot be reduced to numbers. These rules are guidelines, at best, giving the player a feel for the scale of spells, their effects, their Drain, and so on. No rule can take the place of a sense of balance in designing new spells. For instance, a "Hurricane" spell, even with D6 Drain, would let the magician off too easily in return for devastating the countryside. Really tremendous magics, like the Ghost Dance that the Tribes used to attack the old United States, are on another scale entirely from the Sorcery one person can do. Though the Ghost Dancers of Daniel Howling Coyote have remained remarkably close-mouthed about how their rituals worked, researchers have determined that magic on this scale took hundreds of participants and that Drain was measured in the number of magicians who died during the work.

Spell design should be an artistic job, not an exercise in number-crunching where someone tries to get a tactical nuclear whammy for L1 Drain. Even some of the spells in the basic game had to be written on a "that looks good" basis because it was almost impossible to make the rules a perfect fit.

In the last analysis, it is up to the gamemaster what new spells to allow in his game. Players and the gamemaster should confer closely on new spells to make sure everyone buys off on the power involved.

The process of designing a new spell involves several decisions. First, of course, is to decide what the spell does. Next, the designer chooses a purpose that fits that decision. If it heals damage, it is a Health Spell. If it kills someone, it is a Combat Spell, and so on. This can be tricky, as discussed further on. Now the player decides on a Base Drain for the spell, based on the purpose of the spell and the way he wants it to work. Then he decides what modifiers will apply. Finally, with the numbers now more or less plugged in, he writes up the effects in detail. Because the gamemaster has final say on what spells are allowed in his game, he can require juggling the numbers or the description if he does not approve the original version for some reason.

Once the player has designed the spell in these terms, the character who is inventing the spell has to design the formula for it. If the gamemaster is inventing the spell, the spell simply becomes available, either publicly or known only to the non-player character who invented it.

SPELL PURPOSE

The first step in designing a new spell is to decide its purpose: Combat, Detection, Health, Illusion, or Manipulation. The rule of thumb that if it hurts, it's a Combat Spell, if it heals, it's a Health Spell, and so on, does not apply. What about a spell that shoots a rock into someone at bullet speed? Is it a Combat Spell or a Manipulation? How about a spell that sharpens senses? Is that a Detection Spell or a Health Spell?

Sometimes it helps to ask not only *what* the spell does, but also *how* it does it. A spell might be something combat-like ("Zap this scum-bucket...") and do it by way of a Manipulation ("...by zinging this .40 caliber fetish into him!").

MANA OR PHYSICAL

Mana Spells only affect living things or else magical energies in non-living things. Physical Spells affect any material, but increase the Drain of the spell, as explained below.

It is easier on the spellcaster if most spells are Mana Spells. A Mana Spell is useless, however, when the subject is not a living being. A Mana-type Illusion can fool the guards in person, but doesn't do diddly if they are watching the caster via closed-circuit TV.

Some cases are not as clear-cut. One question that has come up is why Mana-type Health Spells work on heavily cybered characters. A partial answer is that it works because the designers fudged a bit on the rules. The other reason is that cyberware, bought and paid for with Essence, is bound so tightly to the organic part of the user that magic can usually be just as effective against a vat-job street samurai as against a pure-flesh fanatic tribesman.

Exceptions, of course, exist. A cybereye, for example, would not perceive a Mana-based Illusion. Cyberears would be immune to Mana-generated sonic attacks or "deafness" spells.

The gamemaster is the final judge on these exceptions, but a good rule of thumb is that a Mana-based spell won't work if the spell's effects are limited to the cybered sense or attribute. It takes a Physical Spell.

Human thoughts, feelings, and so on, are never considered cyber-modified, no matter how much headware a character has. The brain may be so full of wire that a character picks up radio broadcasts, but no matter. The *mind* is pure life force, and thus on the same "wavelength" as Mana magic.

DURATION

Three Durations are possible for spells in **Shadowrun**, as defined on p. 80 of the basic rules.

Instant spells take effect and end in the action during which they are cast. They usually have some permanent effect on reality, but the spell itself only lasts an instant.

Sustained spells last only as long as the caster maintains them, and their effects usually end when the spell does. Most non-Combat Spells fall into this category.

Permanent spells must be sustained for a time, but when this period is over, the effects are lasting. Most healing magics are of this type.

Deciding on the appropriate duration for a spell can be a delicate matter.

A spell that creates a damaging attack should be Instant. A spell that creates a damaging barrier or trap, on the other hand, can be sustained.

Any spell involving sensing, searching, analysis, defense, transformation, or other changes in the world or the way the target of the spell perceives the world, should be sustained spells. The only way such a spell can become permanent is by using Quickening (see **Metamagic**, p.22) or a spell lock.

Only a few spells should be inherently permanent in duration. Spells that heal or repair damage, disease, insanity, the effects of drugs, poisons, and so on are good candidates. They return the target to its natural state, so that the universe will maintain the change once it is established. Minor organic transformations that purify or even create natural compounds from organic sources can also safely become Permanent. A spell that creates food, for example.

Physical cosmetic spells for creating make-up, hair-do, new clothes, even to rearrange the superficial appearance of objects, can be either sustained or permanent. This is the basis of the highly profitable use of magic as a status symbol in these areas.

The gamemaster is the final word on whether it is possible to create a permanent version of a spell in his game. Further, if he approves a spell that turns out to be too powerful, the creator should graciously accept any gamemaster decision to downgrade the spell to sustained, or even instant, duration.

The base time for maintaining a Permanent Spell depends on the complexity of the change the spell makes in the world. An example of how this applies to Health Spells is given on p. 94 of the **Shadowrun** rules. The scale is:

Minor Change	5 turns
Moderate Change	10 turns
Serious Change	15 turns
Drastic Change	20 turns

As with Health Spells, the magician divides this time by the number of successes rolled when he cast the spell.

The staging on Drain for Permanent Spells is increased.

BASE DRAIN

Drain is defined by a Wound Category. Having decided on a spell's purpose, the player must determine its basic Drain. This varies according to the purpose of each spell.

Once Drain is determined, plug in the Drain Category Modifiers, p. 58, and presto, there's the spell.

Combat Spells

The wound category for a Combat Spell's Drain depends on its Staging.

COMBAT SPELL DRAIN

Base Staging	Drain
1	S1
2	M1
3	L1

Detection Spells

Base Drain for a Detection Spell depends on what is being detected and how much information the spell gathers. Detecting non-living things is tougher than working with living subjects.

Spells can simply detect presence. Is the target of the spell there or not? Detect Life simply detects the presence of living beings, for example.

Spells can also analyze the target, providing the spellcaster with information. For example, Detect Enemies analyzes the intentions of a living being.

In addition, Detection Spells can provide hypersenses.

DETECTION SPELL DRAIN

Simply detect living beings or magical energy	L1
Analyze the above or detect non-living things	M1
Analyze non-living things	S1
Minor sensory enhancement (improves physical sense)	L1
Major sensory enhancement	M1
Hypersense or radically new or enhanced physical sense (e. g., ESP, Super-balance, etc.)	S1

Health Spells

Health Spells are hard to quantify because they require keeping track of so many variables.

Remember that spells that treat damage, diseases, poisons, and so on have a maximum Wound Level that they can treat successfully. A spell that heals Light wounds is no help to someone with Moderate wounds. A spell that can cure a Moderate infection will not fix a Deadly one. The Base Drain for these is equal to the level of damage or infection they can treat.

Spells that cause afflictions also base their Drain on what they do to the subject, i.e., a spell that causes Severe disease does Severe Drain.

The Staging on this Drain is always 1. Thus, a spell that heals Light damage has L1 for its Basic Drain.

Health Spells that benefit a character are intended to be unresisted. The usual Drain Reduction Spell does not apply for a spell that only works on a voluntary subject.

On the other hand, harmful Health Spells, which are normally Resisted, increase the Staging of the Drain because the magician is using the powers of healing to bring suffering and death.

All Health Spells are intended to work by the laying on of hands. Health Spells do *not* get a Drain Reduction for requiring the character to touch the target. In fact, any Health Spells that can be cast at a distance *increase* their Drain Code.

All spells that heal damage or neutralize harmful substances in the system are by nature permanent in duration. Their Drain Staging is not increased by this quality.

Illusion Spells

The base Drain for Illusion Spells depends on the senses affected by the Illusion and its overall believability.

ILLUSION SPELL DRAIN

Obvious Single Sense Illusion	L1
Realistic Single Sense Illusion	M1
Obvious Full Sensory Illusion	M1
Realistic Full Sensory Illusion	S1

Manipulation Spells

Base Drain depends on an arbitrary measurement of the overall change in reality that the spell creates. The gamemaster is the final arbiter in setting this.

MANIPULATION SPELL DRAIN

Minor Mental (heighten emotion, suggestion)	L1
Major Mental (mind control, amnesia)	L2
Minor Physical Changes (appearance)	M1
Major Physical Changes (attribute change, shape change)	M2
Minor Environmental Changes (light, darkness, humidity)	S1
Major Environmental Changes (weather, destruction, gravity)	S2

The base drain for Damaging Manipulations is derived from the Staging of the spell, just as for Combat Spells:

Staging	Base Drain
1	S1
2	M1
3	L1

DRAIN CATEGORY MODIFIERS

After determining the Base Drain for the spell, modifiers take their effect. Drain Category modifiers affect the *letter* code for the Drain. That is, if the Base Drain is L2, then a +1 Drain Category gives it a Drain of M2.

If a spell with a Drain of D is modified so that the Drain Category goes up, the *Staging* is increased instead. If a D2 spell gets a +1 Drain Category, it becomes a D3 spell.

The following general modifiers apply to all spell purposes, unless otherwise specified.

Area (+1 Drain Category)

Spells with an Area Effect affect all vulnerable targets within the radius of the spell's effect, which is usually the caster's Magic Attribute in meters (**SR**, p. 80).

Cast At A Range

Any Health Spell that can be cast at a distance has a +1 Drain Category.

Caster Only (–2 Drain Category)

A spell that only affects the caster gets this benefit. A magician is always "touching" himself, so the Touch Required modifier does not apply. Nor does the Voluntary Subject Required modifier apply. The magician does, presumably, want to cast the spell on himself.

Combat Spell Modifier

A modifier that applies only to Combat Spells.

Detection Spell Modifier

A modifier that applies only to Detection Spells.

Drastic Effects (+1 Drain Category)

The spell has lasting impact on the environment or has significant side effects, above and beyond a single main purpose. A Combat Spell that also starts fires would qualify, for example, as would a damaging Manipulation Spell that used flame or gas.

Health Spell Modifier

A modifier that applies only to Health Spells.

Increasing Area

The area covered by an Area-type Detection Spell can be increased by a factor of 10 for a +1 Drain Category modifier. There is no upper limit on this.

Limited Target (–1 Drain Category)

The spell only affects a limited class of target. This might be a single species (e.g., Manaball vs. Elves), a Physical Spell that only affects non-living things (e.g., the Ram Spell), and so on. The modifier is not cumulative with the Very Limited Target modifier.

Stun Only

Any Combat Spell that does Stun Damage gets only –1 Drain Category.

Touch Required (–1 Drain Category)

The caster must touch the target to affect it. If the target does not resist, the magician can touch it without problem, of course. Against a resisting target, the magician must strike with his hands or other body part, using Melee Combat rules (**SR,** p. 70). Because the magician does not have to strike hard, he gets a –1 modifier to the Target Number for his attack as long as he does not do hand-to-hand damage if the blow lands. If he is striking to do damage, the bonus is lost.

Make the Success Test for the attack after declaring the spell. If the blow lands, make the Resisted Tests to see if the spell works. Whether the blow lands or not, make Drain Resistance Tests after the attack.

This modifier is not cumulative with the bonus for Caster Only Spells.

Treats Only Symptoms

Any Health Spell that treats or causes only symptoms gets a –1 modifier. The spell cannot actually affect attribute ratings, heal damage boxes, and so on.

Very Limited Target (–2 Drain Category)

The spell only affects a specific type of target. For example, a Physical Spell that can only blow open doors and is ineffective against other inanimate objects would be limited. The only way to develop a spell with this bonus that affects living things is to designate one against an individual. "Here's a spell with your name on it. No, really!"

Voluntary Subject Required (–1 Drain Category)

This spell only works on a voluntary target. The subject must know that the spell is being used on him *and* must not resist. The magician must still make a Success Test with the usual target numbers, but the target does not make a Resistance Test, so all the magician's successes apply to the spell's effects. Beneficial Health Spells do *not* get a reduced Drain Category for using this modifier.

DRAIN STAGING MODIFIERS

A Drain Staging modifier changes the staging of the Drain Code. For example, a –1 Drain Staging modifier would change a Drain of M2 to a Drain of M1.

- Drastic effects (same definition as above): +1
- Physical Spells: +1 (default spell type is Mana Spell)
- Healing Spell applicable after "Golden Hour" is past: +1
- Health Spell that is harmful: +1
- Non-Health Spell that is permanent in duration: +2

DESIGNING SPELLS

Let's pick a few of these goodies and look at how we arrived at the Drain Codes, applying the rules on pp. 55-8. These examples of how published spells were generated can be of help when players are crafting their own. Happy zapping.

COMBAT SPELLS

Mana Bolt, the magician's standby, is a straightforward, face-stomping Combat Spell. Staging for the spell damage is 1, so the Base Drain is S1. And no other modifiers apply! That was easy: Drain is S1.

Its counterpart, Power Bolt, also has a Staging 1 Combat Spell, so Base Drain is again S1. This is a Physical Spell, however. That increases the Drain Staging by +1, giving Power Bolt a Drain of S2.

A bit further down the list of Combat Spells is Power Blast, with a Staging 1. Its Base Drain is S1. Being a Physical Spell adds +1 to the Staging and Area Spell, so +1 to the Drain Category as well, for a final figure of D2.

DETECTION SPELLS

Moving on to Detection Spells, we chose a few at random. Analyze Device must analyze a non-living thing, so its Base Drain is S1. In addition, it *must* be a Physical Spell or it would not work on non-living things, so the staging is increased +1, for a final Drain Code of S2.

Detect Enemies must not only detect living things, but analyze their mental state and/or actions. That makes its Base Drain M1. It is an Area Effect, and so the Drain Category is increased +1. The typical spell can only be cast on a voluntary subject, however, which reduces the Drain Code to M1. The increased range version is jumped another +1 for the Drain Category, so it has a code of S1.

The personal forms of Detect Enemies should remind players that the basic versions of these spells can be cast on anyone, either the magician or someone else. The personal forms reduce the Drain Code by one Category, because the Caster Only Modifier (–2 Drain) replaces the Voluntary Subject Required Modifier (–1 Drain).

Players must keep in mind that spells to analyze a specific matter or to dig out specific information are considered cast against the thing or person being analyzed and so must overcome its resistance, as in the case of Analyze Device and Mind Probe. General Detection Spells and Hypersenses, on the other hand, are considered cast with the acceptance of the spell's subject. This sometimes requires the gamemaster to make a judgement call.

HEALTH SPELLS

Moving on to Health Spells, note that most of these formulas are pretty ruthless about the "Golden Hour" rule and other special case rules that make Health Spells expensive. This is an attempt to keep the game balanced, so that wounds and combat do not become so trivial a factor in **Shadowrun** that all it takes is a powerful healer to patch up a samurai with the snap of his fingers.

Because the Increase and Decrease Attribute Spells were problematic, the basic rules arbitrarily assigned them Base Drain Codes based on the level of increase or decrease: L for +1 or Minor, M for +2 or Medium, and so on. The Decrease Attribute Spells were then pumped to higher Drain for being harmful and being cast at a distance.

For example, for Minor Cybered (Attribute) Decrease, the Base Drain was L1. Add +1 Drain Category for Health Spell cast at a distance, +1 Staging for Harmful Health Spell, and +1 Staging for a Physical Spell, and voilá, the final Drain Code is M3.

Resist Pain, a new spell in this book, had the same Base Drain Code as a Health Spell. The Drain Category was reduced by 1 because the spell only treats symptoms, and the Staging was increased by 1 because it can be applied outside the Golden Hour. Note that there is no Resist Light Pain Spell. That is because, applying these modifiers, the Resist Moderate Pain Spell came in with a Drain Code of L2, the lowest possible Drain for this spell. A "first aid" version of the spell would be possible, however. It would reduce the pain for an hour at most, keeping it within the Golden Hour and thus have a Drain Code of L1.

The rules for how permanent is relief provided by the Resist Pain Spells were added to make some sense and to apply some limits to the way the spells worked. The rule of thumb was that a Moderate spell does not help Severe damage.

There is no Resist Deadly Pain Spell because there is no reason for it in the game. A character with Deadly Damage is not subject to penalties, but is simply unconscious. A spell that allowed a character to keep going with Deadly Damage was judged too unbalancing.

A spell like Oxygenate is an interesting development. Because this spell does not deal with healing (or hurting), how does one get a Base Drain? Using the values for Manipulation Spells, the spell was evaluated on whether it caused minor or major physical change. So Oxygenate has the Base Drain Code for a major physical change (M2), modified for a voluntary subject (–1 Drain Category), with a final result of L2. A judgement call here determined that the Golden Hour requirement was not relevant, so the spell did not get a +1 Staging even though it can be cast at any time. Spell design is not a cut-and-dried process.

ILLUSION SPELLS

The Illusion spells are fairly straightforward. Chaos, for example, is a realistic illusion affecting multiple senses. Base Drain is S1. It is a Physical Spell, as it can affect sensing devices, so the Staging is increased by +1, for a final Drain Code of S2. Chaotic World is an Area version of the spell, so its Drain Category goes up +1 as well, for a code of D2.

The Drain drops rapidly for the more marketable Illusion Spells, where Voluntary Subject, Touch Required, and other modifiers reduce the wear-and-tear on the caster.

MANIPULATION SPELLS

Last are the Manipulation Spells. The hardest part here is deciding what level of change the manipulation imposes on the target (or the environment) and whether the spell qualifies for the Drastic Effects Modifiers to Drain Category and Staging. Turn To Goo, for example, was judged as quite Drastic, and so costs more than, say, Petrify or Turn To Tree.

Turn To Goo is a major physical change, so Base Drain is M2. It is a Physical Spell (+1 Staging) and has Drastic Effects (+1 to Drain Category *and* Staging), so its final Drain Code was S4.

Turn To Tree is simply a major change: Base Drain M2 and no modifiers. After all, living tissue is formed into different living tissue. So the final Drain Code is also M2.

The Barrier Spells were interpreted as minor environmental changes, and so had a high Base Drain, which was inflated by their Area Effect and the physical nature of some of the spells.

Physical Barrier, for example, has a Base Drain of S1 (minor environmental change) and then gets +1 Drain Category for being an Area Spell and +1 Staging for being a Physical Spell, to give it a final Drain Code of D2. Mana Barrier also gets the +1 Drain Category for Area Spells, but being a Mana Spell, the staging is unaffected and its final Code was D1.

The Anti-Bullet and Anti-Spell versions of the Barrier Spells have lower Drain because they use the Limited Target Modifier, and the personal forms of Barrier are reduced in Drain because they are not Area Spells.

The Damaging Manipulations are also straightforward. Base Drain is derived from the Staging of the spells. A spell doing damage with Staging 1 has a Base Drain of S1. These are Physical Spells, so the Drain Staging gets +1, and they are defined as having Drastic Effects, increasing Drain Category and Drain Staging by +1 each. So a non-Area Spell like Flame Volt has a final Drain of D3. The Area version, Flame Bomb, has a D4. The Area Spell Modifier is +1 to the Drain Category. Because the Drain Category for the spell is already D, this increases Staging instead.

"Hey Horace, there's more drek goin' on out there than you can dig even when you're hotwired. Y'catch?"
—From the hit simsense,* Hamlet 2050, *Elan Vital Productions

Though some discussion of Astral Space appears in the **Shadowrun** basic rules (p. 88), that simple exploration of the Astral Plane only scratched the surface.

Magicians have always believed that Astral Space is divided into many different planes. Like a lot of other magical theories from the centuries before the Awakening, modern research has confirmed that they were partially right.

The description of Astral Space in the basic **Shadowrun** rules refers to the *etheric plane*. This is the level of Astral Space that corresponds to our own physical universe, and is the medium for magical energy that affects the physical world. It is not the only plane in Astral Space, though.

Each of the hermetic elements of Fire, Water, Air, and Earth has its own plane, each a different "dimension" in the universe of Astral Space. Similarly, the shamanic powers fall into one of four planes: those of Man, the Waters, the Sky, and the Land.

These levels of Astral Space are not attainable by just any magician; he must be an Initiate to reach them. Because Astral Projection to these special planes is a type of of metamagic, the levels are called *metaplanes.*

Everything that exists in the material world is at least visible on the etheric plane, even if it is not tangible there. In other words, everything has some kind of Astral Body. The Astral Bodies of magicians can travel to the metaplanes, and in special circumstances, so can those of other beings.

ASTRAL BODIES

When someone is said to "enter" Astral Space, he does not actually move his body onto the etheric plane, or a metaplane. The physical body stays in physical space, but the character's consciousness is transferred into the *astral body*, using its senses (*assensing*), traveling through Astral Space rather than physical space, and so on.

Just what is this Astral Body? Everything has one, to some extent. Some entities such as people, for example, can separate their physical and astral bodies. Others, like Spirits, have nothing but an Astral Body, though they can form a temporary physical vehicle when manifest in the material world.

Most things, living or non-living, have at least an etheric body, that is, an Astral Body that is present on the etheric plane. The more alive something is, the more solid its etheric body will be.

HUMANS ON THE ASTRAL

Let us examine how a player character might be in Astral Space. Presumably he is a member of *Homo sapiens*: a normal Human, Ork, Troll, Elf, or Dwarf. Keep in mind that humanity is not by nature "astrally active." Astral travel is a learned activity, not an instinctive one. When a Human uses Astral Perception or Projection, his Astral Body separates from his physical one. The body is just a little "out of phase" for Astral Perception and entirely separate for Astral Projection. At this point, someone becomes astrally active, because his consciousness can perceive Astral Space and react to it.

Humans in Astral Space use the astral version of their Physical Attributes (**SR**, p. 90). Their Astral Body's "Physical" Attributes are based on their Mental Attributes:

Astral Strength = Charisma
Astral Quickness = Intelligence
Astral Body = Willpower

The Mental Attributes themselves do not change. If someone has an Intelligence 1, he will not get any quicker on the uptake in Astral Space.

Special attributes do not change in Astral Space, and this raises the interesting question of Reaction. Does someone with Wired or Boosted Reflexes get increased Reaction and extra Initiative dice?

The answer is no. Cyberware changes the physical muscles and nerves, which are left behind when someone is active in Astral Space. So Astral Reaction is different from Physical Reaction and is always equal to the Intelligence Attribute.

Initiates will add their grade to their Astral Initiative, however, and as discussed later in **Astral Combat**, action takes place faster in Astral Space than on the physical plane.

When a magician is using Astral *Perception*, he is astrally active. This means he can touch, and be touched by, other astrally active things. And yes, he can engage in Astral Combat if the opponent comes within his physical reach. However, his astral body is still attached to his physical body. He cannot reach through a wall to touch an astral object, because his physical arm cannot penetrate the wall. For such activity, he must switch to full Astral Projection and send his Astral Body away from the physical one.

While astrally perceiving, the magician receives a +2 modifier to all tests that do not involve magic. Remember, his perceptions are split between the mundane plane and the etheric. This also means the gamemaster is free to require the player character to make a physical-based test when attempting a physical action while astrally perceiving.

An astrally *projecting* Human does so by separating his consciousness from his body. He may then travel on the etheric plane. During the time he is projecting, the magician's body is in a state of trance. Only the barest sensory input comes from his body. The magician will be aware of any injury done to his body, but otherwise, he is barely aware of his meatbody at all.

Also, an astrally projecting character can become visible on the physical plane if he wishes. He can speak to people on the physical plane once he is visible. However, he cannot touch physical things, cast spells at them, or in any other way directly influence the physical world. He can still only affect other astrally active beings.

DUAL BEINGS ON THE ASTRAL

Various paraspecies of Awakened critters are noted as having a "dual nature" (**SR,** p.189). They are always active on both the Astral and physical planes, just like a Human using Astral Perception. Their presence is limited to the etheric plane. They cannot travel to the metaplanes just because they are dual beings. As a rule, a dual being would have to learn enough magic to engage in regular Astral Projection to enter a metaplane. Note that travelers to the metaplanes have found creatures that resemble dual beings there, however.

Unlike Humans, dual beings exist naturally on both planes at once. As a result, their Physical statistics are the same in both physical and Astral Space. A Western Dragon has an Astral Strength of 40, not 4. It resists wounds using its Body of 15 and its Armor of 4, whether the damage is inflicted physically or astrally. Best not to mess with a Dragon!

Additionally, natural dual beings do not receive the continuous +2 Target Modifier for non-magical activity and are not required to make any special tests to perform a physical action.

Some dual beings are capable of Astral Projection. That is, they can separate their Astral Bodies from their physical bodies, just as Human magicians do. In this case, their physical body sinks into a trance, but the free-roaming Astral Body *still* has the same attributes astrally that the creature has physically. Only now that body can move freely through the etheric plane to pursue its impudent attackers wherever they may try to flee. Scary, isn't it?

However, the special powers of dual beings, such as the petrifying gaze of Basilisks or the flaming breath of Dragons, are created by the interaction of their twin natures. The astral energy is brought through into physical space through their bodies. These special powers do not work in Astral Space. Of course, the Dragon's astral teeth can still shred someone like fettuccine in one bite, so characters better not get too cocky.

MAGICAL ENTITIES

Magical Entities such as spells, focuses, magical barriers, and so on are all astrally active under the right circumstances.

Spells are active when being cast if they are sustained or rendered permanent by Quickening or spell locks. Their Force is only the Force their caster allocates them. Extra dice from other sources do not make them stronger in Astral Space, but take effect when the spell "grounds" into its target's aura.

Barriers include Medicine Lodges, Hermetic Circles, and a new form of Barrier called a Ward. (See **Astral Security**, p. 68, for details.) Medicine Lodges and Wards are always astrally active. Hermetic Circles are astrally active when being used to do magic.

Focuses are astrally active when bonded to the magician who has activated them for use.

Attributes for these beings are all equal to their actual Force.

ASTRAL BEINGS

As far as anyone knows, Astral Beings are all Spirits of some kind. Though they may manifest on the physical plane, they are native to Astral Space. The only attribute of importance on the astral is the being's Force Rating. When an Astral Being is manifested, it functions as a dual being, but its material form attributes will be different from its astral form attributes.

A Force 6 Fire Elemental would have all its Attributes equal to 6 in Astral Space, though its physically manifested body has Body 7, Quickness 8 x 3, Strength 5, and Mental Attributes all at 6, as defined on the Critter chart, p. 190, **Shadowrun**.

Note that Free Spirits use their real Force Rating. They do *not* get the benefit of their Spirit Energy in calculating Astral Attribute Ratings. They do get to add it to their Initiative in Astral Combat, however (see p. 65).

As with dual-natured beings, the special powers of Spirits are created by the interaction of their astral energies with the physical plane. They cannot use these powers against an astral opponent.

Most Spirits have an affinity to at least one metaplane, their so-called *native plane*. A Fire Elemental, for example, is native to the hermetic metaplane of Fire, a City Spirit to the shamanic metaplane of Man, and so on. Spirits can travel at will to their native metaplane. Indeed, this is where bound Elementals pass the time when not attending on their masters, and this is also where Spirits go when *Disrupted* (see p. 75), that is, driven off the physical plane by magic or damage.

OTHER BEINGS

Other living things, that is, physical creatures who are not astrally active, are visible and tangible on the etheric plane, but immune to Astral Combat. They are obstacles, not opponents.

Note that "living beings" include plants, animals, and rock, sand, or soil. Mother Earth herself is a living being, and thus cannot be passed through. A magician in Astral Space could "fly" easily through pavement because it has been processed, but would not be able to penetrate the ground below.

Such beings have no presence on the metaplanes, as far as present research can determine.

OBJECTS IN ASTRAL SPACE

Manmade objects are visible on the etheric plane, but they are not solid. An astral traveler cannot *see* through them, but he can move or reach through them, unless tied to a physical body the way dual beings are. If tied to a physical body, he is restricted to the movement that physical body can perform. If the meat-body cannot get past an obstacle, he cannot get through, regardless of whether he could do it via Astral Projection. An astrally perceiving character is limited by the constraints of the flesh.

The etheric form is usually a duplicate of its physical form. Of course, if the object were enchanted or otherwise under the influence of magic, that would be detectable to astral senses. Similarly, places that have been the site of extremely powerful magic or events with a powerful emotional charge will retain traces of that information in their etheric form.

Physically, a magician might walk down a somewhat dusty road, glance at a small wood and brick building, and see nothing much. Assensing the scene, he runs away screaming. He is looking at a barracks in Auschwitz. In areas with a high background magic count, the basic nature of the events that created the count can be overwhelming to astral senses. Images of similar intensity, but thankfully, a different nature can be assensed in places where devout worship of the Good has created a high background count. Chartres Cathedral may be equally confusing to the senses, but the sensory images are intensely beautiful.

The traces of a minor spell or a single act of violence, love, or worship would last only an hour or two at most. More potent events would leave more durable traces. It is for the gamemaster to decide just what kind of "atmosphere" a place might have.

Assensing these impressions is not an "instant replay," but as discussed in the next section, an emotional experience, where the astral observer perceives very general information about what happened, not a detailed vision of the past event. An astral detective might determine that a murder took place in a room within the past few hours, but would not be able to tell who was killed, who did it, how the crime was committed, and so on.

ETHERIC TERRAIN

The "terrain" of the etheric plane is made up of the Astral Elements, living beings such as trees, plants, and the Earth, and the visible, but intangible, etheric shadows of things mankind has built.

Fire, Water, and Air in their Astral Forms are somewhat tangible, but not particularly dense, and an Astral Body can move through them, unlike the element of Earth. Of course, a dual-natured creature might have some problems. Its Astral body can move through astral fire safely, but the fire in the corresponding place on the physical plane might make the poor critter's meat body rather uncomfortable.

Air is not a problem. As noted in the basic rules, Astral Bodies can move freely through air on the etheric plane. And the etheric is permeated with the glow of Earth's biosphere, so even on the darkest night or in a deep cavern or at the bottom of the sea, astral travelers can see as though the Sun were shining.

Travel through water or fire does not slow down an Astral Body, but can affect visibility, which modifies tests for Astral Combat, searches, reading auras, and other activities.

ASTRAL PERCEPTION MODIFIERS

Condition	Modifier
Shallow water (50 meters or less)	+1
Deep water (51 – 200 meters)	+2
Deeper water (over 200 meters)	+3
Open flame	+2
Intense flame (e.g., inside a blast furnace)	+3

Besides these phenomena and their effects, Astral Tests can be affected by the "background count" in a given area.

INFORMATION IN ASTRAL SPACE

Information on the etheric plane is a matter of moods, emotions, textures and tones. For example, on the physical plane, a magician sees a sheet of paper covered with hand- or typewritten words. "Dear John, I am fed up. I still care for you but cannot take it any longer. I am leaving. I'll call you. Love, Jane."

In the material world, only the data is present, and the emotional tone must be deduced from the content. Looking at this same letter on the etheric plane, the words would be illegible, appearing as random marks on paper. The astral reader would, however, assense the anger, hurt, and remaining love of the writer for the recipient, the finality of the decision to leave, and get the gist that the relationship was formerly intimate relationship.

If a letter were handwritten, the impressions would be stronger, clearer. If typed, less clear. If it were a piece of electronic mail displayed on a CRT, all would be faint.

Looking at a text that has virtually no emotional content reveals little information on the etheric plane. Assensing a printout of a business report would reveal nothing, for example.

Similarly, listening to live music from the etheric plane, one would pick up the emotional content of the music, but not necessarily be able to hum the melody. A live performance of music crafted with a powerful message, such as Beethoven's *Eroica* Symphony or *Puta* by Maria Mercurial, would present both the composer's emotional content and the mood and purpose of the performers. A recording would mute both of these "signals" down to almost nothing. From the etheric plane, it would be something like muzak, grinding out bland melody over the speakers, a small swirl of meaningless impressions.

A living voice is perfectly understandable, whether the speaker is astrally active or not, but a voice that is recorded or transmitted electronically is just noise. Astral conversations with physical people are possible, but astral phone calls are not.

Similarly, one cannot perceive information from a video screen from astral space.

Players should note that the meatbodies of mundanes are recognizable from Astral Space. If the body has been physically disguised, it would be almost impossible to recognize that person from physical appearance alone. However, all living beings have auras and each aura is as unique as fingerprints or DNA patterns. An aura, once seen, can be recognized again.

BACKGROUND COUNT

The Background Count, a term borrowed from radiation studies, is an optional rule. In science, refers to the normal level of radiation in an area due to cosmic rays, local concentrations of radioactive materials in nature, and so on. In a magical context, the background count refers to the presence of powerful influences that can distort the etheric medium.

Background count is a modifier the gamemaster assigns to all Astral Tests: combat, perception, analysis, and so on. It affects the etheric plane in a given place. The background count is generally rated from 1 to 5. The decision on how high the count might be is a judgement call, though the gamemaster can consult guidelines given here. If a site fits into several categories, only the highest background count would apply.

There are indications that background count can hinder or help magical operations. Reports are not dependable, but background count may be the reality underlying the old legends of "holy ground," "cursed places," and other such beliefs. If a magician is engaged in actions in keeping with the reason for the background count, the modifier might be subtracted from his target numbers instead of added to them.

The level of background count is plotted on something of a bell curve. There is no appreciable background count in a forest where no Human is present for kilometers. There is no appreciable background count on a crowded, filthy, city street, buzzing with life and energy. The highest background count seems to exist in sites where nature and/or the Human spirit have been eradicated, poisoned, or violently warped.

Background count is not a constant. Magical impulses ebb and flow in irregular rhythms. Quite frankly, one reason for this rule is to prevent magicians on the astral from penetrating every secret place in an adventure, or at least to make it more difficult. The gamemaster may choose whether to use this rule or not.

Following are guidelines to assigning the level of the background count intensity.

Level 1

Anyplace where more than three magicians are doing different magical operations or casting spells more or less simultaneously: a magician's convention, a bar frequented by magicians, and so forth. Any site where a violent crime was committed in the last hour.

Level 2

Anyplace where Human presence is rigidly constrained or suffers ongoing misery: a maximum-security prison, terminal ward in a hospital, corporate research facility, most large factories. Anyplace where a large group of people are expressing powerful emotions: a rock concert, an Urban Brawl game, a riot, a revival meeting.

Level 3

Any major battlefield less than a century old. Typical areas exist in Viet Nam, Afghanistan, Europe, Libya, Iran, and large portions of southern and central America. Slashed-and-burned forest areas.

Level 4

A heavily polluted area (slag heap, strip mine, abandoned factory, burned-out residential area, moderately polluted river). Anyplace where a major battle is occurring (site of a corp war, for example). Anyplace that has been the site of intense positive emotions, religious worship, or magic for an extended period: most cathedrals, monasteries, lamaseries, shrines, Arlington Cemetery, Stonehenge. Scenes of sudden, mass death such as transportation disasters, terrorist massacres like the Chicago "Shattergraves," or other similar tragedies.

Level 5

A highly toxic area (lethal toxic waste dump, the Hudson River, radioactive waste storage site). Anywhere within five kilometers of a nuclear blast site, including Hiroshima, Nagasaki, and Alamagordo, New Mexico. Sites of genocide, death camps, gulags, including Auschwitz, Babi Yar, areas of Cambodia, Siberia, the "Native American Re-Education Centers," and so on.

These descriptions mirror the prejudices of this **Grimoire**'s author. Gamemasters may have their own views of what conditions are holy or horrible enough to create a background count.

AURAS

A discussion of auras and the ability to assense information by "reading" the aura with Astral Perception appears on p. 89 of **Shadowrun**. An aura is an energy field within the etheric body. In living beings, the aura is active, generating astral signals that a skilled magician can interpret with often amazing clarity. Non-living beings also have auras, as in the above examples, but these are passive. If they provide information, it was impressed on them by an outside force.

AURA READING

Under normal circumstances, a magician can learn certain basic information from any aura he can assense. To obtain additional information, he must make an Intelligence Success Test. In some cases (see below), he may have to pass this test to gain even the basic information.

The Target Number is 4, plus any perception modifiers and any background count.

Multiple attempts to read an aura are permitted, but the Target Number for the Test goes up by +2 for each additional attempt. A magician can try to get more information or to read an aura after failing at first. No further tries are allowed once the Target Number is greater than the magician's Magic Attribute. He can make a first attempt to read the aura even if the Target Number starts that high, but no additional attempts would be possible.

Because this is a Perception Test, a player might obtain useful information even if he fails to pass the roll of the dice. The gamemaster should consider being the one to make the tests to read auras.

All readings from a Masked aura (see p. 26) fit the false image presented by the aura's owner, unless the assensing magician has penetrated the Masking. Readings may be obtained, but they will be false, appropriate to the disguised aura. The gamemaster should make the secret test to penetrate the Masking when an Initiate tries to read a masked aura.

INFORMATION IN THE AURA

Following is a list of the basic information a magician can read from an aura:

- The relative level of the subject's Essence (low, average, or high).
- Whether the subject is magically active to some extent (a magician or adept). Enchanted items and materials also display a distinctive aura that marks them as magical.
- If someone is under a spell or possessed by a Spirit, that will be visible, with the Astral Form of the spell or Spirit seen bound to the aura.
- The true form of the subject. Beings appear as themselves, despite any disguise or transformation spells. Shapeshifters show their animal forms. This does not apply to beings with masked auras, of course. The "true form" seen in that case will, in fact, be false.

Additional information can be obtained only by an Intelligence Test, as described above. The number of successes determines the amount of additional information. If multiple attempts are made to read the aura, only the best results of the tests are used. If a magician rolls once and scores two successes, then rolls again and gets three, he has three successes, not five.

One success does not give the magician extra information, but is necessary to read the aura at all if conditions prohibit reading basic information at a glance. If trying to interpret the aura of one specific person in a crowd, the magician must make a test to get any information. This rule applies if the subject is less than a meter from other living things, not including plants and the Earth.

If the background count is higher than 1, the magician also needs a successful test to filter out the surrounding interference and get the basic information. The magician must obtain this basic information before using the more sophisticated magical tests possible with auras (**SR**, p.89). Note that those tests are also subject to the modifiers for perception and background count.

With 2 – 3 successes, basic emotions or attitudes can be discerned. It is possible to tell whether someone is physically ill, addicted to drugs or BTLs, and so on.

With 4 or more successes, specific emotional information can be determined. The magician would not only sense someone's emotion, but why he felt that way, in a general sense. "I am angry because of my boss," or "I am sad because of my lover." He can detect what attributes are modified by cyberware, but not the specific type of modification or its rating.

It is also possible to read the aura of a non-living thing or of a place in general. This usually matters only in cases where there is a background count. Success will identify the general reason for the count: violence, magic, toxicity, passion.

AURA READING SKILL

A special skill in Aura Reading exists, and any character capable of Astral Perception can learn it.

ASTRAL COMBAT: ALTERNATE RULES

Though rules for Astral Combat are presented in the basic game, some players may find the alternate system presented here to be more workable. Others may prefer to mix and match concepts between the two systems. Be our guest.

ASTRAL INITIATIVE

Initiative in Astral Combat is handled the same way as normal Initiative. Because no mechanisms exist for getting multiple initiative dice, all combatants roll 1D6 and add it to their Reaction Attribute. In addition, certain beings receive a bonus to Astral Initiative:

•Initiates add their grade.

•Beings astrally projecting receive a +5 bonus.

•Spirits of all kinds add 10 to their Astral Initiative. (They do not, however, also receive the +5 Astral Projection bonus.)

•Free Spirits add their Spirit Energy (and do receive the +10 Spirit bonus).

•Any spell being cast or sustained by a magician, or any focus bonded to a magician and activated as specified on p. 79 of the basic game uses the magician's Reaction to calculate Initiative. (Use Astral Reaction if cast while astrally projecting, Physical Reaction if not). However, a spell being maintained by Quickening or a spell lock would use its own Reaction, which is to say, its Force.

•Beings using Astral Perception use their physical Reaction for Initiative, but may act normally in Astral Space on their action.

When astral and physical actions mix in one Action Phase, resolve those originating on the Astral Plane (not including actions initiated by an astrally perceiving character) first in the Action Phase. If more than one astral action occurs in the same phase, resolve them in descending order, beginning with the character with the highest Reaction.

ASTRAL COMBAT SKILLS

As in the original rules, all Astral Combat is Melee Combat. The constantly fluctuating medium of Astral Space makes ranged attacks impossible. Characters can use one of several skills for Astral Combat:

•Armed Combat Skill if armed with a Weapon Focus.

•Unarmed Combat Skill if not armed with a Weapon Focus.

•Sorcery Skill as a Combat Skill at any time in Astral Space.

Even characters who cannot normally cast spells may use Sorcery in Astral Combat. It is for this purpose that physical adepts and others who might face Astral Combat often study Sorcery.

As a further option, a character can use Conjuring Skill in Astral Combat with Spirits, and he can use Enchanting Skill in combat with focuses. An astral combatant will, presumably, use the appropriate skill for which he has the highest rating.

Dual beings and Spirits use their Essence or Force as their Combat Skill, though a being may choose one of the other relevant skills instead. For example, a Free Spirit with a Force 4 and a Sorcery Skill 6 can use Sorcery in a fight.

RESOLVING ASTRAL COMBAT

The Base Target Number for Astral Combat Tests is 4, as in Melee Combat. Visibility, Weapon Reach, the effects of damage, background count, and possibly the distraction for sustaining spells can modify this Target Number. Movement does not affect it.

When an Astral Being attacks, the target may either counter-attack or try to avoid combat.

If the defender counterattacks, both combatants make a Resisted Success Test, as in Melee Combat. The one who scores more successes hits. On a tie, neither combatant hits. A character's extra successes may increase the damage of the attack. The character who is hit may *not* use dice from his Astral Defense or Astral Dodge Pools to try to augment his Resistance Test against the damage.

If the defender tries to avoid the attack, the attacker makes an Unresisted Success Test. His successes may increase the damage of the attack. In making his Resistance Test, the character hit may augment his Astral Body Attribute with dice from either his Astral Defense or Astral Dodge Pools.

As in Physical Melee, attacks may be split among multiple targets by dividing dice and rolling each attack separately. A character facing multiple astral attackers may choose to counter-attack one, while using his Dodge and Defense Pools to avoid the other attackers.

ASTRAL POOLS

The Astral Dodge Pool is equal to Astral Quickness.

The Astral Defense Pool is equal to any Astral Combat Skill the character wishes. He declares which skill will be used when the pool refreshes. There's a trap here, though. If a character is using, say, Conjuring for his Defense Pool, he cannot use those dice to defend against an attack by something other than a Spirit.

The Astral Magic Pool is the same as the Magic Pool. It is equal to Sorcery Skill and is used only in tests involving spellcasting. It may be used instead of the Defense and Dodge Pools in defending against damage from spells in Astral Combat. All pools refresh at the start of each new action in Astral Combat.

Certain characters also get a special pool called the Astral Pool. NOTE: This is *not* the very large Astral Pool described on p. 90 of **Shadowrun**.

Dice from this Astral Pool may be used to enhance any test, offensive or defensive, related to Astral Combat.

A magician can use this Astral Pool in place of the normal pools for some non-sentient magical item he is controlling in Astral Space. This might be any spell he is casting or maintaining, any barrier within which he is working, or any focus he has activated. In order to do this, the magician must be assensing the combat, either via Astral Perception or by fully projecting his own Astral Body, and dice he uses from his Pool to aid his magical item are spent as though he had used them himself. That is, if the magician is attacked in Astral Combat, those dice are not available to him.

Magicians may *not* use the Astral Pools in this way to support Spirits bound to them.

Initiates get an Astral Pool equal to their grade. Free Spirits get an Astral Pool equal to their Spirit Energy.

ASTRAL DAMAGE

Astral Damage may be physical or mental, at the choice of the character inflicting it. An exception exists in the case of mundanes encountered in Astral Combat. They can only do Stun Damage.

Non-sentient astral entities not being controlled by a magician (permanent spells, barriers, and so on) will usually "choose" to do physical damage. Similarly, non-living magical items take all damage as Lethal Damage. This means a mundane doing Stun Damage cannot harm such entities.

The Damage Codes for astral attacks vary (see the **Astral Damage Codes Table**). Extra successes from the Success Test for the attack increase damage normally.

Additional extra successes above Deadly cancel out armor if striking a being with astral armor (see below). Once any armor is cancelled, extra successes can counter successes the target made on his Resistance Test.

Extra successes equal to the Staging of the attack have this effect. For example, an attacker with a 4M2 attack rolls 6 extra successes. Four of these push the damage code up to 4D2. The last two act to counter one success from the target's Resistance Test. If the target rolled 4 successes, only three would count. The target would only reduce the damage to S instead of all the way back down to M. Against a being with astral armor, the same results would reduce its armor by 2 points.

These effects only apply to the attack being resolved. They do not permanently reduce the armor or test successes of the character.

Charisma (Astral Strength) is important to Humans in Astral Combat because it is used as the power of their attack, that is, the Target Number their opponents must resist. Initiates may choose to use their grade instead of their Charisma for this purpose. That is, a Grade 6 Initiate with Charisma 4 would do 6L1 Unarmed Damage instead of 4L1.

Dual-natured beings do the same damage astrally as physically. See the **Attacks** column of the **Critters Table**, pp. 190 – 1 of **Shadowrun**. Note that dual beings also have the same Reach bonus as in their physical forms. Beings noted on the table as doing "Special" or "Humanoid" damage use the same Damage Codes as do Humans.

Resistance Tests against Astral Damage are always made using the Astral Body Attribute (i.e., Willpower, in the case of Humans).

Note, too, that a physical adept is able to use his special power, Killing Hands, on the etheric plane to full effect.

ASTRAL DAMAGE CODES

Unarmed Human Magician	(Strength)L1
Unarmed Human Initiate	(Strength or Grade)L1*
Unarmed Human Mundane	(Strength)L1 Stun
Armed Attacker (using Weapon Focus)	(Strength)M(Rating of Focus)**
Dual-Natured Being	**SR** rules, pp. 190-1
Spirit	(Force)M2
Spell	(Force)Drain Code
All others	(Rating or Force)L1

* Use Strength or Grade, whichever is higher.

** For example, a magician with Charisma 4 swinging a Weapon +2 Focus would do 4M2 damage.

ARMOR ON THE ASTRAL

Dual-natured beings that have physical armor enjoy the benefits of that armor in Astral Space as well. See the **Critters Table** on pp. 190–1 of the basic rules.

Research to develop magical armor effective in Astral Space is underway at several universities and corporate R&D centers, but so far, without success. As of this writing, no spell or focus can provide armor on the etheric plane.

CONDITION MONITORS

In the case of living beings, there is no separate Astral Condition Monitor. Damage inflicted on one plane affects the body on the other by the phenomenon of repercussion. Then, if a character suffers moderate physical damage in Astral Combat, he is moderately wounded. It does not matter whether it is his physical body or his Astral Body, for both share one life.

Wounds a character has when he projects into Astral Space are still in effect while he is there. Wounds received in Astral Space cause equal wounds to the physical body, and are still present when the character returns to normal consciousness. First aid or Health Spells that cure the physical body while its owner is on the astral are effective in healing the Astral Body.

Any living thing uses only its usual condition monitors to keep track of damage when in Astral Space. It is entirely possible for a magician to half-kill an opponent in Astral Combat, and for someone else to finish the job with damage in physical combat in the same turn.

Non-living magical entities (spells, barriers, and focuses) have *only* a single condition monitor measuring Lethal Damage. They are immune to attacks by beings that can do only Stun Damage. In addition, these things regenerate all "wounds" instantly if an opponent lets an action pass without attacking. This tends to depend on the attacker, because such entities do not generally initiate combat. As long as the attacker makes an attack, successful or not, its wounds remain in force every action until he "kills" the thing. If he fails to destroy it, the thing "heals" all its damage at once. Attackers can "take turns," however. If a second attacker starts in on a non-living target, the first can withdraw from combat without letting the target regenerate.

ASTRAL EVASION

Given the great speeds at which astral bodies can travel (**SR**, p. 90), Astral Evasion is a pretty simple matter, with only a few options to consider.

A dual being, shackled to its flesh, can only move at speeds and in ways allowed physically. An astrally projecting opponent can break off combat with such an opponent by moving out of its reach, dodging through a wall, and so on.

When both opponents can move with equal freedom, however, Astral Evasion Tests may be needed to break off combat and evade pursuit. Use Unresisted Quickness Tests for movement at the normal rate or Resisted Magic Tests for fast movement. Normal movement would let one break off a fight without leaving the general area. Fast movement is involved if running for it or pursuing. Success Tests are required unless one opponent chooses to let the other flee.

The Target Number for each opponent is the Attribute of the other. For example, if a magician with a Magic Attribute 5 was trying to evade a Spirit with a Force of 7 using fast movement, the magician rolls 5 dice with a Target Number 7, and the Spirit rolls 7 dice with a Target Number 5.

Tests to keep the opponent in sight or to catch up are subject to Astral Perception Modifiers. (See page 63).

The opponent with the higher number of successes decides what happens. At normal movement rates, he can move a distance equal to his full move away from his opponent. At fast movement, he can evade his opponent completely, leaving the area. Alternatively, the winner can maintain combat range and can attack. A character who tries to break off combat and fails can try to avoid combat, but cannot counterattack.

ASTRAL COMBATANTS

Any astrally active being or thing can fight in Astral Combat. Only sentient beings such as Humans, dual beings, or Spirits can attack, however. Focuses, barriers, and other astrally active non-sentient things can only counterattack. Leave them alone, and they leave you alone. Spells that are cast at an astrally active being will initiate attacks against their target. Against other opponents, spells only counterattack.

The following rules clarify or modify the published rules for Astral Combat with various beings, bringing them into line with the new system presented here.

BARRIERS IN COMBAT

Magical Barriers only counterattack when attacked. An attacker has two options. First, he can try to pass the barrier alone. In this case, the damage he does the barrier only "counts" for him. If a character "kills" the barrier, it lets him pass through, but the damage done does not affect the barrier when anyone else fights it. On the upside, the barrier only does Stun Damage when fought this way.

If a character attacks the barrier to destroy it, the damage is Lethal. If anyone kills the barrier this way, it is gone.

DUAL BEINGS IN COMBAT

Dual-natured beings can include Awakened critters, Humans using Astral Perception, and Spirits manifesting on the physical plane (see **Spirits**, p. 74). A being that is astrally active but also has an active physical body can fight on both planes, with all astral activity resolved before the physical activity takes place in the Combat Turn.

FOCUSES IN COMBAT

A focus must be bonded and activated by its owner (**SR**, p. 79) to be astrally active, and thus is subject to Astral Combat. When such a focus is attacked, the owner is aware of it, whether or not he is astrally active.

SPELLS IN COMBAT

A magician who is not astrally projecting or astrally perceiving can cast a spell at any target he can see in the mundane world. One who is astrally perceiving may cast at any target he can see on either the etheric or mundane planes. A magician who is astrally projecting can only cast spells at astrally active targets on the etheric plane. Spells cannot be cast at other spells. They ignore each other.

If the target is not astrally active, the normal spellcasting rules apply. Astral Combat does not come into play. If the target is astrally active, then Astral Combat can take place. If the spell wins the fight, it "grounds" into the target's physical body and takes effect. It will ground no matter where it is, be it halfway across the planet or only a meter away.

The spell's Attributes, by the way, are equal to its real Force, and are not affected by additional dice due to focuses, Spirits, and so on.

If the target has no physical body, then only Mana-type Combat Spells can be used. Sorcery like "Mind Control" cannot affect a Spirit. Spirits cannot be destroyed by spells, but they can be "Disrupted" (see p. 75).

If a spell grounds successfully, that is, wins the Astral Combat, the target of the spell does *not* get its usual chance to resist the caster's Success Test. All the caster's successes count toward the spell effect on the target.

If an Area Spell grounds into a target, its effects strike everyone else in range on the physical plane, using normal spellcasting rules. Even if other targets are astrally active, they cannot try to block the spell astrally. It has closed the circuit to the physical plane, and so bypasses their defense. Guarding an astrally projecting magician's body can be risky, because an Area Spell thrown at his Astral Body would ground out into his physical body. No one likes a Fireball in the living room.

Spells cast at magical items must be able to physically affect the item, and must, therefore, be Physical Spells. If an Area Spell is cast at a magical item from Astral Space, it will ground out to the physical portion of the item, as described above.

A spell in Astral Combat takes damage normally. Only Lethal Damage affects it. If it wins, its wounds do not reduce its effect on the target. If it is killed, it is gone.

Damage done to the target's Astral Body in this fight is not permanent. Damage only counts to see if the spell overcomes the Astral Body. When the fight ends, any damage the spell did is cancelled out, no matter who won. Physical Spells do damage measured on the Physical Condition Monitor. Mana Spells do damage measured on the Mental Condition Monitor. Existing damage *does* affect the fight. A target with 4 boxes filled in on the Condition Monitor would be overcome when the spell did 6 more points of damage, but those 6 points of damage would "heal" at the end of the fight.

An astrally active magician who can reach the target of a spell can intercept a spell and engage it in Astral Combat. In other words, he can try to kill the spell in Astral Combat. He can also do this to sustained spells and spells held in place by Quickening or a spell lock. Damage done to the magician by the spell is real damage and does not go away at the end of the fight.

If all the attackers let up on a spell for even one of their actions, the spell regenerates all the damage it has taken.

If the target of a spell is given spell defense dice, they are added to his Astral Body Attribute when resisting the spell's damage.

The magician who casts a spell or is sustaining a spell can use his Astral Pools in place of the spell's own in Astral Combat. He still checks for Drain in the action when the spell is cast, and if he is knocked out, the spell vanishes. If the spell is intercepted, he can keep it attacking, but this counts as sustaining the spell for purposes of distraction and blocks doing exclusively magical actions.

Similarly, a magician who wants to give dice to someone fighting off a spell in Astral Space would have to reallocate them if his next action comes up while the fight is going on.

Complex? Yes. Though these rules are cleaner than in the first version, unfortunately, the subject just ain't simple.

ASTRAL SECURITY

Just as the invention of Matrix technology led to the rapid development of IC, so the rebirth of magic has led to techniques for securing areas from astral invasion.

The best security is provided by a powerful magician or magicians patrolling a secure area. As magicians do not work cheap and their time in Astral Space is limited to a few hours at a time, magical security is expensive.

Spirits can also provide astral patrolling. A bound Elemental can be assigned to astrally guard a given site for 24 hours. This counts as a service. If the master pays Karma equal to the Spirit's Force, the Elemental is bound to watch the site forever, or until it is banished or killed in Astral Combat. Once the Karma is paid to set the Elemental on astral guard duty, it no longer counts as bound to its summoner. A shaman can summon a Nature Spirit and ask it to guard the site of the summoning from astral intrusion until the Spirit's services are complete, i.e., at the next sunrise or sunset. A Spirit can patrol an area of about 10,000 square meters.

Watchers can also be summoned to act as astral guards.

Passive astral security, or barriers, exists in Medicine Lodges and Hermetic Circles. A Medicine Lodge provides a barrier against astral travelers all the time. A Hermetic Circle is an effective barrier only when in use. If a magician casts a Hermetic Circle for summoning a Fire Elemental, it is an astral barrier only when a mage is within it, summoning Fire Elementals. It is not astrally active the rest of the time. Astral barriers are opaque.

WARDS

Another form of astral barrier against astral travelers is the *ward*. A magician of any tradition who is capable of Astral Projection (not just Astral Perception) and of using Sorcery can set up a ward. A ward is an astral barrier that has no other magical application. It only blocks movement by characters using Astral Projection, dual-natured beings, and Spirits. It cannot serve as a working area for Ritual Sorcery, for example. It also provides "Hard Cover" from spells.

The maximum area a magician can ward is equal to his Magic Attribute times 100 square meters. A group of magicians can use Ritual Sorcery to ward an area that is 100 square meters times the sum of their Magic Attributes.

Warding requires a Sorcery Test with a Target Number equal to the desired Force of the ward. The result becomes the ward's rating as an astral barrier. The number of successes is the number of days the ward will last before dissolving. The magician may choose not to use all his successes, which makes it easier to Resist Drain for setting the wards.

The ritual of warding takes a number of hours equal to the Force of the ward and consumes special ritual materials costing 1,000 nuyen per unit. One unit is required for each point of Force the ward will have, and the materials are used up, whether or not the ritual succeeds.

Drain for casting wards is (Force)L(Days). Drain is *never* Lethal, but the maximum Force a magician can use in setting a ward is equal to twice his Magic Attribute. Centering may be used to Reduce Drain.

A magician can perform the ritual of warding to increase the lifespan of existing wards. He uses the same Force Rating as for the existing barrier and must use up additional ritual materials. The lifespan of the wards increases by the number of successes scored. If this ritual fails, the existing wards are not harmed unless the die results were all 1s, in which case the barrier is destroyed.

A number of firms and freelance magicians contract to maintain wards for those who value their astral privacy.

METAPLANES

There are realms beyond the etheric plane, levels of Astral Space known only to their inhabitants and to Initiates, who alone among Humanity have the power to travel to them. These are the *metaplanes*, or "higher" planes of Astral Space.

The scientists, the occultists, all the theory-wiz-boys, argue long and loud about the "real" nature of the metaplanes. Meanwhile, the magicians come and go among these planes of Astral Space without worrying much about the outcome of these arguments. For the purposes of **Shadowrun** gaming, the metaplanes are real places, inhabited by real beings. A character can die there. How much more real can it get?

There are eight known metaplanes. Four correspond to the hermetic elements: Fire, Water, Air, and Earth. Four correspond to the major classes of natural domain used in shamanism: the realms of Man, the Waters, the Sky, and the Land. Initiates of either tradition can travel to any metaplane.

In game terms, these metaplanes do not differ much from one another. However, they are traditional in magical literature, and the "theme" of a metaplane can help set the scene and the mood of an Astral Quest.

ASTRAL QUEST

Every time a magician enters a metaplane, he is committed to an *Astral Quest*. He cannot return to his body until he either completes this quest successfully or fails because he has taken too much damage.

Every task requiring an Astral Quest must have a *Quest Rating*, though the questing magician may or may not know the rating. If his quest involves a rating he controls (e.g., invoking a Great Spirit), he will know the Rating. In a case such as seeking the True Name of a Free Spirit, he would not know the Rating.

The goal of an Astral Quest is to reach the *Citadel*, the heart of the metaplane. Once there, the magician obtains whatever he came to the metaplanes to find.

Idle travel among the metaplanes is not possible. The magician must choose the metaplane to which he will travel when he leaves his body; once there, he cannot move to any other plane. If a magician wants to visit a metaplane without having a specific task to accomplish, the quest has a Rating of 1D6, and he will not know what it is!

METAPLANAR GEOGRAPHY

Though the vistas of the metaplanes vary wildly from one to the next, and indeed, can change from moment to moment, they have a common structure.

A metaplane is made up of *Places*, which correspond to human experiences. The same Place, on the same metaplane, visited on two different quests, can be entirely different.

A Place can be an abstract "landscape" of magical energy or seem as real and solid as the material world. It can be populated by creatures out of nightmare, empty of all life, or filled with Humans going about their concerns. It may appear as any scene from history, fantasy, myth.

A magician may find himself changed from Place to Place. He may face battle as a medieval knight in one Place, then in another, tackle a deadly challenge on the streets of the Sprawl in his own form. The astral medium is infinitely flexible.

There may be many other Places besides the ones discussed here, but they relate to aspects of the metaplanes that Humans cannot comprehend directly.

At each Place he visits on a metaplane, a traveler faces a challenge of some kind. The encounter may leave him wounded or even killed. If he overcomes the challenge, he will be able to forge deeper into the metaplane toward his goal.

Damage suffered in a Place can be physical or mental. Such damage is real, affecting the physical body as well as the astral. If the physical body, in trance in the material world, is healed, then the astral body is healed as well. Each use of healing magic this way uses up one *shift*, however, reducing the time that the magician can stay on the quest.

If the magician is knocked out by Mental Damage, he returns to his body, unconscious, just as though he had been knocked out in the physical world. If the magician is killed, that is, takes a fatal amount of Physical Damage, he is also back in his body and dying of his wounds! Again, this is real damage, as fatal as though the victim had been shot! In either case, the quest has failed.

It is because all Astral Projection into a metaplane follows this pattern that journeys into these realms are called *Astral Quests*. Once a magician enters a metaplane, he is stuck there until he completes the quest or fails at it.

QUEST TESTS

The challenge of each Place can be resolved by a simple test. Unfortunately for the character, it is a Damage Resistance Test. He must use a skill or attribute to resist a damage code specific to the Place, as though it were his Body Attribute. He can use his Astral Pool to augment the dice for this test. In this case, the Astral Pool renews every time he moves to a new Place.

As described later, it is possible to set up roleplaying challenges in a Place instead. This is more dangerous and more challenging, but when handled fairly and with an eye toward a good story, it is more satisfying. A gamemaster can even design Astral Quests with structured plots and encounters, rather than using the random system given in these rules. In general, fulfilling one of these challenges will automatically let a magician travel directly to the Citadel, but the risks can be much greater than simply taking his chances on the Resistance Tests.

DWELLER ON THE THRESHOLD

To begin an Astral Quest, the character must astrally project onto a metaplane. Initiates with the ability to use Astral Projection can do this under their own power. Others must gain access to Astral Space by a Free Spirit using the Astral Gateway Power (see p. 95). Either way, the character must project directly onto the metaplane. He can make no side trips on the etheric first.

If several people are carrying out a Quest together, they can start from different places, as long as it is at the same time and with the intention of working together. A magician in Manhattan can accompany a colleague from Seattle and another in Tokyo as easily as though they were all in the same room.

The magician always finds himself in the same place at the beginning of a Quest: floating in the dark void where the Dweller on the Threshold lives. He should get used to the view because every Astral Quest starts here.

The Dweller guards the metaplanes. He (it?) has no objection to Humans entering those realms, but he likes his little joke first. Some traditions say the Dweller is the crystallization of all that is negative or dark within the astral traveler. In any case, the Dweller will propose a test before the traveler can pass on to the metaplanes.

The Dweller also knows everything about the traveler: every crime, every secret, his real name, his numbered bank account, and so on. If the magician goes on a Quest with companions, he should be prepared to hear the Dweller announce some choice tidbit of information to them. The Dweller is fair, of course, revealing something about every member of the group. It is impossible to get around this by projecting into the Metaplanes separately and then joining up after passing the Dweller. All must begin the journey together, and once someone is hurled back to his body, he cannot rejoin the Quest.

After airing the travelers' assorted dirty laundry, the Dweller requires each to pass a test of some kind. The Dweller (that is, the gamemaster) chooses one of the character's skills or attributes, and the player makes a Success Test, with a Target Number equal to the Rating of the Quest. Any successes rolled count as "armor," that is, automatic successes in resisting damage from Quest Tests. They may also serve as armor in combat if roleplaying scenes are set up in the Places instead.

If the traveler fails the test, the Dweller sneers at him and sends him on his way.

METAPLACES

Each metaplane has many Places known to Humanity. As mentioned earlier, the metaplanes may include Places that Humans cannot comprehend. A Dragon on an Astral Quest may face challenges inconceivable to lesser beings.

Known Places are described below, but others can exist. Each Place tests a skill or attribute or may be used for a roleplaying scenario. The gamemaster can also create Places for one quest that never appear in other quests. If the gamemaster wants to create the Place of Booze where a quester must survive a drinking contest in one adventure, he need not worry about having a Place of Booze in all future Astral Quests.

When moving past the Dweller on the Threshold onto the metaplane, roll 1D6 and consult the Metaplaces Table. The traveler's Quest begins in that Place. If he survives the challenge of the Place, make a note that he has been there, keeping track of all the Places the character visits as the quest continues.

Next, roll 2D6. Starting from the character's current Place, count down the Metaplaces Table for the indicated number of Places. The result is the next Place on his quest. He must move to this Place.

If the dice say he moves to the Citadel, he achieves the goal of his quest. Otherwise, he deals with the challenge of the new Place and repeats the process. As mentioned above, it is important to keep track of Places he has been.

The gamemaster may also decide to design an Astral Quest in detail instead of using this random system of movement. If so, the traveler moves from Place to Place according to that scenario.

When a random movement dice roll lands the traveler in a Place he has been before, he moves instead to the place just before it on the table. If the character has been *there* before, he moves up to the next higher place, and so on. If this process takes him around the "top" of the Metaplaces Table, he does *not* reach the Citadel. Instead, he would move to the Place just before the Citadel.

For example, the traveler starts in the Place of Battle and survives combat there. The next rolls land him in the Place of Courage, and then the Place of Charisma, and then in the Place of Courage again. At the Place of Courage, he counts up the table to the Place of Charisma. But nope, he's been there. Next up is Battle. He's been there, too. "Rolling around" the top of the table, he arrives at the Citadel. No, again. Not allowed. Finally, working his way up the table, he reaches the Place of Spirits. As he has not been to this Place before, it becomes his next destination.

If random movement sends the traveler to every Place on the table without him either blowing the Quest or reaching the Citadel, he automatically goes to the Citadel on his next shift.

NOTE: The intent of these rules is that if a character successfully overcomes a roleplaying challenge that a gamemaster designs for a Place, the character can move directly to the Citadel. If he does not come up with a successful solution, the character moves on to the next place normally.

METAPLACES TABLE

1	Place of Battle
2	Place of Charisma
3	Place of Destiny
4	Place of Fear
5	Place of Knowledge
6	Place of Magic
7	Place of Spirits
8	The Citadel

Place of Battle

The challenge in the Place of Battle requires combat.

The Quest Test uses the character's best Melee Combat Skill to resist (Quest Rating)S2 Lethal Damage.

If the combat is roleplayed, the traveler must overcome some creature, preferably one appropriate to the metaplane, in combat. This can be a Spirit, an apparently real normal critter, or a type of paraspecies. Even other Humans are possible foes.

The Quest Rating should not affect the scores used in "real" combat too much. A fight is a fight, after all. If the Quest Rating is 3 or less, it means a fairly easy combat. An opponent of equal strength is appropriate for quests rated from 4 to 6, and Quests of 7 or higher should weight the fight somewhat in favor of the opposition.

Combat may be Astral Combat against a Spirit with a Force equal to the Quest Rating, or it may be real combat fought with physical weapons. In the latter case, spells, focuses, and so on work normally. The character can even use Astral Projection as though he were fighting the battle on the physical plane.

The gamemaster may allow the character to carry his usual weapons or may decide to arm and armor him in a particular manner. If the character has weapon focuses, however, they will always be with him. Because they are "real" on the metaplanes, they cannot be twisted by the energies of the Place.

In all fairness, Astral Combat is usually the way to go if a single magician is on the quest. If he has two street samurai with him, then physical combat is more likely.

Winning an actual battle allows the character to move directly to the Citadel. If he merely survives, he takes his next move randomly, as usual. If he runs away from the combat, he must still take the Quest Test before moving on to the next Place.

Place of Charisma

For a quest in the Place of Charisma, the traveler must use a Social Skill to resist damage of (Quest Rating)M2 Stun.

If it is a roleplaying scenario, success means that the magician can move directly to the Citadel. The scenario involves a social situation, but that does not mean a tea party! The character might have to stop a lynching, plead for his life in a trial, or preach a crusade. In this case, success means resolving the situation using charisma or social ability, or showing courage in making a compassionate decision. Solving a lynching scene by shooting everyone in sight is not a success, and would mean the questers must move on to the next Place.

If the situation breaks down, a combat can occur. Whether the character wins or loses this combat, he has not successfully resolved the situation. The gamemaster may decide otherwise if the quester made a really good try, however. To escape from the combat, he must take the Quest Test. Otherwise, winning the fight is the only way to move on to the next Place.

Place of Destiny

The Place of Destiny Quest Test uses the character's Magic Attribute (or Essence, if he is not a magician or adept) to resist (Quest Rating)S2 Stun.

For a roleplaying challenge in this most mystic Place, the character must overcome *himself* in some way. It may be in combat, either astral or real, or in some other area. He and his astral double may have to carry out a task such as spell design, Enchantment, or other. The one who carries it out best is the winner.

Alternatively, the character may be sent "back in time" to prevent or cause some historical event.

If he succeeds at this challenge, he moves to the Citadel. If he fails, he moves on to the next Place.

Place of Fear

The Place of Fear Quest Test uses Willpower to resist damage of (Quest Rating)D2 Stun.

Roleplaying this Place pits a character against something he fears or otherwise tests his courage in some way. Examples of successful solutions are resisting torture, swimming through stormy, shark-infested waters to save a drowning friend, or otherwise demonstrating bravery in the face a danger.

If the character flees the challenge, he must take the Quest Test to move on to the next Place. It is no small matter to turn away from Fear.

Place of Knowledge

The Place of Knowledge Quest Test here uses Science to resist (Quest Rating)M3 Lethal Damage. The knowledge area should be related to the metaplane.

Appropriate skills are:

Fire: Magical Theory, Military Theory
Water: Biology
Air: Psychology, Sociology
Earth: Physical Sciences
Man: Psychology, Sociology
Waters: Biology
Skies: Physical Sciences, Magical Theory
Land: Biology

If the character does not have the right skill, use the one closest on the Skill Web. To avoid charges of cruel and unusual punishment, the Target Number of the Resistance Test goes up by only +1 for every circle passed on the web, not the usual +2.

As a roleplaying challenge, the Place should require the character to solve a puzzle or to fulfill a task using a science or intellectual ability. Alternatively, the challenge can depend on *any* skill appropriate to the metaplane. This usually applies to shamanic planes, where skills in Wilderness Survival, Mountain Climbing, even Piloting Skill, can be relevant. Success permits the traveler to move to the Citadel. If he fails to unravel the puzzle, he must move on to the next Place.

Place of Magic

The Place of Magic Quest Test uses a Magical Skill to resist (Quest Rating)S2 Damage. The exact skill depends on the purpose of the quest.

Use Conjuring if the quest is intended to summon a Great Spirit or to learn the true name of a Free Spirit.

Use Magical Theory if the quest is intended to fulfill an Ordeal for Initiation.

Use Sorcery for all other purposes.

If roleplayed, the challenge involves some magical challenge, task, or test. The character may, for example, have to overcome a danger using spells (and Resist Drain) or banish a Spirit, or construct a formula.

Place of Spirits

In the Place of Spirits, the character must use Astral Combat or banishing to overcome a Spirit of the metaplane. There is no Quest Test. The character either defeats the Spirit or it defeats him. If he succeeds, he goes directly to the Citadel.

The Spirit's Force is equal to the Quest Rating.

If a group is present, increase the Spirit's Force by 1 for every two people on the quest. If mundanes are present, the gamemaster has the option of making this a physical combat, as in the Place of Battle. Modern weaponry is permissible; that is, game it as though the spirit were attacking the questers in the physical world.

The Citadel

The Citadel is the heart of the magical energy of the metaplane. Once a character reaches it, he has fulfilled whatever was the goal of his Quest. He receives the knowledge, the insight, the power, he needs. He then returns to his body.

TYPES OF QUEST

Why go through all this agony? What are the rewards of a successful Astral Quest?

Astral Concealment

Various items can be traced to a magician astrally: spell locks, material links for Ritual Sorcery, the linkages of a Thesis, and so on. Watchers can track him down in Astral Space. Whenever one of these tracers is on a character, he can "conceal" the linkage by way of an Astral Quest to any plane he chooses. Using this to throw a Watcher off his track is effective, since the pursuer cannot cope with the "impossible" direction the character's astral trail takes. Other linkages can be reestablished only by a Quest to the same metaplane.

This Quest is at any rating the character chooses. If he reaches the Citadel, he conceals the astral link there. Someone wishing to use this link to track him down must fulfill a Quest of the same rating to the same plane. Detecting the correct plane uses the same test as penetrating a Masked Aura (see p. 26).

The time required for this quest is equal to (Rating)D6 hours.

Great Summoning

As specified on p. 75, summoning the Great form of a Spirit involves an Astral Quest with a Rating equal to the Force of the Spirit. This quest is performed after completing the basic Summoning Ritual and Resisting Drain. The magician need not undertake the quest, however. Should the summoning fail, the magician take more Drain than he wishes, or simply think it better not to increase the Spirit's power, he can decide not to go. Otherwise, the Quest takes no time on the physical plane. To an observer, the magician would simply freeze for a moment after the Spirit materializes, and then the Spirit either grows into its Great form, or the magician collapses, wounded and unconscious, as the Spirit (still in its regular form) becomes uncontrolled.

Initiation

An Astral Quest (or Quests) can fulfill an Ordeal for Initiation (see p. 19). Shamans must carry out the Quest on the metaplane of their totem. Urban totems are always native to the metaplane of Man.

Mages must perform Quests on all *four* hermetic metaplanes. Failure in one Quest does not require that the mage repeat quests he has fulfilled. For example, if a mage succeeds at the quest on the Fire plane, but then fails on the Water plane, he does not have to repeat the Fire Quest.

The Quest Rating is equal to two times the grade being sought.

These Quests occur in deep trance, and the magician's Spirit can travel far. In physical time, the quest lasts for the Quest Rating in days.

Spirit Battle

A Spirit can be destroyed utterly if a character makes a Quest to its native plane and engages it in Astral Combat at the Citadel. This applies to Free Spirits, bound Elementals, Allies, or anything else with a native plane. It is even possible to destroy Spirits with a Hidden Life in this manner. Of course, the character must know where to look (see p. 81, **Native Planes**). Once the character reaches the Citadel, the Spirit will appear and Astral Combat *to the death* takes place.

This Quest lasts (Rating)D6 hours.

True Aura

An Astral Quest allows a magician to read the aura of an Initiate using Aura Masking. The Quest is equal to the magician's Initiation Grade. It takes no time on the physical plane, but the quester must be assensing the Masked Aura (and must know it is masked) when he projects to the Threshold.

True Name

A character can make an Astral Quest to learn the True Name of a Free Spirit (see p. 92). The Quest Rating is equal to the Spirit's Force. This quest takes (Rating)D6 hours on the physical plane.

Wisdom

A magician can learn certain spells by making an Astral Quest to the appropriate metaplane.

Mages must visit the metaplane of the element that governs the spell's purpose:

Fire for Combat Spells
Water for Illusion Spells
Air for Detection Spells
Earth for Manipulation Spells

Mages cannot learn Health Spells in this way.

Shamans can make a Quest to the native plane of their totem to learn any spell for which their totem gives them an advantage.

The Quest can also be undertaken to gain insight into formula design for any Magical Skill. The magician chooses the Quest Rating. After completing it successfully, he receives extra dice equal to the Rating for use in the Success Test for designing the formula. For example, a magician with Magic Theory 5 carries out a quest rated at 3. If it succeeds, he can roll 8 dice for a specific piece of formula design for a spell, a focus, an Ally, and so on.

Shamans can make this Quest on the native plane of their totem. The nature of the formula does not matter, for their totem is the source of all their magical understanding.

Mages must Quest on the metaplane of the element most appropriate to the subject of the formula. This would be to the metaplane governing Spell Purpose or the native plane of the Ally they wish to create. In the case of focus formulas that do not fit a particular element (power focuses, weapon focuses, and so on), the gamemaster selects an element at random, based on the astrological influences or some similar tide in the universe.

The Quest Rating is equal to the Force at which the spell is learned. The Quest takes physical time equal to (Rating)D6 hours.

"Catch the Spirit at Astral Associates. Call 4206-VASTY-DEEP."

—From an advertisement on the Business Thaumaturgy Datanet, October 12, 2050

he philosophers don't know what to make of them. Some theologians turn faintly green when the subject pops up. But when magicians call, they come. They are Spirits.

Conjuring Skill unlocks the gates between the planes to admit them, and they can swim in the energies of magic like dolphins—or sharks—in the bosom of the ocean.

The **Shadowrun** basic rules already presented Elementals and Nature Spirits. This **Grimoire** introduces several other types of being. It explains how magicians can summon Watchers, simple little servants and messengers who can carry out tasks in Astral Space. It reveals how to create Allies, the powerful familiar Spirits of legend, each one either a unique companion or a slave. The next chapter is a full description of the powers of Free Spirits, those who have become their own masters, pursuing their own mysterious ends in the Sixth World.

Before examining these new forces, some rules expansions and clarifications are needed to put Spirits into better perspective.

SPIRIT FORM

Nature Spirits and Elementals can appear in one of three forms: Astral Form, Manifest Form, and Great form.

ASTRAL FORM

The *Astral Form* is the one Spirits most favor. In this state, the Spirit is present astrally, just barely perceptible on the physical plane by a faint shimmering like heat haze on a summer's day. In Astral Form, Spirits can communicate with the magicians who control them and can be sensed by those using Astral Perception. The Spirit is also visible to normal sight while remaining in its Astral Form, but this does not constitute actual presence on the physical plane and so the Spirit is not vulnerable to physical weapons.

Spirits in Astral Form can only be attacked by banishing or Astral Combat. To keep the game balanced, gamemasters should limit the powers they can use in Astral Form. It is recommended that Spirits in Astral Form only use powers and services that defend or aid people.

They may use hostile powers (such as Alienation or Confusion) on targets that are astrally active. These powers can "ground" like spells (see **Astral Combat**, p. 65). Of course, Spirits in this form can engage in Astral Combat.

MANIFEST FORM

Spirits assume *Manifest Form* when they must use a power not available to them in Astral Form. Spirits usually manifest only if necessary to carry out their orders. They dislike Manifest Form because it makes them vulnerable to physical attacks.

There is much confusion about just how to "kill" a Spirit without the aid of a magician, and that is because it is so difficult. If mundanes have enough courage, however, they can attack and disrupt a Spirit appearing in its Manifest Form.

When an attacker uses a mundane weapon to strike or shoot at a Spirit in Manifest Form, use Willpower instead of his usual Attack Skill. Against Spirit foes, unshakable strength of will is more important than weapon skill. Attacks with weapon focuses, other magical attacks, and attacks using a Spirit's Vulnerability are not subject to this rule.

In addition, Manifest Spirits have the power of Immunity to Normal Weapons against Fire Combat Attacks, for these do not carry the full "charge" of the attacker's will. That is, against firearms, Spirits have "armor" equal to twice their Force. They do not, however, have this power against Melee Attacks, as there is nothing to attenuate the effects of their opponent's courage in close combat.

A Spirit in Manifest Form can use its powers against any target in its line-of-sight. Each such attack is a separate service. However, summoning a spirit to perform the physical service of fighting a group of enemies is a single service, no matter how many foes it must engage in that fight.

GREAT FORM

An Initiate can conjure a Spirit in its *Great Form*. To do this requires that the Initiate successfully summon the Spirit and survive the Drain of the summoning. He must then undergo an Astral Quest, as described in **Metaplanes**. This Quest takes no measurable time by physical-world clocks, no matter how long it may seem to the magician. The Quest Rating is equal to the Spirit's Force.

A Great Spirit can exercise its powers over a far greater area and with greater effect than can a Spirit in Astral or Manifest Form.

Great Spirits also have the power of Immunity to Normal Weapons. The armoring effect of this power is treated as Impenetrable Cover: small arms fire (any firearms with an effective Power under 5) merely bounces off (or passes through). Melee Attacks are fully effective, however, as are attacks that use any Vulnerability the Spirit has. As with Spirits in Manifest Form, the attacker uses Willpower instead of his usual weapon skills for all attacks with normal weapons. Resolve magical attacks and attacks exploiting a Vulnerability normally.

SPIRIT INITIATIVE

Creatures of quicksilver and shadow, Spirits move with great speed compared to bags of mud and blood like the rest of us.

Spirits in Astral Space receive a +10 Initiative bonus to their calculated Reaction. They can, however, only receive new commands on their summoner's actions.

In Manifest and Great Form, Spirit Initiative is equal to 5 plus its Reaction. This is used only to determine Initiative for action on the physical plane.

DISRUPTION

When a spirit is "killed" by banishing or by Lethal Damage in Astral Combat, only the most powerful magic can keep it from being destroyed. Some Free Spirits can actually survive this fate, as described in the next chapter.

If a Spirit's form is destroyed by Stun Damage in Astral Combat, a spell, or mundane weaponry, the Spirit is *disrupted*. A disrupted Spirit cannot appear on the etheric or physical planes in any form for 28 days minus its Force. The timing suggests a lunar influence at work, but no rigorous theory has yet emerged to account for this. The minimum time in which a disrupted Spirit can appear again is 24 hours.

Bound Elementals not available to a mage because they have been disrupted still count against the limit on the number of Elementals he can bind at one time. A mage who has bound his limit of Elementals and whose entire "stable" of Spirits has been disrupted would have to release one of the beings from the bond before he could conjure up reinforcements.

Watchers are never merely disrupted. If they are "knocked out," it destroys their fragile energies permanently.

The only way to bring a disrupted Spirit back from its exile before the time is to make an Astral Quest to its native plane with a Quest Rating equal to the Spirit's Force.

HEALING SPIRITS

If a Spirit is wounded while performing a service, its wounds are healed the next time it is called upon to perform a service.

The magician who summoned a Nature Spirit or Elemental can "heal" it. It takes an action to do this, and uses up another service owed by that Spirit. This does not heal the effects of banishing, which does not do damage in the normal sense of the word. It takes the magician an action to do this. If the last service that the Spirit owes is used up healing it, it will complete the service it is carrying out and then vanish.

Spirits also recover 1 point of damage on each monitor per minute after they are out of combat. After all, a few bullet holes can't do much against something made from the very fabric of the universe.

ELEMENTALS

If a mage wishes to increase the number of services owed him by an Elemental he has already bound, he can perform a new summoning ritual specifically to conjure that Spirit to new obedience. If the Conjuring Test succeeds, the new successes are added to the remaining services that the Spirit owes, extending its bond to the magician.

If an Elemental has lost Force Points, they can be restored by conjuring the Spirit in the same way, using its original Force as the Target Number. Instead of services, the successes are added to its Force to return the rating to its original value. Any successes left over from this process are lost. They do *not* increase the number of services the Spirit owes the magician.

In both cases, the magician must Resist Drain; if he passes out or is killed, the Spirit goes free at once. Similarly, a Conjuring Test that scores all 1s would free the Elemental.

When Elementals of opposing types engage in Astral Combat (Fire versus Water or Air versus Earth), the combat is resolved in a single clash. The Elemental with the lesser Force is destroyed utterly. The Elemental with the higher Force has its Force reduced to the difference between the ratings of the two. Elementals of opposed elements and equal Force destroy one another.

Free Elementals are not so vulnerable. They engage in normal Astral Combat with Elementals of the opposing element, but each spirit is exposed to its Vulnerability when struck.

BOUND ELEMENTALS

This section attempts to clarify just what a bound Elemental is and when and how to call one for a service.

Any Elemental that is doing a task for a magician or who can be ordered to do so counts against the limit on bound Elementals, i.e., the magician's Charisma Rating. This includes Elementals sent on a remote service. On p. 87, the **Shadowrun** basic rules state that Elementals used for remote service cannot be bound, which was intended to mean that the summoner does not get additional services from an Elemental when on remote service. It will do the job or be destroyed trying, and thereafter owes the summoner nothing. The summoner cannot call it away from its job by demanding a service.

Elementals on remote service *do* count against the Charisma limit, until they either carry out their orders, are destroyed, or are taken over by another mage.

A mage cannot "release" an Elemental on remote service prematurely in order to make room for another Spirit. This is why this service is not lightly chosen; one must take on an awful lot of Karma for it.

Any Elemental that is not sent on a remote service is considered truly bound. It owes the summoner services.

It takes an action for a character to call a bound Elemental to attend him. At that time, he must specify the service he desires, whether it will take place in that action, or whether the Elemental is to keep its power in reserve until the mage is ready to use it. If he expects to be juggling many spells, he can call up a bound Elemental and tell it to stand by until he is ready to use

ELEMENTALS

	B	Q	S	C	I	W	E	R	Attacks
Air	F–2	(F+3) x 4	F–3	F	F	F	(F)A	F + 2	Special
Powers: Engulf, Manifestation, Movement, Noxious Breath, Psychokinesis.									
Weakness: May Be confined, Vulnerability (Earth)									
Earth	F + 4	(F–2) x 2	F + 4	F	F	F	(F)A	F–2	4S3, +1 Reach
Powers: Engulf, Manifestation, Movement									
Weakness: Vulnerability (Air)									
Fire	F + 1	(F + 2) x 3	F–2	F	F	F	(F)A	F + 1	3M4
Powers: Engulf, Flame Aura, Flame Projection, Manifestation									
Weakness: Vulnerability (Water)									
Water	F + 2	F x 2	F	F	F	F	(F)A	F–1	6D2 Stun
Powers: Engulf, Manifestation, Movement									
Weakness: Vulnerability (Fire)									

Aid Sorcery. Calling up a bound Elemental is an exclusive act, i.e., no other magic may be cast or maintained in the same action. The mage can use the Elemental's service in that action if it does not involve casting or maintaining spells, however. If he ordered up a Fire Elemental for Aid Sorcery, and in the same action were hit with a Combat Spell, the mage could use the Elemental's Force to resist the spell.

Changing the Spirit's orders also takes an action and uses up a service.

Some magicians and a few impudent samurai have complained that it seems unreasonable that Spirits would hang around for hours, or even days, on standby without getting bored and ticked off. Putting aside the anthropocentric arrogance of believing that time means the same thing to an immortal Spirit that it does to transients, Spirits will eventually get fed up. Twenty-four hours on duty uses up a service, even if the Spirit does not accomplish a task in that time.

ELEMENTAL POWERS

Elementals have certain powers unique to them as Spirits. These powers and some clarifications are discussed below. Note that all Spirits may manifest, as mentioned previously.

ENGULF

The Engulf attack is a Melee Attack. The Spirit uses its Quickness to hit the target. Targets must counterattack successfully to avoid engulfment. If a victim is engulfed, the effects vary.

Each time it is the *victim's* action, he can try to escape. Make Resisted Success Tests, with the victim's Strength versus the Elemental's Force, Base Target Number 4. If the victim wins, he breaks free.

On each of the *Spirit*'s actions, engulfed victims must resist damage, as follows.

Fire Elemental

The effect here is the same as being struck by the Elemental in combat. Damage is 3M4, +2 Staging for Flame Aura, with 3M6 damage. (Impact Armor helps against damage; Ballistic, which tends to melt, does not).

Note that a Great Fire Elemental's Engulf attack will have a Rating equal to its Force.

Water Elemental

Resist (Force)M(Actions) Stun Damage. The Staging is equal to the Spirit's number of actions since engulfing the victim. This is rougher than normal drowning, because the Spirit is able to exert great pressure on Engulfed victims. Victims who pass out are still exposed to damage during the Spirit's actions, and will take Lethal Damage as a result. Eventually, they will drown.

Air Elemental

Resist (Force)S2 Stun effects of the Noxious Breath power, using Willpower or Body, whichever is greater. Because the Elemental can astrally penetrate breathing gear or other protective systems, these items provide no defense. The Engulfed victim continues to take damage after being rendered unconscious, which will do Lethal Damage, eventually suffocating him.

Earth Elemental

Resist 4S3 damage from crushing weight of the Spirit. Impact Armor defends against this, not Ballistic.

FLAME AURA

Flame Aura gives the Elemental the power to make its surface ripple with flame, burning any who touch it. The aura extends out from its Manifest Form for a distance equal to the Spirit's Force in centimeters. Intense forms of this power may make wooden objects burst into flame at a touch or even melt plastic or metal weapons.

Any successful Melee Attack against an Elemental with Flame Aura means that the attacker may take damage from the intense heat. The attacker must make a Body Resistance Test against a Damage Code of the Spirit's (Force)M2. Impact Armor does count in resisting damage if the gamemaster rules that the character in question struck the Elemental with an armored part of its body.

Any successful Melee Attack by a Spirit with Flame Aura increases its Damage Code Staging by +2, including Engulf.

FLAME PROJECTION

With this power, a Spirit can project flame. This attack has a Damage Code of (Force)L1.

An Elemental Spirit may sustain this attack, but will suffer Drain the way a magician does: Drain (Force)S2. When the attack is sustained, the Spirit spreads the effects over a number of square meters equal to its Force.

Highly flammable items may be ignited by a Flame Projection attack.

MOVEMENT

The Spirit may increase or decrease its victim's movement rate within the terrain it controls, multiplying or dividing the rate by the Spirit's Force.

NOXIOUS BREATH

The nauseating effects of the Spirit's "breath" incapacitate the victim. The victim makes a Willpower or Body Resistance Test (whichever is greater) against the Damage Code, which is (Force)S2. Neither Armor nor Dermal Plating help in making this Resistance Test.

PSYCHOKINESIS

Psychokinesis works in a manner similar to the magic spell, Magic Fingers, with a Strength equal to the Spirit's Force.

GREAT ELEMENTALS

Great Elementals appear as large versions of their Manifest Form (**SR**, p.182). Great Elementals can use their Engulf power as an area attack, affecting all within a radius equal to their Force in meters. The Spirit is the center of this area. It can choose not to attack friendly characters within the area.

Great Elementals can also produce showy and often dangerous special effects appropriate to their element within their line-of-sight. A Great Fire Elemental can ignite highly flammable materials. A Great Water Elemental can burst water mains and sewer pipes, cause plumbing to flood and so on. It can direct masses of water like a fire hose. A Great Air Elemental can generate fierce winds, causing all movement in the area to be as though on treacherous ground. A Great Earth Elemental can set up a series of minor earth tremors (.4 or .5 on the Richter Scale), which can cause damage to fragile structures or items and also create treacherous ground for all in the affected area.

NATURE SPIRITS

Some questions have also arisen about Nature Spirits since publication of the basic rules. Following are the four main classifications of Nature Spirits, with a listing of the powers of each.

SPIRITS OF MAN

City Spirit
Accident, Alienation, Concealment, Confusion, Fear, Guard, Search

Hearth Spirit
Accident, Alienation, Concealment, Confusion, Guard, Search

Field Spirit
Accident, Concealment, Guard, Search

SPIRITS OF THE LAND

Desert Spirit
Concealment, Guard, Movement, Search

Forest Spirit
Accident, Concealment, Confusion, Fear, Guard

Mountain Spirit
Accident, Concealment, Guard, Movement, Search

Prairie Spirit
Accident, Alienation, Concealment, Guard, Movement, Search

SPIRITS OF THE SKY

Mist Spirit
Accident, Concealment, Confusion, Guard, Movement

Storm Spirit
Concealment, Confusion, Electrical Projection, Fear

SPIRITS OF THE WATERS (LAKE, RIVER, SEA, SWAMP)

Lake Spirit
Accident, Engulf, Fear, Guard, Movement, Search

River Spirit
Accident, Concealment, Engulf, Fear, Guard, Movement, Search

Sea Spirit
Accident, Alienation, Concealment, Confusion, Engulf, Fear, Guard, Movement, Search

Swamp Spirit
Accident, Binding, Concealment, Confusion, Engulf, Fear, Guard, Movement, Search

DOMAINS

One rule to keep in mind is that any given place is in only one domain. A step away, and another domain might hold sway. The gamemaster decides in which domain a shaman is when he wants to cast a spell. A recent case in Seattle boiled down to whether the shaman was sitting in the front seat of the limousine (which was inside the bakery's plate glass window and therefore in the domain of a Hearth Spirit) or the back seat (which was still over the sidewalk, thus in the domain of a City Spirit).

Domains are sharply restricted. A City Spirit can exercise a power like Search on the streets, squares, and plazas of the city. It cannot find the object of a Search if it is inside a building (Hearth Spirit territory), a park (Forest Spirit), on a boat on the river (River Spirit), or Puget Sound (Ocean Spirit, most definitely).

Great Nature Spirits can cross domain lines, but lesser forms cannot leave their domain nor can their powers extend into a different domain.

Nature Spirits in Astral Form can only use powers that directly protect or benefit the shaman, such as Concealment, Guard, and Movement. To use their powers on others, for good or ill, the Spirit must assume a Manifest Form.

The descriptions of Manifest Forms in the basic rules should make it clear that Nature Spirits take many different manifestations. Some tend toward more naturalistic forms: clouds, masses of earth or water, whirlwinds and dust devils, and so on. Others may assume the more humanoid forms that gave rise to legends of "little people" in cultures around the world. Spirits of Man are most likely to assume a Human form, but that by no means implies they are all cute little munchkin types. Spirits of the deep wilderness, the storm, and the open sea are the least likely to assume such Human forms.

MULTIPLE SPIRITS IN A DOMAIN

Nature is a pool of infinite energy, which Human magic cannot exhaust. If many shamans are in the same place and each wishes to raise a Nature Spirit, he can. However, no one shaman can raise more than one Spirit at a time in one domain.

Nature Spirits can fight one another in Astral Combat, of course. Similarly, any two Nature Spirits in the domain can oppose one another with their powers. The Spirits can also use offsetting powers, with one trying, say, to strike a target with Accident, while the other protects the target with Guard. The Spirit with the higher Force will win such a contest. Its power takes effect with a rating equal to the difference between the higher Force and the lower.

Alternatively, one Spirit could simply try to prevent the other from using a power. Instead of opposing Accident with Guard, the defending Spirit would simply use its Force to block its opponent's use of the power. In such a case, make Resisted Force Tests. The Target Number for each Spirit is the Force of its opponent. The winner can use its powers freely. The loser is unable to use its powers until its next action, when it can try again.

NATURE SPIRIT POWERS

A Manifest Spirit can only use a power on an individual target. Each use of a power generally uses up a service, though having a Spirit fighting on behalf of its summoner only counts as one service, regardless of the number of foes involved.

Beneficial powers do not require a test, but instead use the Spirit's Force to measure their effects.

The use of a harmful power requires an Unresisted Force Test, with the victim's Body or Willpower (whichever is higher) as the Target Number. If the victim has Conjuring Skill, that may substitute for the attribute, because the skill includes numerous traditional charms used over the centuries to turn away the malice of the "fair folk." If the Force Test succeeds, the power takes effect with a rating equal to the Spirit's Force. In cases where the Spirit can produce an Area Effect, it makes a Force Test once. Note the highest Target Number it scores. Anyone in the area who does not have a resisting Attribute (Body, Willpower, or Conjuring Skill) is affected. The Spirit can choose not to affect "friendly" characters in the area, if the summoner orders it to spare them.

A simple ranged attack, such as Electrical Projection by a Storm Spirit, is handled exactly like Fire Combat, except that the Target Number is derived from the target's Attributes instead of range. Successes can increase the Damage Code of the attack.

In the case of other powers, note the number of successes rolled. They act as a rating used to measure the effects of the power.

Following are descriptions of the powers appropriate to Nature Spirits, including some clarifications.

Accident

A character hit with Accident must make an Unresisted Quickness or Intelligence Test, whichever Rating is higher, with a Target Number equal to the Force of the Spirit. If he fails the test, his action is lost as he trips and gets a faceful of leaves—or cream pie, for that matter. Accident is not intrinsically dangerous, but the environment can make it so. A fall in a narrow mountain ledge can be most unfortunate.

A Great Spirit can cause a dangerous accident, doing (Essence)L3 damage.

Alienation

Alienation power as used by Nature Spirits is not intended as a beneficial power of invisibility. Victims of this power are invisible, intangible, and inaudible to those around them. It is as though they are not there. They are *alienated* from other people. Drivers do not stop for them. Their friends shoot through them to hit targets, lob grenades or powerballs around them, and so on. The Spirit's Force is the victim's Target Number in a Success Test of whatever Attribute or Skill seems appropriate to avoid dangerous situations or to get someone's attention, if only out of the corner of his eye.

A Great Spirit can alienate anyone in its domain whom it can see or who can see it.

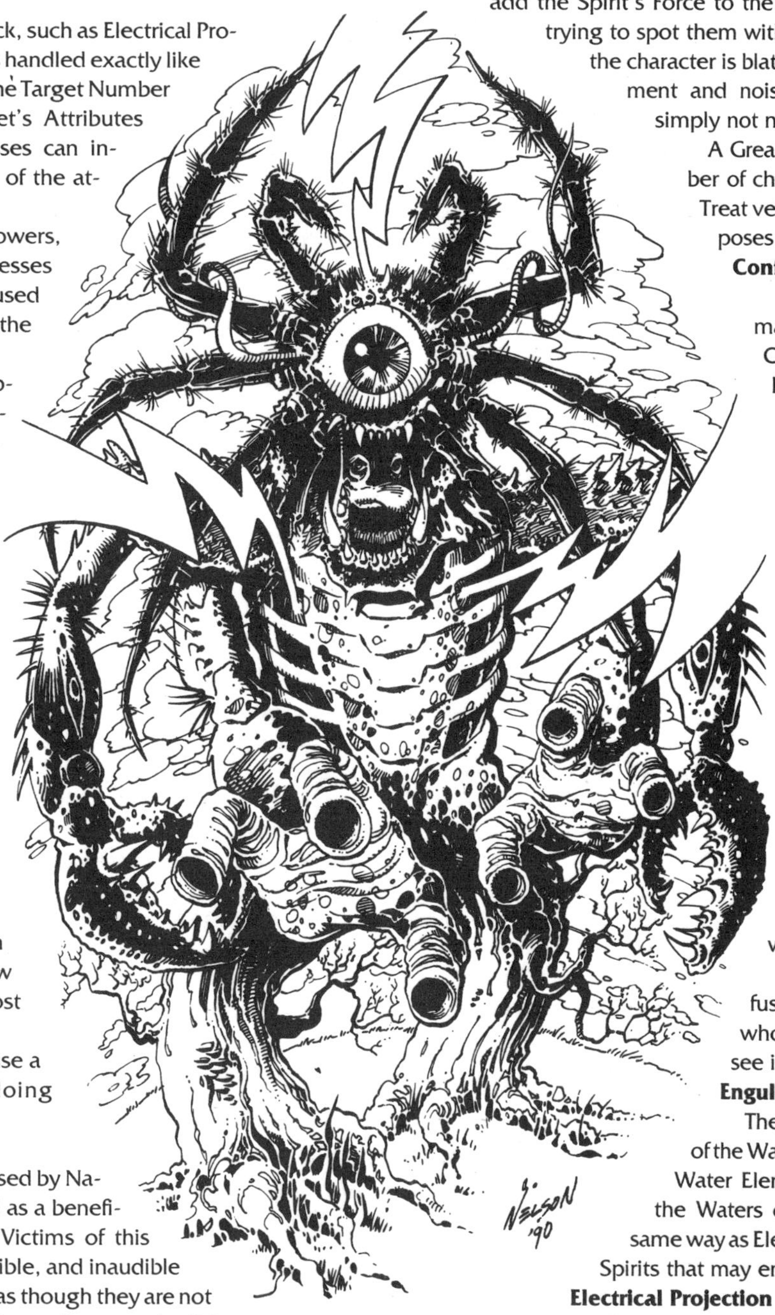

Binding

Binding gives a Spirit the power to make its victim "stick" to a surface or to itself. The binding has a Strength Rating equal to twice the Spirit's Force.

Concealment

Characters under the Concealment power of a Nature Spirit add the Spirit's Force to the Target Number of anyone trying to spot them with a Perception Test. Unless the character is blatantly obvious about movement and noise, a casual observer will simply not notice him at all.

A Great Spirit can conceal a number of characters equal to its Force. Treat vehicles as characters for purposes of this total.

Confusion

If Success Tests must be made when a victim is under Confusion, add the Spirit's Force to all Target Numbers. In addition, when the victim must make any decision, he must make an Unresisted Willpower Test with a Target Number equal to the Spirit's Force. If this fails, he dithers, unable to make up his mind, and will stay that way until something happens to remind him of the need for a decision. An attack, a verbal reminder from a companion, or something similar allows another test. If left alone, a character in this state will eventually wander off.

A Great Spirit can confuse anyone in its domain whom it can see or who can see it.

Engulf

The Engulf power of the Spirits of the Waters work the same way for Water Elementals. A Great Spirit of the Waters can engulf an area in the same way as Elementals. They are the only Spirits that may engulf.

Electrical Projection

Electrical Projection gives the Spirit the power to strike a target with a discharge of electricity. Depending on the being, results may range from a mild shock to a lightning bolt. A victim can neither dodge nor defend against Electrical Projection attacks. This attack does (Force)M3 damage and disorients the target for a number of turns equal to one-half the Spirit's Force.

Fear

Fear power works as described on p.176 of the **Shadowrun** rules. If the Spirit overcomes his target's resistance, the victim is filled with overwhelming fear and must flee. A Great Spirit can induce fear in anyone in its domain whom it can see or who can see it.

Guard

Guard does *not* increase defenses against attacks or magic, but the Spirit's Force is used as automatic successes in any tests against damage from accidents or natural phenomena in the domain. Someone falling (or even jumping) off a cliff while under the guard of a Mountain Spirit would get its Force as automatic successes in resisting damage from the fall.

Normal dangers of the domain, e.g., drowning in water, dehydration in the desert, freezing in the cold, and so on, are cancelled altogether. A person guarded by a Lake Spirit cannot drown in the Spirit's lake at all.

Note that *all* Spirits of Man, the Land, and the Waters should have Guard as a power. (This was omitted from some of the descriptions on p.185 of the basic rules).

A Great Spirit can guard a number of characters equal to its Force.

Movement

Movement works as specified in the basic game. A Great Spirit can modify the movement of a number of characters equal to its force.

Search

The summoner must be able to envision the subject of the Search very clearly. Because of the astral connection between them, the Spirit can then read the image from the summoner's mind. A vague command such as "locate every corporate security guard within two blocks" may not be carried out completely, if at all. The magician does not have to know all the guards by sight, but must be able to give the Spirit something to go on: the look of a uniform or a "generic" image of heavily armed plainclothes corp goons.

Nature Spirits do not deal well with high-tech. A Hearth Spirit sent to search an office building for a secret file can probably locate a printed file if the summoner knows the title (and is interested enough in Humans to handle such concepts), but will have trouble with electronic data. It might know how to log onto a workstation (after all, it is the Spirit of an office building), but will not be any great shakes as a hacker.

The Spirit makes an Unresisted Force Test using a number of dice equal to twice its Force. The Target Number is 4 for finding a living thing. For other things, use the Object Resistance Ratings for Sorcery (**SR**, p. 81).

The basic area a Spirit can search is 1,000 square meters times its Force. A Spirit can double the search area for +2 to the Target Number. Double it again for +4 and so on. Each doubling adds +2 to the Target Numbers.

To determine the Target Number for a search:

1) Calculate the area to be covered. A city block, for purposes of scale, is about 50 by 50 meters, or 2,500 square meters. Say the Spirit is to search a 40-story office building. The building is about a quarter-block across (about 400 square meters on a floor). 400 x 30 = 12,000 square meters.

2) Divide the area by 1,000. Divide the result by the Spirit's Force. Round any fractions up. Multiply the result by 2. Add that to the Base Target Number. A Force 4 Hearth Spirit examining a 12,000 square-meter building in search of someone the summoner believes is held captive there, has a Base Target Number of 4 (looking for living person). The modifier is: 12,000/1,000, or 12. 12/4 = 3. 3 x 2 = 6. 4 + 6 gives a final target of 10.

If the Spirit scores no successes, it does not find its quarry. It will take the full base time for the search to come up empty.

The base time for a search is the area to be searched divided by the Spirit's Force x 5 (its normal speed in Astral Space). This is the figure in minutes. Great Spirits divide the area by Force x 10. After calculating the base time for the search, divide it again by the Spirit's successes in the test. This is the time it will actually take for the Spirit to find its quarry.

If the object of the search is not in the Spirit's domain, a successful search will reveal that fact. An unsuccessful search means the Spirit does not know whether the quarry is present or not.

Storm

Storm is a new power, and one only available to Great Nature Spirits. Spirits of Man cannot have this power. The Spirit can cause a storm anywhere in its entire domain, whether it be a tiny waterspout on a lake or a storm covering a vast area created by a Great Storm Spirit. The upper limit is a radius equal to the Force of the Spirit x 100 meters. Storm Spirits, by the way, can create a storm regardless of the domain on the ground.

A storm can do massive damage, depending on its type. Each time the magician calls down this kind of destruction, however, he must Resist Drain as though conjuring the Spirit. Each storm strike also counts as a separate service.

If an uncontrolled Spirit is causing the Storm power, it must resist (Force)D2 damage each time it throws a storm strike, as it is severely draining its energies.

The damage for a storm strike is (Force)S3. Armor is no help and this damage is effective against vehicles, but at half-Force and only M3.

Everyone and everything in the area of a storm is subject to damage from a storm strike, unless protected by the Guard power of a Spirit of equal or greater Force. This can be the Spirit causing the storm or another. It need not be a Great Spirit. Note that a Spirit of the domain where the Storm Spirit's targets are located could guard the victims or oppose the Spirit's use of this power. If a character were under attack by a Great Storm Spirit in the mountains, a Mountain Spirit could protect him.

Storms can be the kind with howling winds, lightning, rain, and twisters or equally devastating phenomena proper to the domain such as tidal waves, earthquakes, avalanches, and flash floods.

TOXIC DOMAINS

A river streaked with a half-dozen poison-bright strands of chemicals. A wood where toxic waste leaches into the soil, killing the trees where they stand. An abandoned factory, concrete graveyard of rusting machinery and waste tanks, without a single pulse to show that once Humans lived and worked here.

These are toxic domains, places where the order of nature has been twisted, raped, or ground flat and embalmed in plastic and concrete.

The Nature Spirits in these areas are warped by the damage done to their domain and cannot be summoned by any sane shaman. An insane shaman is another matter, discussed more fully in the section on **Toxic Shamans**, p. 101.

The question of toxicity is fairly straightforward when dealing with natural domains, but what about Spirits of Man? If it were just a question of pollution, City Spirits would all be toxic, right?

The Spirits of Man flourish where Human love, liberty, and the energy of life are found. Even in the squalor of the Barrens, these qualities exist. Spirits of Man become toxic at two extremes of the Human condition. The first is where misery, poverty, and cruelty reduce Humanity to hopelessness, and the second is where Humanity itself is twisted by regimentation, repression, and the denial of life, no matter what the level of material comfort.

Examples of the first condition are the great urban slums where there is no hope, no drive, nothing but bleak days, one after the other. Plague zones or areas smashed by famine or in a chaos of natural disaster that mixes the domains would also fall into this category. And no shaman has ever reported successfully raising a Spirit on the site of a former death camp, whether in Auschwitz, Kampuchea, or Abilene.

The second condition admirably describes most high-security corporate facilities: the land smashed flat, suffocated by concrete and asphalt, sterilized, and populated with ranks of mindless wage slaves, good little salarymen.

The powers of the hermetic magician are dispassionate. Elementals neither weep nor rejoice at Human misery. Shamanic Spirits, however, can only echo that which creates them, whether it is the pulse of life in a normal domain or the twisted poison of a toxic one. And a shaman cannot safely traffick with the latter.

NATIVE PLANES

All Spirits seem to have a *native plane*, with the possible exception of Watchers. It has been argued that the etheric is their native plane, but who cares?

More powerful Spirits are native to a metaplane. Elementals are native to the metaplane of their element, and Nature Spirits to the metaplane appropriate to their domain. The importance of native planes is referred to in many areas of the rules, but this section spells out just what the term means.

ALLIES

A magician conjures an Ally Spirit to provide extra power or to create a servant or perhaps a companion. An Ally can be a valuable source of extra punch, both physically or magically. Magical tradition also calls Allies "familiar spirits," from the Latin *famulus*, meaning a trusted family servant.

Each Ally is unique, created according to a special formula using the rituals of Conjuring Skill. The magician gives life to the Spirit by giving it 1 point of his own Magic Attribute. He also gives it attributes and skills, paying Karma for these ratings. At first, Allies have little personality and unquestioningly obey the commands of their creator. As they grow in power, Allies can become more independent, perhaps even too strong for their creator to control.

If an Ally escapes from its master's control, it becomes a Free Spirit (see p. 90). Because its master retains great power over it, a Free Spirit may devote itself to bringing about the death of its former master. Most magicians must struggle with the question of whether they should banish the Ally while they can still control it, thus losing access to the Spirit's abilities, or try to maintain control over an increasingly willful being.

When a magician wants to create an Ally, the player running the character designs its characteristics and the magician must expend time, power, and Karma—lots of it—to create it.

Allies are created in a Ritual of Summoning, and may be modified later by a Ritual of Change. Knowledge of these rituals is part of Conjuring Skill.

Allies have no inherent appearance, for all their characteristics are designed by the magician who creates them.

NATIVE PLANES OF ALLIES

The magician must specify a native plane for his Ally. Shamans must draw their Allies from a shamanic plane and mages from a hermetic metaplane. The Spirit does not receive any powers or abilities by virtue of originating from a given metaplane, but a magician could destroy an Ally by making the appropriate Astral Quest to that plane.

POWERS OF ALLIES

Allies can have many powers, though some powers preclude others.

Inhabitation

The Ally can inhabit a physical body prepared for it by the summoner. This is not the same as possession, which allows the Spirit to try to inhabit any living body. Rather, the magician makes a suitable host body available to the Spirit. This power actually limits the Spirit in some ways, but makes it more powerful on the physical plane.

The Ally cannot leave this body while it still lives. When inhabiting its body, the Ally functions as a dual-natured being and is still astrally active. The Spirit cannot use Manifestation power, because it is locked into the host body.

The magician can provide an animal host. Any normal critter may be used for this purpose. Paranatural animals are too magically powerful to be used as hosts, as are sapient beings (such as people). The Ally adds its Force to all the Physical Attributes of the host animal. The animal body receives the additional powers of Immunity to Age and Pathogens.

More impressively, the magician can make or commission a unique focus (see p. 49) to create an *homunculus* as a host body. This is an enchanted item, a statue. It adds its Enchantment Rating to the Spirit's Physical Attributes and has "external" armor (both Ballistic and Impact) based on the material from which it is made (see **Homunculus Materials Table**). The focus formula for an homunculus requires a copy of the formula for the Ally (see below).

If the host body is destroyed, the Ally retreats to its native metaplane. The magician has a choice. It can procure a new host body of the same type and perform a Ritual of Change to conjure the Spirit back into the new body. There is no Karma cost for this ritual. Alternatively, the magician can try to summon the Spirit back and permanently give up its power of Inhabitation. This requires an Astral Quest to the native metaplane, with a rating equal to the Ally's Force. If the Quest fails, the Spirit goes free.

If the Spirit becomes free while inhabiting a host body, it must remain in that body. If the body is destroyed, it must be "rescued" by a Ritual of Change or an Astral Quest by some friendly magician. As the magician must know the Ally's true name to do either of these, the Spirit must trust the magician completely.

HOMUNCULUS MATERIALS TABLE

Material	Armor
Clay*	2
Wood**	3
Bronze	5
Iron	8
Stone	6

* Severe allergy: Water (i.e., will soften and melt. Treat immersion as 4M2 damage per action. Treat high-pressure stream such as fire hose as 6S1 weapon.)

** Severe allergy: Fire

Immunity To Normal Weapons

When in Manifest Form, Allies, like other Spirits, have Immunity to Normal Weapons, as described on p. 176, **Shadowrun**. Allies with Inhabitation power do *not* have this immunity.

Manifestation

Manifestation is described on p.177 of **Shadowrun**. When creating an Ally, the magician chooses a true form for it. He may also choose additional Spirit forms. The Ally may manifest in any of these forms, but its Attributes will always be at the ratings specified in its formula. See **Designing The Ally** below. Allies with Inhabitation power do not have Manifestation, for they are bound to their host body.

An Ally cannot appear in a Great Form.

Sense Link

The magician can choose to "buy" Sense Link power for his Ally. If he does, one of the services the Spirit can provide is allowing its master to perceive with its senses, no matter how far apart the two may be. The magician's own senses are shut down while using Sense Link. The power may be used to view the physical plane if the Ally is manifesting or inhabits a host body. If the Ally is in Astral Space, the magician assenses what the Spirit can without being astrally active. He is, therefore, not vulnerable to astral attack.

Sorcery

An Ally has Sorcery Skill, with a rating equal to its creator's own at the time of creation. Allies cannot learn spells on their own as long as they are bound to a master, however. A Free Spirit can learn its own spells.

The only way an Ally can learn a spell is when its master learns the spell specifically for the Ally. Note that if a magician learns a spell for his Ally, he does not learn it himself. The Ally knows it, not the master, who must learn it all over again if he wants to know the spell, too.

Allies are subject to the normal rules for Sorcery, including Drain. If they are knocked out by normal Drain, they disrupt (see p. 75). If they are killed by lethal Drain, they are gone for good.

Telepathic Link

This power allows an Ally to communicate telepathically with its master. Communication is limited to line-of-sight. If there is a background count on the Astral Plane when the Ally tries to communicate with the magician, the Spirit must pass a Force Test, with a Target Number equal to the background count. Make this test in each action that the two try to communicate. The test is always made by the Spirit, no matter which of them is trying to send thoughts.

Three-Dimensional Movement

Allies in a manifested form or an inhabited body can move in three dimensions. They can "walk on air" at their normal movement rate. Allies active only in Astral Space can, of course, do this anyway, plus moving at the blindingly fast rates of travel available to Astral Beings.

SERVICES OF ALLIES

As a rule, Allies are always astrally present in the company of their master. If the Ally is inhabiting a physical body, it may not necessarily be where its master is. Of course, if the magician sends it off to do a job for him, the Ally cannot be with him at the same time.

It takes an action to order the Spirit to perform a service, though the magician can always tell the Spirit to be ready to perform a specific service for him. As a Spirit becomes more independent, it may perform some needed service without being told. A Spirit that resents its treatment is unlikely to do this.

Astral Watch

The Ally will watch Astral Space for its master, and will attempt to contact him telepathically if anything happens on the astral. The Spirit can also be ordered to guard a specific site and to attack astral intruders. If the Ally must make a Perception Test, use its Force for the test.

Aid Power

The Ally acts as a power focus, adding its Force to its master's Magic Attribute and to his Magic Pool.

Resist Drain

The magician may have the Ally Resist Drain for spells he has cast. Resist Drain as though the Spirit had cast the spell at the Force the magician used. It may use its Magic Pool to aid in Resisting Drain.

Alternatively, when the magician has tried to Resist Drain himself, he may permanently sacrifice the Ally's Force to buy additional successes. Each point of Force sacrificed buys an extra success. If the Spirit's Force is reduced to 0, it is destroyed.

If a character uses this option much and the Ally later becomes free, he'd best watch out. This service is agonizing to the Spirit, and it may decide to take that out on its former master. Hey, no one likes to have their own Essence burned off to save someone else's butt!

In addition, the magician may send the Ally off to perform physical services, do astral spotting for Ritual Sorcery, engage in Astral Combat, and so on.

DESIGNING THE ALLY

Before the Ally can be conjured by the character, the player must decide on its attributes, skills, and levels of power, and how much Karma he can spend.

Appearance

The magician may choose one Manifest Form for the Ally free of charge. If it will have Inhabitation power, this form is the same as its host body. Otherwise, the true form and any of the Spirit's additional forms can be anything at all, subject to gamemaster approval.

The Spirit can manifest physically in any of these forms, but its attributes will not be affected by its form. They remain the ratings assigned by its creator. An Ally with a Body 5 has that rating whether it appears as a gurgling infant or a two-meter white rabbit.

Karma Cost

True Form (i.e., First Form): 0

Additional Forms: 1 Karma Point each

Attributes

Like all Spirits, an Ally has a Force Rating. The magician gives up 1 Magic Point to create this 1 point of Force for his Ally.

To raise the Ally's Force to the next higher Rating costs 5 Karma Points times the current Force Rating. For example, raising the Force from 1 to 2 costs 5 x 1, or 5 Karma Points. Raising it from 2 to 3 costs 5 x 2, or 10 Karma Points and so on. Force may be increased either in the initial design of the Spirit or after it has been conjured by a Ritual of Change.

Physical Attributes at the time of the Ally's creation are equal to its Force. Later increases in Force do not affect the other attributes. It is possible to increase a Physical Attribute at any time, either when designing the Spirit or in a later Ritual of Change, at a cost of the current Rating for a +1 increase. For example, raising Strength from 4 to 5 costs 4 Karma Points.

Mental Attributes are equal to the magician's own at the time the Ally is created. They may not be changed. If the magician's Mental Attributes change after the Ally's creation, this does not affect the Spirit's ratings.

Karma Cost

Force: First point paid for by 1 Magic point sacrificed by creator

Per +1 to Force: 5 x current Rating

Physical Attributes: Initial Attributes equal to Force: 0

Per +1 to an Attribute: Current Rating

Mental Attributes: Initial values equal to creator's: 0

Cannot be changed.

Skills

As noted, an Ally receives Sorcery Skill equal to its creator's at the time of conjuring. Other non-magical skills may also be purchased at that time. The Spirit's master may increase its skills at a later time by paying Karma and performing a Ritual of Change. The magician can never increase the Ally's Skill Rating higher than his own.

Increasing any skill rating by +1 costs the current rating in the skill (1 Karma Point to buy the first point). Raising an Ally's skill rating from 3 to 4 would cost 3 Karma Points, either at initial design or in a later Ritual of Change.

Cost

Per +1 to a skill: Current Rating

Powers

The basic powers listed above for an Ally cost no additional Karma, with the exception of Sense Link, which costs a flat 5 Karma Points.

Cost

Sense Link: 5

Other Powers: 0

Walks-With-Spirits, an Eagle shaman, decides it is time to seek an Ally Spirit to aid him along the paths of power. The player who runs Walks-With-Spirits sits down to design the Spirit's abilities, as the magical process in the game cannot proceed until this is done.

He decides that the Ally's true form will be that of the shaman's totem: a great eagle. He also gives the Ally two additional forms (cost: 2 Karma Points). The Ally can also appear as a powerfully built warrior, armed and painted for battle, and a beautiful woman, wearing a cloak and headdress of eagle feathers.

He gives the Ally an initial Force of 4. The first point is free. The additional points cost 5 x (3 + 2 + 1) = 5 x 6 = 30.

All of the Ally's Physical Attributes are also rated at 4, as that is its Force. The player decides to increase its Strength to 7, which costs 4 + 5 + 6, or 15 more Karma Points.

The total cost for conjuring this Ally will be 2 + 30 + 15, or 47 Karma Points.

ALLY FORMULA

Before he can summon the Ally, the magician must now design the formula for the ritual. This requires a Magical Theory Test with a Target Number equal to the *complexity* of the Ally.

The complexity is the Karma cost of designing the Ally divided by 10. Round fractions to the *nearest* whole number.

The base time to design the formula is the complexity times 3, in days. Divide this by the number of successes rolled. If no successes are rolled, the design will take twice the base time. On a roll of all 1s, the magician is stumped. Before he can try to task again, he must either reduce the complexity of the Ally design, that is, create a less powerful Ally, or increase his Magical Theory Skill.

A shaman must perform the design in a Medicine Lodge with a rating at least equal to the formula's complexity. A mage needs a Conjuring Library with a similar rating.

The formula is specific, and may be used only to conjure an Ally with specific traits of forms, attributes, and so on. The native plane may be changed if the formula is translated from one tradition to another, and that is all.

Once the formula is designed, the magician may proceed to the Ritual of Summoning. The ritual requires a copy of the formula, for it is too complex to be memorized.

Walks-With-Spirits is going to summon an Ally costing 47 Karma Points. The complexity of this Spirit is 47/10, or 4.7, which rounds to 5. Walks-With-Spirits has Magical Theory Skill 4. Rolling 4 dice, he scores only a single success. The base time for the design is 3 times the complexity: 3 x 5 = 15 days. After 15 days of dancing, chanting, violent exercise, and much resorting to the beer pot (remember, shamanic ritual can make a frat party look like study hall), he puts the finishing touches on a shield ornately beaded with shells and adorned with two feathers from a mountain eagle. Its complex spiral designs seem to throb with meaning, though it may only be the after-effects of that last all-nighter he spent getting the energy patterns just right.

RITUAL OF SUMMONING

The Ritual of Summoning uses a Conjuring Test with a Target Number equal to the Ally's Force. A shaman must conduct the rite in a Medicine Lodge whose rating is at least equal to the Ally's Force. A mage must have access to a Conjuring Library with a similar rating.

In addition, units of ritual materials equal to the Spirit's Force are required. One unit costs 1,000 nuyen.

The base time for the ritual is a number of *days* equal to the Spirit's Force. Make the test and divide the base time by the successes, as usual. If the test fails, the ritual takes the full base time and then fails.

Every day the ritual continues, the magician must check to see if the constant demands on his energy are taking a toll. Resist (Force)L(Days) Stun Damage. That is, each day it gets harder and harder to resist the fatigue.

Make the Drain Resistance Tests as usual for Conjuring (**SR**, p. 87). Centering may be used to combat Drain. A failed or interrupted ritual may be repeated at some later time, starting over from the beginning.

If the magician passes the test with one or more successes, the Spirit appears at the end of the rite. The magician now pays the Karma for the Ally and also pays 1 point of his Magic Attribute to bring the Spirit into full manifestation.

Make the test to Resist Drain. If the magician is not incapacitated by Drain, the Spirit is controlled, bound to him as his Ally. If he is knocked out or killed by Drain, the Spirit goes free at once. (See **Free Spirits** p. 90.) The magician does *not* get his Magic Point back!

Walks-With-Spirits enters the lodge of the Eagle totem, armed with medicine bags full of rare herbs and the medicine shield bearing the formula for the Ally he hopes to draw to him. Because the Ally will have a Force 4, the shaman has 4 units of ritual materials: 4,000 nuyen worth.

Walks-With-Spirits makes a Conjuring Test with his Skill Rating of 5. The Target Number is 4, the Force of the Ally. The shaman scores 2 successes. The base time for the ritual is 4 days. Divide this by 2, for a result of 2 days.

After the first day, Walks-With-Spirits must resist 4L1 Stun Damage. He has Body 4 and so manages that handily. After the second day, he must resist 4L2 Stun Damage. Walks-With-Spirits only manages 1 success, suffering Light Stun Damage.

After 48 hours in the confines of the Medicine Lodge, he feels a blast of cold mountain air cut through the thick haze made by the herb-fed fires, then a Great Spirit eagle swoops down through the smoke-hole to land on the young shaman's shoulder. Its cruelly curved talons grip but do not break the skin. The piercing eyes of the hunting bird regard the fatigue-reddened eyes of the magician who called it.

Walks-With-Spirits has Charisma 6, suitable for one who wishes to excel at Conjuring. Because his Charisma is greater than the Ally's Force, the Drain is 4S1 Stun. Even with the fatigue he suffered from the ritual, this does not incapacitate the shaman, so the Spirit is automatically controlled.

The sharply hooked beak dips toward the young magician's face, then with a soft chirrup, the great raptor rubs its head fondly against the magician's cheek. Disciplining his reeling senses, Walks-With-Spirits greets the Ally politely and asks if the name Sky Warrior would please it. The Ally settles more comfortably onto his shoulder, making small sounds of pleasure. Unable to completely erase a triumphant grin from his sweat-streaked features, Walks-With-Spirits leaves the lodge, chanting the medicine songs of his people.

RITUAL OF CHANGE

All the requirements and ratings used for the Ritual of Summoning apply to the Ritual of Change. The Target Number for the Conjuring Test is increased by the total number of points this ritual will add to the Spirit's Ratings. If adding 2 Attribute Points and 1 Skill Point to a Force 4 Spirit, the Target Number would be 7.

This ritual is used whenever the magician is going to change the Ally's Ratings. The magician must have the Karma to pay for the changes before starting.

Even though the Spirit's design is being changed, the original formula is used for the Ritual of Change. No changes to it are either required or even allowed. A copy of the original formula is needed to perform the ritual.

If a Ritual of Change fails, with no successes rolled, the Ally will attempt to go free. Moreover, the magician must still Resist Drain, and if it knocks him out, the Spirit will attempt to go free *again*.

Similarly, if the ritual works, the magician must pay the Karma for the changes to the Ally, and then Resist Drain. If he is incapacitated, the Spirit can attempt to go free.

Unlike the Ritual of Summoning, where the Spirit always goes free if Drain overcomes the magician, the Spirit can only try to do so in a Ritual of Change. This is described in the next chapter, **Free Spirits**.

An Ally Spirit need *not* provide services to help its master succeed or to Resist Drain in its own Ritual of Change. It can help if it wishes, but this is one time it may refuse a service to its master.

After some time has passed, Walks-With-Spirits decides to increase Sky Warrior's Body Attribute, which is currently Body 4. The shaman has enough Karma to raise this to 6. To raise the Rating to 5 costs 4 Karma Points and to raise it to 6 costs 5 Karma points: 4 + 5 = 9 Karma Points required in all.

Again, the ritual is prepared in a Medicine Lodge with a Rating 4, and Walks-With-Spirits procures 4 more units of the necessary materials. He also removes the medicine shield bearing Sky Warrior's formula from its place of safe concealment.

Walks-With-Spirits makes his Conjuring Test, rolling 5 dice, with a Target Number 6, because he is adding 2 Body Points to a Force 4 Spirit. He scores a single success. The ritual will take 4 days. The shaman must resist damage 4 times, against Damage Codes of 4L1, 4L2, 4L3, and 4L4 in turn. Even if he fails all four tests, the combined fatigue and Drain damage does not knock him out. The worst he would get is 9 points of Mental Damage. The ritual is a success, and Sky Warrior now has a Body Attribute 6.

LOSING THE ALLY

As long as an Ally's Force is less than or equal to its master's Charisma, it can only try to escape from control if the master is dying of wounds, that is, if all ten boxes are filled in on the character's Physical Condition Monitor.

If the Ally's Force is greater than the magician's Charisma, the Spirit will also attempt to go free whenever the magician is rendered unconscious by wounds, fatigue, Drain, or the like. That is, when the magician is down because all ten boxes are filled in on either condition monitor, the Spirit can try to break free of his control.

In either case, make a Resisted Success Test. The magician rolls dice equal to his Conjuring and Charisma Ratings, with a Target Number equal to the Ally's Force. The Ally rolls dice equal to its Force Rating, with a Target Number equal to the magician's Charisma. If the Spirit rolls more successes than the magician, it is free. The magician loses his invested Magic Point as well as access to the Spirit's other abilities.

Note that the Spirit does not *have* to try to escape control. If the magician has treated the Spirit well and courteously set aside Karma regularly to improve the Spirit's scores, learned spells for it, and otherwise been a good friend as well as a good master, it is possible that the Spirit will not want to go off on its own. Or, having become free, the Spirit may choose to stay with its former master as a companion. A Free Spirit can perform services for anyone it chooses. Only if the Spirit truly loves the magician would it sacrifice Force to save him from Drain, however.

This is a roleplaying decision, not something that can be determined by a roll of dice.

Walks-With-Spirits dives to the side, but too slow, too late. A burst of chattering machine gun fire cuts him down. Spouting blood, the shaman sprawls bonelessly into the filthy gutter, mortally wounded. As his companions frantically apply first aid, trying to get the abused body to cling to life, a dim shape appears, hovering on mighty wings above the scene. It dips uncertainly, its outlines taking on definition in the wan urban twilight. It hovers, as though unsure whether to descend or rise into the winds of freedom. With a piercing cry, Sky Warrior begins to climb toward the skies that call to its inmost nature.

Walks-With-Spirits has taken a Deadly amount of damage. This means that Sky Warrior may escape from control and go free. The magician rolls 11 dice: 6 for Charisma and 5 for Conjuring Skill. His Target Number is 4. Sky Warrior rolls 4 dice, with a Target Number of 6. Not surprisingly, the Ally loses the Resisted Test.

Out of the shadows, a mighty figure again swoops down, diving unseen past the shadowrunners clustered around its fallen master. Landing lightly on the pavement next to Walks-With-Spirits, the great eagle brushes its beak lightly against the injured shaman's cheek.

"I've got a pulse," one of the runners says in a relieved voice. "I think he'll make it."

BANISHING THE ALLY

An Ally can be banished like any other Spirit. As the creator initially summoned the Ally, he gets the usual bonus, rolling dice equal to his Charisma Attribute and Conjuring Skill for banishing tests. He gets this bonus even if the Spirit goes free.

If a magician banishes an Ally he created, he gets his invested Magic Point back, but nothing else. If the Spirit is destroyed by any other means, the point is lost.

If the banishing is unsuccessful or the Spirit vanquishes its creator, the Ally goes free at once.

The magician may also try to destroy the Ally in Astral Combat. The same conditions apply if he loses or breaks off combat.

When an Ally goes free, its former master often spends much time chasing the Spirit down, trying to banish it and get back his Magic Point. Note that the magician must learn the Free Ally's true name to banish it (see **Free Spirits** p. 90) or else overcome it in Astral Combat on its native metaplane. Similarly, a Free Ally that is threatened by its former master may spend its time trying to kill him off.

WATCHERS

The double-domed docs at MITM have come up with a new way to use Conjuring, and word on it has now trickled down to magicians all over the world. These days, every magician in the Sixth World who can use Conjuring knows how to summon a Watcher.

A Watcher is a simple little Spirit. Some say it is just a bit of the summoner's consciousness, impressed onto the fabric of Astral Space. Be that as it may, a magician can conjure one up and give it simple tasks to perform.

The summoning ritual usually requires no special equipment and can be performed at any place and time. The Target Number is the number of hours the magician wishes the Spirit to serve him. The number of successes becomes the Force of the Spirit. The summoner may choose to make the Spirit of any Force less than the number of his successes, making Drain easier to withstand.

Drain for summoning a Watcher is always (Force)L(Hours). It is *always* non-lethal Stun Damage. *Never* Physical Damage! As always, to Resist the Drain of Conjuring requires a Charisma Success Test. The metamagical power of Centering can be used to reduce this Drain (see p. 24).

A magician can maintain a number of Watchers at one time equal to his Charisma Attribute. Watchers do not count against the similar limit on the number of Elementals a magician can bind at one time. Keep separate track of these two totals if necessary. The summoner can dissolve a Watcher that he has conjured anytime he wishes, even before its time is up and whether or not the Spirit is near him.

Watchers can be summoned for longer times either by expending Karma or using ritual materials, or a combination of the two. The summoner can conjure a Watcher that lasts for days, either by paying Karma equal to its lifespan in days or expending that many units of ritual materials. These cost 1,000 nuyen per unit. Summoning a Watcher for 5 days could be paid for with 5 Karma Points, or by using up 5 units of ritual materials, or any combination of the two (3 units and 2 Karma, for example).

Whether its lifespan is measured in hours or days, the Watcher will simply dissolve back into the boundless energy of Astral Space when the time runs out.

Sister Susan summons Spirits smartly, with a Conjuring Skill of 7. She wants a Watcher to do an errand for her, and estimates it will take it 4 hours to take care of business. So she makes a Conjuring Test with a Target Number of 4. She decides to roll 5 dice, saving the other two to help Resist Drain. The dice come up 1, 2, 4, 4, 6. That's three successes, which give the Watcher a Force of 3. Now she must Resist Drain. (Force)L(Hours) means she is resisting 3L4 Drain. Susan has Charisma 4 and saved 2 dice from her Magic Pool (based on Conjuring) so she rolls 6 dice, scoring 1, 2, 2, 4, 5, 5. Three successes isn't quite enough, so Sister Susan takes Light Drain (filling in one box on her Mental Condition Monitor).

CHARACTERISTICS OF WATCHERS

Watchers exist on the Etheric Plane in Astral Space. They can never leave the etheric, either to manifest physically in the material world or to ascend to a metaplane.

They can see the physical plane and hear what is being said, and can even manifest visibly and speak to physical beings. They cannot touch material things, however, or affect the physical plane directly, rather like the Apparition Class of Ghosts.

All of a Watcher's Attributes are equal to its Force Rating. No matter how high the Spirit's Mental Attributes may be, however, it tends to be rather, er, slow. Watchers are single-minded, possibly even clever, about carrying out their assigned tasks, but everything else tends to be over their little astral heads. Their level of intelligence might be compared to a well-trained, loyal dog.

Watchers are better at recognizing living things and magical energies than at complex navigation in Astral Space. Energy is their strong suit, not geography.

Watchers move through Astral Space at a normal rate of 5 x Rating, or a Fast Rate of Rating x 1,000 KPH.

Watchers do not deal with unforeseen difficulties very well. For example, if a Watcher is sent somewhere and finds access blocked by an astral barrier it cannot crack, the poor thing is likely to sit there, quivering, until its time runs out and it dissolves.

Watchers can be banished normally and/or engaged in Astral Combat. Another magician *cannot* take control of a Watcher, though. It is bound strictly to its summoner.

WATCHERS AND ASTRAL TRACKING

A Watcher can track down any person or place known to its summoner. It cannot find a non-living thing, even if the summoner knows the object well. It can, however, find an enchanted item or other magical object if the summoner has ever assensed the item's aura.

The Watcher makes an Unresisted Force Test with a Target Number 9 minus the summoner's Intelligence Rating. If the Spirit is looking for an Initiate, then *increase* the Target Number by the subject's grade, for a Watcher cannot deal well with the complex patterns of metamagical energy. Do not apply this modifier if the Initiate the Watcher is looking for is its summoner.

The Spirit is using its magical power to track the mental image it got from its summoner down through Astral Space. Divide the number of successes the Spirit rolled into 120 minutes if the Spirit is looking for a living being, into 240 minutes if it is looking for a magical item, and into 360 minutes if it is looking for a place. If the test fails, the Spirit will hunt around in confusion until its time runs out. The gamemaster makes this test in secret.

If the target object enters a magical barrier at any time during the search, the Watcher will lose the trail at that barrier. If a subject happens to project into a metaplane during this time, the Watcher loses the trail. The track is going in a direction the poor thing cannot follow. Make a Force Test with a Target Number 4. If the Watcher succeeds, it will try to return to its master to report its failure. Otherwise, it will wander around Astral Space fruitlessly until it dissolves.

The Watcher can track down its own summoner, if it must. The Target Number for this is 6 minus the magician's Magic Attribute. Divide the number of successes into 120 minutes to see how long it takes the Watcher to pick up its boss' trail.

Janos needs to send a message fast and quiet to his friend Katzchen. He knows she's in town, but not where. Janos is a magician, so he summons a Watcher. Figuring that 3 hours ought to do it, he makes his Test and gets a Force 3 Spirit. He orders Spirit to give Katzchen a message, get her reply, and bring it back to Janos, wherever he may be.

Probably mumbling the message over to itself, the Watcher starts casting around for Katzchen's astral trail. Rolling 3 dice, with a Target Number of 4, the Spirit comes up with 1 success, so it takes 120 minutes. "Ohhhh, I am going to be so laaaate," it whines, as it finally locks onto her aura-trail. Katzchen is only 100 klicks away, so it takes the Watcher but a few minutes to reach her. The little Spirit delivers Janos' message, gets her answer (about 20 minutes involved here), and then starts looking for the boss. Janos has a Magic Attribute 7, so the Watcher's Target Number is 2 (no Target Number can ever be less than 2). Rolling 3 dice, the Spirit scores 3 successes, meaning it can find Janos in 120/3, or 40 minutes. Let's see now: 120 + 20 + 40 = 180 minutes. Ooops. As the Watcher comes bounding back to Janos, he says, "I found her, boss. She says...gleep!" The Spirit's time runs out and it vanishes.

JOBS FOR WATCHERS

Watchers are useful. They can serve as astral guards or alarm systems or to bug a place magically. They can deliver messages and bring back replies. Just don't load them down with too many instructions, or they might get confused!

Air Cover

The Watcher is sent to follow some magician around and attack him immediately if the mage uses Astral Perception or Projection. If the target of this attack enters a magical barrier or projects into a metaplane, the Watcher will lose track of him and wander off, lost.

Alarm

The Watcher is assigned to guard some place in Astral Space. The Spirit will only react to intruders in Astral Space. The Watcher can patrol a maximum area equal to 10,000 square meters times its Force Rating and can be instructed to allow specific individuals to pass unchallenged. The maximum number of people the Watcher can recognize this way is equal to its rating. The Watcher will patrol the assigned area at its normal Movement Rate (5 x Force Rating meters per action). If it observes an unauthorized person on the astral in its area, it will hurry to inform some specified person. If this specified person is not in the area it is guarding, the Watcher will track him down and inform him. It is also possible to order the Spirit to allow any person it finds in a specified location (like a security office) to know about the intrusion instead.

A Watcher can also be ordered to guard an area from physical intrusion. One Watcher cannot guard both the Physical and Astral Planes against intrusion at the same time, however.

Attack Dog

The Watcher is assigned to guard some place in Astral Space. It will only react to intruders in Astral Space and attacks them ferociously. The Watcher can patrol a maximum area equal to 10,000 square meters times its rating and can be instructed to allow individuals to pass unchallenged. The maximum number of people it can recognize this way is equal to its Rating. The Watcher will patrol the assigned area at its normal Movement Rate (5 x Rating meters per action).

Bug

The Watcher can be sent to some place or to follow some person known to the summoner. It will observe all that goes on for some specified length of time, then return to its boss and report. It can give very clear reports on magical things that happen or on conversations between living persons. It is vague about anything involving technology, comm calls, printed matter, or arithmetic.

Alternatively, one can order the Spirit to observe the place or person until some specific event occurs. For example, "Follow her until she picks up a leather attaché case, then see where she takes it. Then come tell me." With this type of command, however, it is always a danger that the Spirit will get confused and/or run out of time before completing the task.

Courier

The Watcher will go to some specific place and/or to some specific person known to its summoner and deliver a spoken message. It can also display simple pictures, up to the complexity of a two-dimensional, non-moving photograph of something shown to it by its summoner. The Spirit will get a reply if required, and return to its master with that answer.

If the master cannot give exact directions on how to get from where he summons the Spirit to the delivery site or if he does not know the recipient's location, the Spirit has to track it down. It can then deliver the message and get a reply (if any). If the summoner has since moved elsewhere, the Watcher has to track him down before it can deliver the answer.

Irritant

The Watcher can be ordered to find someone and to follow him around, loudly repeating some slogan, insulting the victim, or even carrying on an argument. The Watcher will manifest visibly and audibly upon the Physical Plane for this job. For example, a magician who is irritated with a Mr. Johnson might send a Watcher to follow the corp around. "You know, it's really an honor to meet the guy who spread that rumor about Mitsuhama just in time to louse up their acquisition of Garuda Aircraft. How much did the decker get for the run, anyway? I guess you showed those goons that they can't mess with Boeing, huh!"

Alternatively, the Watcher can be sent to some specific place and ordered to hang around, sounding off on its assigned theme. "Hey, there! Welcome to Hannibal's Grill. I hear the ratburgers are really tasty today. Hiya, welcome to Hannibal's Grill. Got your DocWagon card paid up?" And so on.

This little trick can be used as anything from a practical joke to a protection racket to a declaration of war.

"Living in the material world would be a real drag if it weren't for people. You guys are just so darn funny!"
—Interview with Artsnletters, Free City Spirit, Paranatural Proceedings, Vol. 4, Number 8

hen a Spirit escapes from its summoner's control (**SR**, p. 87), it may decide to hang out in the material world instead of vanishing back to its place of origin. Spirits who do so are called Free Spirits, and ever since the Awakening, a small but growing number of them have chosen to live on the physical plane. There are even Free Spirits who claim they've been around for hundreds, even thousands, of years, before the Awakening.

Allies, Elementals, and Nature Spirits have all been known to become Free Spirits, but as far as anyone knows, Watchers are not robust enough to survive as Free Spirits.

From the gamemaster's point of view, a Free Spirit is a non-player character, with free will, its own goals and tastes, and everything else that makes a unique character. Not too many are running around, however, and no standard Contact or Archetype exists for a Free Spirit.

BORN FREE

In one sense, the moment when a Spirit becomes free may be regarded as its "birth."

Whenever a Spirit becomes uncontrolled, the gamemaster may decide whether it becomes free or simply vanishes from the physical world. Most powerful Spirits, those with a Force higher than 6, tend to become free. In addition, Spirits that have a long history of association with mankind tend to go free: Elementals who have been bound for more than a few weeks, Allies, and Spirits of Man.

To decide this question randomly, roll 2D6 when a Spirit becomes uncontrolled. If the die roll is less than or equal to the Spirit's Force Rating, it goes free. Otherwise it vanishes.

If the Spirit is one of those listed as more likely to become free, add +2 to its Force for this test.

MOTIVATIONS

No one knows why Free Spirits choose to stay in the material world. It may be that all uncontrolled Spirits become Free, but only some of them stay here, while the rest go off to some other plane entirely.

Free Spirits seem to fall into one of several general categories. These are not hard and fast classifications, but provide convenient ways to describe particular behaviors.

TRICKSTERS

Tricksters enjoy the increased abilities they have as Free Spirits, seeing the physical world as a big playground. They tend to interfere in Human activities, often engineering complicated practical jokes for their own private hilarity. They can be ruthless, destroying someone's reputation, his career, even driving a victim to suicide in pursuit of what they call fun. Or they may adopt more or less humane attitudes, acting rather like spiritual Robin Hoods, using their powers to take down the arrogance of the corps and other "stuffed shirts" of Human society.

Tricksters can be any kind of Free Spirit: Elemental, Nature Spirit, or Ally.

SHADOWS

Shadows are darker, more menacing. They enjoy causing Human fear and suffering, and may enlist psychopathic Humans as their assistants. Some occultists and paranaturalists theorize that these Spirits are in some way addicted to the psychic energy of Humans (and other beings) in torment. Like Trickster Spirits, some Shadows may set up complicated situations for no reason that the Human mind can fathom. Others revel in simple bloodletting: violence and terrorism feed their "habit."

Shadows are usually Free Elementals or Allies.

GUARDIANS

Guardians are Spirits who seem motivated to protect the living Earth from exploitation. They rarely have much use for Humans, though Guardians have been known to form alliances with nature-oriented tribal peoples to hold off resource-hungry corporations. Guardians have also been known to enlist shadowrunners to help derail corporate plans for invasion of an unspoiled environment.

Guardians are almost invariably Free Nature Spirits.

ANIMUS/ANIMA

The Animus/Anima Spirits identify strongly with Metahumanity, and often help people in trouble or danger. As their name suggests, these Spirits tend to assume one gender or another. Even in Astral Space, their auras take on a Human-like form, though they are still obviously Spirits. Animus types assume male characteristics. Anima Spirits assume female characteristics. There are very vague rumors of such Spirits becoming romantically involved with Metahumanity. Others tend to be wanderers, moving about the Earth seeking to satisfy an intense curiosity about Human behavior.

Any kind of Free Spirit can be so motivated, but it is more usual for Elementals, Allies, and some Spirits of Man.

PLAYERS

The final group of Free Spirits are the Players. Players, like Animus/Anima Spirits, identify with Humans, but their orientation is toward the power, wealth, and pleasures of the material world. Players seem to be Spirits with mortal "vices." This may be as innocent as an appreciation of luxury food and drink or as perverse as a taste for BTL chips or other Human addiction. Players also tend to form organizations to guarantee access to the resources they need, and the head of at least one criminal organization is rumored to be a Player.

Any kind of Free Spirit can become a Player.

FREE SPIRITS AND KARMA

Free Spirits need Karma to grow in power, but there is a catch: Free Spirits cannot get Karma on their own. They have to get it as a willing sacrifice from living, physical beings. Karma is, after all, akin to luck and the power of a living soul to influence its own destiny. Karma is also related to the experience of life, and such things are unique to an embodied soul. The Spirit cannot take the Karma; it must be given. Sure, there are rumors of magicians with hot skills and not-so-hot ethics who've found a way to transfer Karma from unwilling victims to Free Spirits, but no evidence exists to prove these are more than scare-stories.

When shadowrunners must negotiate a deal with a Free Spirit, Karma is the usual payment. Of course, some Free Spirits have a taste for resources such as services, contacts, rare goods, unique enchantments, and even plain old nuyen. Some Free Spirits even have credstik accounts, managed by Human agents, of course. It all depends on the Spirit's goals. Karma is not the only thing Free Spirits want, but it is what they most value.

Magicians can give Karma to Free Spirits more effectively than to mundanes. For that matter, full-blown magicians are better at it than adepts.

- Fully capable magicians can give Karma to a Free Spirit at 1:1. That is, if the magician gives up a point of Karma, the Spirit gets a point of Karma.
- Adepts of any kind can give Karma to the Spirit at 2:1. The Spirit gets 1 point of Karma for every 2 points the adept spends.
- Mundanes can give Karma to the Spirit at 3:1. The Spirit gets 1 point of Karma for every 3 points the character spends.

Someone who knows Conjuring Skill can try to do a simple ritual to improve this ratio, even if the character cannot use the skill for other purposes. Even a mundane can do this trick. Make a Conjuring Test with a Target Number equal to the Force + Spirit Energy of the Spirit (see below). If the test succeeds, improve the ratio by a step, i.e., an Adept can give Karma to the Spirit at 1:1 and a mundane at 2:1. For every point the magician gives, the Spirit gets 2 points of Karma.

Mundanes and adepts can only use their Conjuring Skill to help themselves here, but fully capable magicians can use their Conjuring Skill on behalf of other characters. They get a +2 penalty to the Target Number, however. Note that if a magician performs the ritual for some one else, the benefit depends on who it is for. That is, if a magician tries to improve the ratio for a mundane, the mundane pays Karma to the Spirit at 2:1 if the rite succeeds, not 1:2.

The Conjuring Test can be made anytime a character is making a "payment" to the Spirit. But it's a gamble, and the character gets only one try. He makes a deal with a Free Spirit to "pay" it, say, 3 points of Karma. That means the Spirit ends up with 3 Karma Points. A mundane character would have to pay 9 Karma Points, at 3:1, to give the Spirit 3 points. If the mundane makes the test and succeeds, he pays the Karma at 2:1, or 4:5 Karma. Because **Shadowrun** rounds down any fractions, he only loses 4 points. If he blows the test, though, he loses the full amount. Free Spirits are not big on revolving credit plans. They won't take the payments a point at a time while a character tries to hold onto his Karma. It's all or nothing, chummer.

TRUE NAMES

Each Free Spirit has a true name, which it gets at the moment it becomes free. The true name of a Spirit, however weird or ordinary it may sound to Human ears, is a complex astral formula that defines the Spirit's essence. The theory is that the local conditions in Astral Space at the time and place where the Spirit went free are what "generates" the true name. Maybe so. No one knows much about the Free Spirits who have been identified so far, and the Spirits sure don't give researchers their true names.

Anyone who knows the true name of a Free Spirit can try to enslave it through use of Conjuring Skill. The magical tradition of the magician does not matter. For example, a mage could try to capture a Free Nature Spirit. Even a non-magician can try this stunt if he knows Conjuring.

And *only* someone who knows a Free Spirit's true name can kill or banish it. Whether a character uses Astral Combat, combat on the native plane, or banishing, if he does not know a Spirit's true name, he cannot destroy it. The most he can do is disrupt it for a time.

So Free Spirits protect their true names. When a Free Spirit tells someone its "name," it is actually using a handle, just as shadowrunners do, and probably for some of the same reasons.

LEARNING A TRUE NAME

There are several ways to learn a Free Spirit's true name. The Spirit can reveal it (fat chance). A character may find it written or recorded by someone who knew it. The Spirit cannot destroy such records itself, but it would probably try to get a Human agent to wipe out the information. A Free Spirit would tend to be careful about this kind of project, though. If it hired a shadowrunner to destroy the information, the runner might end up learning its name.

A magician can use his powers to learn a true name, which is the problem Free Spirits face most often. The mage does so in two steps.

DETERMINING THE NATIVE PLANE

First, the magician must determine the Spirit's native plane (see p. 81). The magician may be able to deduce this logically. For example, it does not take a genius to guess that the gigantic thunderbird that rained all over the magician's convertible while the top was down may just be a native of the Metaplane of the Skies. Lacking such subtle clues, the magician has to assense the Spirit, or closely assense some place it has recently been or

some object it has touched intimately. The subtle traces usually wear off from a place or item within a few days, but some place or some thing the Spirit contacted frequently and/or over a long period of time may carry its "signature" permanently.

If the magician assenses the Spirit's personal aura, he immediately knows its native plane, but this will not work if the Spirit has *Aura Masking* power (see p. 95). Only an Initiate can overcome this power, which lets the Spirit "hide" its true aura from any observers on the etheric plane.

Of course, the Spirit may notice that it is being studied astrally. It makes a Resistance Test with a Target Number equal to double the magician's Magic Attribute. If the test succeeds, the Spirit knows the magician is trying to read its aura.

If the magician is assensing a place or item, the Spirit makes no test, but the magician needs to spend 1D6 hours studying the subject to get the information. If interrupted, he must start over from scratch. Typical subjects for this kind of study include:

- Some item the Spirit has affected with its magic.
- Some person the Spirit possessed.
- Some place where the Spirit manifested physically.
- The Spirit's Personal Domain (see **Powers of Free Spirits**, p. 95).

QUEST FOR THE TRUE NAME

The magician must journey to the Spirit's native metaplane on an Astral Quest to learn its true name. The Quest has a Rating equal to the Spirit Energy of his quarry. Having completed this Quest, the magician knows the Spirit's true name. If he has sought the information on the wrong metaplane, he must complete the Quest to discover his error. That is, only when he "succeeds" at the Quest will the Powers of the metaplane inform him that he is barking up the wrong astral tree.

BINDING A FREE SPIRIT

Conjuring Skill can enslave a Free Spirit if the conjuror knows the Spirit's true name. Anyone who knows Conjuring can try to pull this off, whether they can conjure other Spirits or not. True names are powerful magic and can provide the energy needed to summon its owner, even if a mundane is performing the ritual. The effective Force of the ritual is equal to the Free Spirit's own Force *plus* its Spirit Energy.

Mages need access to a Conjuring Library and must prepare a Hermetic Circle, with rating. Shamans must perform the ritual in a Medicine Lodge, with rating.

Adepts and non-magicians usually use hermetic techniques, as though they were mages. At the gamemaster's discretion, someone from a tribal culture might use shamanic techniques.

If the Spirit is aware of the magician's plan to control it, it will almost certainly try to keep the conjuror away from the resources he needs. The Spirit would be wary of a magician who knows its true name, for he would have the power to banish the Spirit forever. A mundane or an adept is at greater risk in attempting to learn a Spirit's true name. Because neither can banish a Spirit, the Spirit would not fear him as much.

The ritual itself takes only a few minutes because the power of the true name forces the Spirit to appear. Indeed, the ritual will summon the Spirit whether or not the conjuror succeeds at his test or not. The use of the Spirit's true name compels it to appear. Once it appears, the question is whether it is under the summoner's control.

Make an Unresisted Conjuring Test, with a Target Number equal to the Spirit's Force *plus* its Spirit Energy. Simple success forces the Spirit to submit. On a failure, the Spirit can attack immediately, and usually will, unless the foolhardy summoner can negotiate a deal with the Spirit instead. This is not a task for magical dabblers with only a few points of skill, however. Free Spirits whose freedom is threatened are not happy campers.

If the summoner fails this test, he can never try to bind the Spirit again. For this reason, the Spirit might not automatically try to slaughter the audacious clown. However, the Spirit is in danger as long as the character has its true name, for the would-be summoner can give that information to someone else.

If the character succeeds at the Conjuring Test, the Spirit cannot disobey specific orders from the conjuror, nor can it directly attack or harm him. It must come when he calls, just like a bound Spirit, and it *never* runs out of "services." It is trapped as a loyal slave until the magician dies or lets it go deliberately. The Spirit can work *indirectly* against its master, though, setting up plots or involving him in schemes likely to get him killed. Free Spirits are valuable allies, but dangerous servants.

Once a magician lets a Free Spirit go, he can never bind it again. Of course, he still knows its true name, so he could try to banish it (that is, destroy it) if he had to. Perhaps he might put the name up for sale or give it to someone for some service. Before turning the Spirit loose, a smart magician will make the Spirit swear an oath not to kill him or try to get him killed. The Spirit cannot break this oath, but must keep it to the letter. Of course, if will look for any loopholes.

All in all, it is better to befriend a Free Spirit than try to boss one. Just because a magician knows a Spirit's true name does not necessarily make the Spirit and the magician deadly enemies. Many runners know lethal secrets about their teammates.

OTHER USES OF TRUE NAMES

Any magician who knows the Free Spirit's true name can try to banish it, just as with any other Spirit (**SR**, p. 88). Similarly, two magicians who know the true name of a Spirit could compete to control it, as described in the same section of the basic rules. If a Free Spirit becomes "uncontrolled" as a result of such a contest, neither magician can ever bind it again. If one of the magicians involved in the contest had already freed the Spirit from his service and he ends up winning the contest, the Spirit will be free of any bonds to either magician.

A magician must be able to use Conjuring Skill to banish or try to control, but the tradition of the magician does not matter. A shaman could try to control or banish a Free Elemental, for example. However, an adept who cannot use Conjuring usually cannot try to banish or take over a Free Spirit.

If a character knows a true name, he could use Enchanting Skill to make a Spirit focus that is effective against the Spirit. Normal Spirit focuses are useless in trying to bind or banish Free Spirits. Various "unique" enchanted items can be made to threaten or reward a Free Spirit if a character knows its true name (see p. 49).

NELSON

SPIRIT ENERGY

One of the things that make Free Spirits more powerful than other Spirits is their ability to build up *Spirit Energy*. This augments their Force Rating in various ways to give them more power in the material world. Indeed, Spirit Energy is a measure of how much material power the Spirit has accumulated.

When used by a Free Spirit, all the normal powers of Spirits (**SR**, pp. 174–8) that are measured using Force have a Rating equal to the power's Force *plus* the being's Spirit Energy. A Free Fire Elemental, for example, that has a Force of 4 and Spirit Energy of 3, would use its Flame Projection power as though it had a Force of 7, doing 7L1.

Physical manifestations of the Spirit also benefit from this bonus. A Free Forest Spirit, a Spirit of the Land, with a Force and Spirit Energy of 5, would have Attributes based on a Force of 10, not 5. Some special manifestations, described below, have different attributes and powers than those normally assumed by the Spirit.

All Free Spirits get 1 point of Spirit Energy at the moment of becoming free. They can build up more Spirit Energy using Karma. Raising Spirit Energy by 1 point costs Karma equal to its new value. A Spirit with 1 point of Spirit Energy could raise it to 2 by spending 2 Karma Points. A Spirit can have a maximum Spirit Energy equal to its Force.

A Free Spirit can increase its Force as well, but must sacrifice Spirit Energy to do so. Increasing its Force Rating by 1 costs Spirit Energy equal to the being's current Force. To increase its actual Force, the Spirit would have to build up its Spirit Energy to maximum, then wipe it out. The Spirit could then start again to accumulate Spirit Energy.

POWERS OF FREE SPIRITS

Besides the normal powers for Spirits of their class, Free Spirits gain special abilities in the physical world. A Free Spirit automatically receives 1D3 of these Spirit powers at "birth," that is, when it goes free. It may gain additional powers when it increases its Force. Roll 2D6. If the result is greater than or equal to the Spirit's new Force, it gains another power. It should be obvious that an upper limit exists here, a spiritual "law of diminishing returns." The more powerful the Spirit becomes, the more fixed is its manifestation and the more difficult it is to gain new powers.

Free Spirits that start at lower Force Ratings and grow gradually are potentially more powerful than those very strong when they go free.

ANIMAL FORM

The Spirit can appear in the form of a non-magical animal (See the Critters list, **SR**, p. 190). When in animal form, the Spirit is like a Shapeshifter, appearing as a larger and stronger version of the beast. Add its Spirit Energy to the critter's normal Physical Attributes and use its real Force in place of the critter's Mental Attributes. The animal form also has Immunity to Normal Weapons (**SR**, p.176), with a Rating equal to the Spirit's Spirit Energy. The Spirit has all its other powers while in this form and can speak if it wishes.

Nature Spirits usually appear in the form of an animal typical of their domain. Elementals rarely have this power, but when they do, they seem to use a single animal form that is usually big and powerful.

If the animal form is "killed," the Spirit is disrupted.

ASTRAL GATEWAY

The Spirit can bring the planes into closer contact. It can permit anyone—magician or non-magician—to project into Astral Space, either on the etheric plane or the Spirit's native metaplane. The traveler is in a trance, his physical body remaining on the material plane. Also, as long as the Spirit maintains watch over the body, the traveler does not suffer Essence loss.

Should the Spirit leave off guarding the magician's body, however, the gateway closes. A magician can try to find his way back to his body the normal way, but non-magicians will die at once. Non-Initiates on a metaplane also die instantly.

AURA MASKING

The Spirit can mask its aura in two ways. It can match its aura to its present physical form (animal or Human) or it can make it look like that of a summoned, that is, non-free Spirit. It does this by raising its true aura to its native metaplane.

The effect of this power is similar to the metamagical ability of Masking (see p. 26). Only an Initiate can determine the true nature of a masked aura. For purposes of the Magician's Success Test, treat the Spirit's Force as its Magic Attribute and its Spirit Energy as its grade.

If an Initiate succeeds at this test, he knows that the Spirit's aura is masked and on which metaplane its true nature is located.

This will usually be enough information to identify the type of Spirit. If the mage wants more information about the Spirit, that is, if he wishes to view its true aura, its true nature, he must undertake an Astral Quest with a rating equal to the Spirit's Force.

If the magician completes this Quest successfully, he will know the Spirit's true name. From viewing the true aura of the Spirit, he also gains the usual information available in Astral Space (see **SR,** p. 89 and p. 64 of this book).

Free Spirits with Aura Masking can also perceive the true nature of masked auras. The gamemaster makes a test to see if this occurs, as described on p. 26, or he may simply decide to let the Spirit pierce the mask automatically. Imagine the dismay of some carefully disguised Initiate when the Spirit he is trying to fool chuckles and asks the character why he hides his power from the world.

DISPELLING

The Spirit has the metamagical power known as *Dispelling* (see p. XX). The Spirit uses this with an effective skill equal to its Spirit Power and a grade equal to its Force.

HIDDEN LIFE

The Spirit hides its life force in some place or thing. Having done this, it cannot move its life again. If the hiding place is destroyed, so is the Spirit. As long as the hiding place is safe, however, the Spirit can never be permanently banished or destroyed by any means, and all its physical forms and manifestations possess the power of Regeneration (**SR**, p. 178). Even when this power fails, however, the Spirit is not destroyed, but merely driven away for a time. Even someone who knows its true name cannot destroy the Spirit utterly if it has hidden its life.

The hiding place is protected from most normal harm, but much depends on its nature. All hiding places are protected from magical or mundane damage, with "armor" equal to the Spirit's Force. It gets that many automatic successes in resisting harm, along with the normal resistance.

A Spirit can also hide its life in an animal, which gives the animal Immunity to Age, Normal Weapons, Pathogens, and Toxins. Its attributes are all increased by the Spirit's Force, as well. Such animals are puppets of the Spirit.

There are rumors that a very powerful Free Spirit can use a Human as the hiding place for its life. The Human would, presumably, receive the same advantages as does an animal hiding place, but what effects such a relationship would have on the mind and will of the Human are unknown.

HUMAN FORM

The Spirit can assume any Human or Metahuman form it desires. While in this shape, its attributes are those normal for its type, with the usual bonuses for being a Free Spirit. That is, its effective Force is equal to its Force plus its Spirit Energy. In addition, this form has Immunity to Normal Weapons (**SR,** p.176), with a rating equal to its Spirit Energy. The appearance of its Human form, whether male or female, old or young, beautiful or hideous, is entirely up to the Spirit.

If the Human form is "killed," the Spirit is disrupted.

PERSONAL DOMAIN

The Spirit selects some limited area where its powers will be greater than usual. A Nature Spirit must choose a site in a domain appropriate to its type. The personal domain may have a maximum area of 10,000 square meters times the Spirit's Force.

When a Spirit is in its personal domain, its Spirit Energy is doubled. This bonus applies to all powers influenced by Spirit Energy, including those added to its Force. A Spirit with a Force of 4 and a Spirit Energy of 3 would have an effective Force of 10 when using powers that receive the bonus in its personal domain.

Once a Spirit chooses a personal domain, it cannot change it. If the domain is physically destroyed or even drastically altered, the Spirit loses this power. For example, if a Swamp Spirit chooses a particular marsh as its personal domain, it would be destroyed as a domain if turned into a landfill. The Spirit will, of course, fight ferociously to prevent such interference with its domain.

Some speculation exists that Free Spirits whose personal domains have been so destroyed sometimes become Toxic Spirits, especially when the domain becomes badly polluted.

POSSESSION

This power allows the Spirit to possess a living being. It is usually possible in three types of circumstances.

The Spirit can attempt to possess anyone it defeats in Astral Combat. The victim must have a physical body in order to be possessed.

The Spirit can inhabit a willing host, whether or not the host is capable of astral travel. Though the host invites the Spirit to enter, the Spirit decides when it will leave, unless it is exorcised unwillingly.

A Free Spirit with a personal domain can attempt to possess anyone, willing or not, astrally active or not, who is in that domain. It forces the victim to engage in Astral Combat, and can possess him if it wins.

The possessed character has his own knowledge and skills as well as the skills of the Spirit. All his Physical Attributes are increased by the Spirit's Spirit Energy and all his Mental Attributes are replaced by the Spirit's own.

If the victim is immune to Stun Damage, and if incapacitated by Lethal Damage, the Spirit is unharmed but driven back into astral form. Banishing the possessing Spirit disrupts it instead of killing it, even if its true name is used. Spells cast at the Spirit always ground into the host's body.

In addition, if the host did not willingly submit to possession, all his Target Numbers while possessed are at +2.

When a possessing Spirit departs from a body, the former host must resist (Force)D2 Stun Damage using Willpower.

SORCERY

If the Spirit has Sorcery Skill, it uses it exactly as a magician does. Allies *always* have this power.

The Spirit increases its skill and learns spells like any other character (**SR,** p.150), which costs Karma Points. The Spirit does not need the usual tools and props of mages and shamans, however. Because it is always in tune with Astral Space, the heart and source of magic, neither does the Spirit need a teacher or a spell formula, but it must to spend the same amount of time it would take a Human magician to learn the spell. When casting a spell, the Spirit must abide by some special rules:

•The Spirit is not subject to Drain. It cannot, however, give the spell a Force greater than its own Force Rating.

•It cannot gain additional dice for its Magic Pool from focuses; it cannot use fetishes for a power advantage; and it cannot gain dice from other Spirits.

•The Spirit's Magic Pool is equal to its Sorcery Skill *plus* its Spirit Energy.

•The Spirit must manifest physically to use Sorcery on the physical plane. It cannot cast spells that affect the physical plane while it remains in Astral Space.

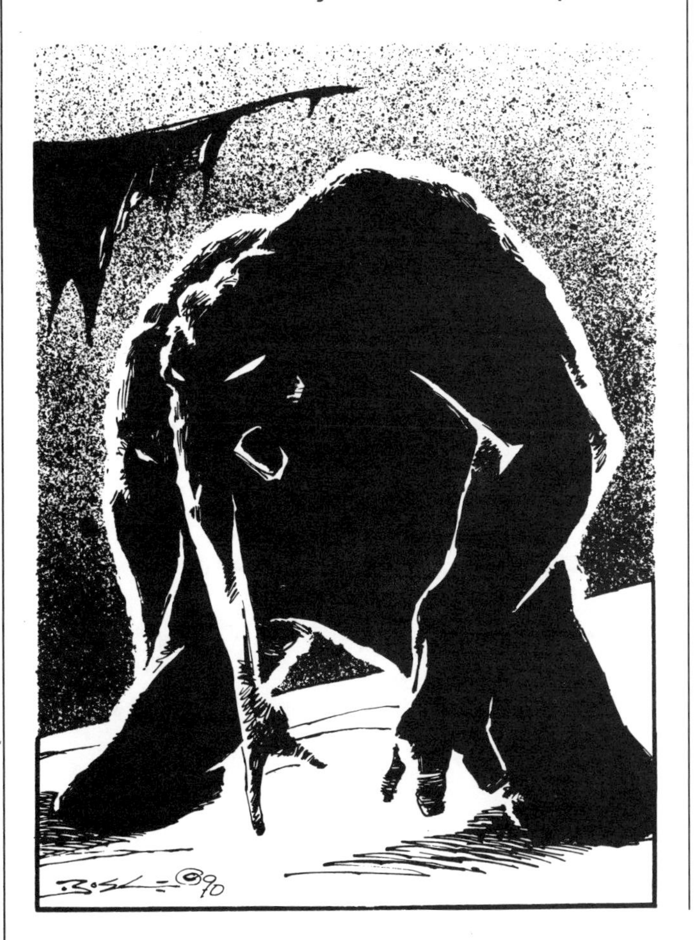

WEALTH

Wealth gives the Spirit the power to create precious stones or metals. A Spirit sophisticated in the ways of Humans may, like a genie from the *Arabian Nights*, even produce exotic fabrics, artworks, and so on. Material so created will register as magical spells and will show a magical element if assensed.

Market conditions vary, of course. What was a fortune in the days of legend may only be a moderate charge on the credstik in 2050. The gold, jewels, and other precious items a Spirit produces may not be so easy to sell. Even if a character finds a buyer who is not going to make him pay fences fees, people are going to wonder where he came up with this stuff.

The Spirit produces wealth with a base value of 1,000¥ times its Force. Roll a number of dice equal to its Spirit Energy and multiply the result by the base. For example, a Spirit with Force 4 and Spirit Energy 3 can cough up 3D6 x 4,000¥.

The Spirit must wait a month before it can do this trick again.

A Free Spirit that is very active in Human society—a Player, for example—tends to use this power to bankroll its operations. Other Free Spirits do not generally use it for themselves, and may even be contemptuous of the excitement Humans display when a Spirit demonstrates Wealth power for them.

DESIGNING FREE SPIRITS

There are two cases where a gamemaster may have to design a Free Spirit. First, he may need to make one up from scratch for an adventure. It is best if he designs the Spirit to fit his story, but he can certainly use the random system given below if inspiration fails.

The second case arises when a Spirit summoned during an adventure becomes uncontrolled. It does not matter whether or not the player character summoned the spirit. The gamemaster can simply decide whether the Spirit goes free or goes home (wherever that is). If the being stays on the physical plane as a Free Spirit, what powers does it get? What is its motivation? How will it behave?

SPIRIT TYPE

When designing a Free Spirit, the gamemaster asks himself how it came into the material world. The answer may eliminate the need for random dice rolls. If not, roll 1D6 and consult the **Spirit Generation Tables**.

Making random rolls is no problem for Elementals, because they can go anywhere and do fine. If the gamemaster is dealing with a Free Nature Spirit, the Spirit will likely be most comfortable in the setting where the story happens. If the gamemaster needs a Free Nature Spirit to guard an old mine in the middle of the Desert, what need is there to roll dice to find out what kind of Spirit it is?

After determining the type of Spirit, proceed to the next section on determining its Force and Spirit Energy.

SPIRIT GENERATION TABLES

Table 1: Spirit Type

Die Roll	Spirit Type
1 – 3	Elemental. Roll 1D6 and consult Table 2.
4 – 5	Nature Spirit. Roll 1D6 and consult Table 3.
6	Ally.

Table 2: Elemental Type

Die Roll	Spirit Type
1 – 3	Fire or Water. Roll 1D6: 1–3 = Fire. 4–6 = Water.
4 – 6	Air or Earth. Roll 1D6: 1–3 = Air. 4–6 = Earth.

Table 3: Nature Spirit Type

Die Roll	Spirit Type
1 – 2	Spirit of Man. Roll 1D6 and consult Table 3A.
3 – 4	Spirit of the Land. Roll 1D6 and consult Table 3B.
5	Spirit of the Sky. Roll 1D6 and consult Table 3C.
6	Spirit of the Waters. Roll 1D6 and consult Table 3D.

Table 3A: Spirits of Man

Die Roll	Spirit
1 – 3	City Spirit
4 – 5	Hearth Spirit
6	Field Spirit

Table 3B: Spirits of the Land

Die Roll	Spirit
1	Desert
2 – 3	Forest
4	Mountain
5 – 6	Prairie

Table 3C: Spirits of the Sky. Roll 1D6.

Die Roll	Spirit
1 – 4	Mist
5 – 6	Storm

Table 3D: Spirits of the Waters

Die Roll	Spirit
1 – 2	Lake
3 – 4	River
5	Sea
6	Swamp

Randomly designing a Free Spirit, Joe Gamer rolls 1D6 and scores 2: an Elemental. Rolling another 1D6, he gets a 3, and rolling again, a 1: A Fire Elemental.

SPIRIT ATTRIBUTES

Having determined the kind of Spirit, the gamemaster next works out its Force and Spirit Energy.

Unless he wants a particular rating, assume that Free Spirits have a Force of 2D6.

Its Spirit Energy will be 2D6 x 10 percent of their Force. If the Spirit scores an 11 or 12 (110 percent or 120 percent), raise its Force by +1 and calculate its energy as 10 percent or 20 percent of the new Force.

The Spirit gets a break here, with fractions rounded to the nearest whole number instead of the usual round-down convention.

After determining its attributes, proceed to choosing the Spirit's powers.

Joe Gamer rolls 2D6 for his Free Fire Elemental, scoring 8. A hefty little bugger, isn't it? He rolls 2D6 again and scores a 7. The Elemental's Spirit Energy is 70 percent of its Force. 8 x.7 = 5.6. Rounded to the nearest whole number, the Spirit Energy becomes 6. A Free Fire Elemental with a Force of 8 and a Spirit Energy of 6 should inspire an attack of politeness in any character who encounters it.

SPIRIT POWERS

Free Spirits have all the usual powers of Spirits of their type. A Free City Spirit would have Accident, Alienation, Concealment, and so on. These are listed in the basic game.

Allies have the powers their designers gave them (see p. 83). Being he can design a Free Ally, the gamemaster has to design the Ally as it would have been when first conjured. As a rule of thumb, roll a number of dice equal to the Spirit's Rating. The result is the amount of Karma needed to design the Ally.

Now roll 1D6 to determine how many powers the Spirit has. The gamemaster can select the powers or randomly roll 3D6 for them, consulting the appropriate table below. If the result indicates a power the Spirit already has, roll again.

POWERS OF FREE ELEMENTALS

Die Roll	Power
3 – 4	Animal Form
5 – 7	Astral Gateway
8 – 9	Aura Masking
10 – 11	Human Form
12	Possession
13	Dispelling
14	Wealth
15 – 16	Hidden Life
17	Sorcery
18	Personal Domain

POWERS OF FREE NATURE SPIRITS

Die Roll	Power
3 – 4	Human Form
5 – 6	Possession
7	Astral Gateway
8 – 9	Aura Masking
10 – 12	Animal Form
13 – 14	Personal Domain
15	Hidden Life
16	Wealth
17	Dispelling
18	Sorcery

POWERS OF FREE ALLIES

[**Note:** Allies *always* have the Sorcery power.]

Die Roll	Power
3 – 5	Animal Form
6	Astral Gateway
7 – 8	Dispelling
9	Human Form
10 – 11	Hidden Life
12 – 14	Aura Masking
15	Possession
16 – 17	Wealth
18	Personal Domain

Joe rolls 1D6, scoring 3. His Free Spirit has three powers. Rolling against the table for Elemental Powers, he scores a 9, 4, and 14. The Spirit has the powers of Aura Masking, Animal Form, and Wealth.

FILLING IN THE BLANKS

At this point, random die rolls cannot do much more. The gamemaster will have to decide what motivates the Spirit, either inventing its characteristics from scratch or using the guidelines from earlier in this chapter. Decide how the Spirit fits into the adventure and then give it habits, quirks, goals.

These need not be particularly logical, for a Spirit is an *alien* intelligence. If the gamemaster wants a City Spirit that wears a trench coat and appears as Humphrey Bogart, he's got it.

Add little powers to the Spirit for color. The music of a lonely saxophone or a muted trumpet blowing the blues as the fog rolls in from the Bay, and the streetlights glistening on the rain-swept streets might, for example, always accompany a gumshoe Spirit.

Having sketched in the attributes for the Free Fire Elemental, Joe starts the important work of telling its story. Conjured by a mage, of course, the Spirit went free when enemies killed its summoner. It flamed them down, and then stayed in the physical world. The mage had treated it politely enough, however, and the Spirit became rather intrigued by its glimpses of Human activity when called upon for services. Now, as its own master, the Elemental decides to find out more about these Humans. Because its conjuror always favored calling it up as a beautiful, red-headed woman, it becomes an Anima. Under the handle of Rebecca, the Spirit has been free for five or six years now. She (it is very difficult to think of a typical Anima as "it") sometimes reveals her existence to a simpatico Human, and if the host is willing, possesses him or her for a time, living life through the host's experience. Rebecca is troubled, though, because her last host was murdered by the Yakuza. She does not understand why Humans behave so. She has heard about shadowrunners and is trying to find some who will help her locate the yak who did the killing.

"I'll face gunnies, samurai, BTL-freaks with choppers, anything ya send. But ain't enough nuyen in Geneva-Orbital to make me face them toxics again, chummer."
—Nameless Street Samurai

agical Threats are two non-player types of magician. These are not "character classes," but stand halfway between Critters and Archetypes/Contacts. The Critter aspect comes in at times because some Magical Threats can do things "normal" magicians cannot. They can handle contacts with power that would either kill a sane Human or drive him mad. Indeed, some Magical Threats doubtless start life as perfectly respectable magicians with "normal" powers and abilities, then…who knows? Perhaps the magician suffers a trauma that breaks his mind open to sinister forces, or perhaps he arrogantly attempts a ritual for power Humans were not meant to touch. Whatever happens, it is something that leaves the magician no longer entirely Human.

These special traits are in addition to the formidable powers of a magician. Threats are still magicians capable of spells, enchantments, Initiation, and any other thing their player character countertypes can do. Gamemasters should not throw too many of these guys at the players, however, or they'll end up with a lot of dead characters instead of interesting plot twists.

THREAT RATINGS

One measure of a Magical Threat is his *Threat Rating*. This score flat out augments his Magic Pool. The energy he taps from his abnormal Astral contacts acts like a living focus to enhance his abilities above the level of normal magicians.

The Threat Rating may vary during an adventure. Magical Threats must often carry out strange tasks that often spell disaster for anyone nearby. When the magician carries out the task successfully, his Threat Rating increases. If he is thwarted, it goes down. The magician may try to do these things on his own or have his nefarious agents carry them out. Either way, a major part of an adventure involving Magical Threats will involve discovering and foiling these activities in order to weaken the enemy.

The gamemaster should assign an initial Threat Rating to a Magical Threat in an adventure, then design a series of tasks they are to carry out. Each task the Threat fulfills increases his Threat Rating by +1. Each one foiled decreases the Rating by the same amount. Each task should have a loophole that allows the player characters to attempt to disrupt the evil scheme.

Each type of Magical Threat has his own unique abilities as well.

TOXIC SHAMANS

Toxic shamans may have tragic elements, but they are actively hostile and are valuable villains for adventures.

The most common type is the Avenger. This is a shaman who has, for one reason or another, been turned against Humanity by the horrible damage that the species has wreaked on the planet. One type of Avenger might say, "I shall track and destroy the poisonous race of man until it is gone. When only I am left alive, I shall slay myself happily. Only then can the Mother heal Herself, free of the ravening cancer of mankind."

There are also toxic shamans who revel in the blight, who spread the poison to feed their power. They have little to recommend them except that they make really wiz villains. These are known as Poisoners.

Both kinds of toxics are essentially loners, driven by hatred of their species and themselves. Avengers might form temporary alliances with groups such as Greenwar or the government of Amazonia. A Poisoner might be co-opted by a corp, perhaps one trying to undercut some ecological preservation scheme but with a show of "plausible deniability." They can give their dirty work to the loony tune. In either case, however, the toxic shaman is only loosely bound by any group ties.

A cabal of Avengers is rumored to be among the more effective border security forces of Amazonia, living in the eroded ecological ruins of the worst areas of slashed-and-burned rain forest. They operate as terrorists making ferocious attacks magically and militarily on any who attempt further damage to the fragile ecology on the fringes of the rain forest. Meanwhile, the more balanced magicians of Amazonia work feverishly to restore and expand the habitat.

Someone might say these types don't sound so crazy. Remember, however, that a toxic shaman has no compassion. A peasant family trying to scratch out a living from the eroded soil at the fringe of the rain forest is found horribly slain by magic. After a merchant in a border village secretly dumps some waste oil in the forest, the whole village is massacred the next night. For that matter, there are reports of magical attacks on Amazonian tribes for using what the toxics consider "inappropriate technology" within the habitat. The keynote to the Avenger is an intolerant and vicious response to any perceived threat to nature. They consider Humanity to be a parasite upon the Earth. As long as Humans are relatively benign, they may live. If they threaten their host, they must be exterminated.

Poisoners may also come in groups, but are more likely to be loners. The magical grapevine is rife with rumors that recent disasters in Pennsylvania, where fires ravaged a half-dozen abandoned coal mines, causing over 100 deaths from cave-ins and smoke inhalation in the towns built over them, are the work of a Poisoner.

TOXIC TOTEMS

A toxic shaman chooses a totem just as a normal shaman does. Avengers tend to choose Wilderness totems, while Poisoners prefer Urban totems. This does not represent a moral judgement on the relative merits of totems, but reflects the psychologies of the two types of toxic shamans. Toxic shamans receive all the normal benefits of the shamanic tradition, and must abide by the taboos and customs of their totem. These are always interpreted in light of their toxic alignment, however. A toxic Eagle shaman views it as his sacred duty to destroy polluters as supreme examples of evil.

Poisoner shamans may reverse the normal mandates of the totem. A toxic Dog shaman would be a rabid thing, literally a ferocious destroyer of Humanity, ravening for the lives of those he would normally protect.

TOXIC SPIRITS

On p. 81, this **Grimoire** mentioned that normal shamans cannot conjure Nature Spirits from badly polluted domains. Guess who *can* summon such spirits? That's right. Only a toxic shaman can summon or control a Toxic Spirit. They can be banished by another magician, but a control contest will only free the Spirit if its original summoner loses control.

Toxic Free Spirits do exist, and are very, very bad news. Besides the other powers of Free Spirits, such a being can grant a shaman a Threat Rating equal to its Spirit Power. If this Human Ally can increase the Threat Rating, the Spirit Power goes up, too. If the magician fails his tasks, losing Threat Rating, the Spirit also loses Spirit Power. Shamans who lose their twisted master too many points are often discarded in some painful manner.

Toxic Spirits are twisted and crippled-looking, warped by the pollution of their domain. Their nature is apparent to any astral onlooker. When a toxic shaman summons such a Spirit, its Force may be increased. His tests for summoning and Resisting Drain are based on the Force he allocates to the conjuring. However, the Spirit's actual Force is increased by the background count of the area that is due to its pollution level (see p. 63). Facing these guys on their "home turf" is a remarkably bad idea.

And that turf can *move*. A toxic shaman can summon a Spirit and send it, in Manifest Form, outside the domain. If a toxic shaman in a blasted area of the Barrens (a Toxic City Domain), summons up a Street Spirit, the latter cannot escape by running into a house (Hearth Domain). The thing can follow him there, or anywhere.

TOXIC THREATS

A typical toxic shaman starts with a 1D6 Threat Rating. His tasks might include the following examples:

•Destroy a community that is clearing wilderness land (suitable to Avengers).

•Assassinate executives in an organization, either one that is polluting the land or one trying to repair the damage, depending on the type of shaman involved.

•Foment riots and destruction in an urban area or strike such an area with a plague, fatal levels of toxic waste, or other disaster.

INSECT SHAMANS

The **Shadowrun** rules (p. 75) note that insects are rarely used as totems. This is true in most, though not all, shamanic cultures. Some societies consider insects "power animals," but even in these, such shamans are regarded as beings of special power.

Most insect shamans hold themselves aloof from Human affairs. They are in touch with powers of nature that do not impinge upon our consciousness. The typical Astral Quest of an insect shaman would probably drive another magician insane.

Most is known about insect totems of the communal insects: Wasp, Ant, and Termite. There are rumors of shamans dedicated to Spider and Mantis, the terrible, solitary hunters of the insect world. However, nothing is known of their cults.

An insect shaman may concern himself with Human society and its affairs. In some cases, a shaman may contact the insect totem, seeking to use its power for his own ends. For a time he may succeed, but the alien nature of the totem will inevitably begin to take over. The shaman finds his plans are more and more mysterious, even pointless, to himself and to everyone else. He becomes a tool of the power he sought to turn to his own ends.

The hive mentality of the known insect totems seeks food, security, the expansion of the nest. By carrying out tasks designed to procure these things, or their analogues in society, an insect shaman can increase his Threat Rating as well as gain material wealth.

THE HIVE

Prior to summoning the Queen Spirit, the shaman may only control a number of True Form Worker or Soldier Spirits equal to his Threat Rating x 10. The maximum number of total Force Rating Points they may possess is equal to the sum of his Magic Rating plus his Threat Rating x 5. Flesh Form Spirits do not count against this total. All these Spirits are loyal to the shaman and will act under his direction, unless their Queen directly and explicitly orders otherwise.

Once the Queen is present, she may boost the shaman's effective Threat Rating for the purpose of increasing the number of Spirits he directly controls. If she later uses that same Spirit Energy to boost her own Force, he loses the bonus to his Threat Rating.

Working together, the Queen and the insect shaman may summon a number of points per day in Spirits equal to the Queen Force, plus his Magical Attribute, plus his unmodified Threat Rating. A Soldier is worth twice its Force in points, and a Worker half that.

The maximum number of True Form Spirits in a Hive is equal to the Queen's Force multiplied by the Shaman's Body Attribute for Soldiers and the Queen's Force multiplied by the Shaman's Willpower, multiplied by 10 for Workers.

The Shaman gains 1 Karma Point for every number of Spirits in the Hive equal to his Magic Attribute x 10. This Karma could be used for his own ends, but the Queen, of course, demands it to raise her own Spirit Energy.

INSECT SPIRITS

An insect shaman can summon Insect Spirits in any domain where insects can survive, which is to say slottin' near everywhere. Regardless of the domain, he may summon a Worker, a Soldier, or a Queen.

When summoned, the Insect Spirit must be incubated in a host body, a Human body. During a period of time in weeks equal to the Force of the Spirit, a transformation occurs. The lower the host's Willpower compared to the Force of the possessing Spirit, the greater the transformation. A Worker always reaches an intermediate stage between its original body and the ideal shape of the possessing insect. A Queen always manifests as a True Form. A Soldier's form, on the other hand, may vary considerably.

A Resisted Success Test between the host body and the Spirit is necessary to determine the extent of the transformation. The host pits its Willpower against twice the Force of the Spirit, and vice-versa. If a Queen participated in the summoning of the Spirit, the host receives an additional +2 to his Target Number. Consult the following table:

Successes	Result
0	The host is destroyed and a True Form Insect Spirit emerges.
1 – 2	The host body acquires primary resemblance to the True Form, such as changes in body shape and mass, additional limbs, and so on.
3 – 4	The host body acquires some True Form characteristics, such as the appearance of chitinous armor, multifaceted eyes, underdeveloped extra limbs, and so on.
5 – 6	The host body acquires only one of the physical aspects of the True Form.
7+	The host body retains its original form and acquires the Free Spirit power of Aura Masking. It is not, however, a Free Spirit, and does remain under the control of the Queen or shaman.

WORKERS AND SOLDIERS

Worker Spirits

Workers are useless in combat, but can produce fine products, make chemicals, build things, and so on day after day, without stopping.

Soldier Spirits

Soldiers have one job: combat. That is all they know and all they do, but they do it terrifyingly well.

TRUE FORM INSECT SPIRITS

The True Form Insect Spirit is a Spirit as described previously in this book. It has the ability to operate in Astral Space and to manifest in the mundane world.

It appears as the actual insect, but near man-size and perfect in form.

True Form Soldier Spirits

B	Q	S	C	I	W	E	R	Attacks
F + 1	F + 4 x 4	F + 4	—	F	2	(F)A	F x 2*	(Str)M2 or Special

*In Astral Space, it receives a +10 initiative bonus, and a +5 when physically manifest.

Powers: Enhanced Senses (Smell), Paralyzing Touch, Venom

Weaknesses: Reduced Senses (Sight), Vulnerability (Insecticides)

True Form Worker Spirit

B	Q	S	C	I	W	E	R	Attacks
F – 2	F x 3	F+ 2	—	F – 2	1	(F)A	1	None

Powers: Enhanced Senses (Smell), Skill

Weaknesses: Reduced Senses (sight), Vulnerability (Insecticides)

FLESH FORM INSECT SPIRITS

A Flesh Form is some bizarre cross between the host's Human body and the insect appearance of the actual Spirit. The extent of the transformation in the Flesh Form Soldier varies and could range from barely noticeable to unconcealable. The Flesh Form Worker always reaches a halfway point.

The will of the Insect Spirit always consumes that of the original host.

All Flesh Form Spirits are Dual Beings

Flesh Form Workers

The Flesh Form Worker's Physical Attributes are 1 point less than the host's. Their Mental Attributes are per the True Form Worker.

Flesh Form Workers have the Power of Skill and the Weakness of Reduced Senses (Sight). They do not have the Power of Enhanced Senses (Smell) or Vulnerability to Insecticides.

Flesh Form Soldiers

The Mental Attributes of the Flesh Form Soldier are per the True Form Soldier, while its Physical Attributes are equal to the host body's plus the Spirit's Force.

Flesh Form Soldiers do not have the Powers of Enhanced Senses (Smell), Paralyzing Touch, or Venom. They also lose their Weakness of Reduced Senses (Sight) and their Vulnerability to Insecticides.

QUEEN SPIRIT

The Queen Spirit is the conduit of power to the shaman. Even before being summoned, she acts as the focus of his magic, his personal totem. Once she is in the physical world, the Queen will chafe under the yolk of the shaman. Besides the normal ways that a Spirit can go free, she can try to break control like an Ally (see p. 86), or try to go free whenever the shaman increases or decreases his Threat Rating. Because these are non-player characters, the gamemaster can, of course, decide when the Queen goes free to suit his adventure.

The Queen will work to make her nest on Earth stronger and safer and to extend its influence. This can be a brutally direct effort to bring through more Spirits, possess more Humans, and take over territory, or a subtle matter involving use of Compulsion-laden substances, political influence, wealth, and so on.

The original shaman (or a more competent replacement) is used as the nest's principle representative in the Human world.

The Queen is larger than Human-sized, usually four to six meters long.

An insect shaman can summon only one Queen. If she is banished or destroyed, all his magic power departs forever. If she is disrupted, he loses the use of his Threat Rating (and thus of all his other Spirits) until she can return to the world.

If the Queen goes free, the shaman retains his power only if the Queen wills it. If a Queen makes this kind of alliance with a shaman, she can grant him a bonus to his Threat Rating equal to her Spirit Energy. As noted above regarding Toxic Free Spirits, if the insect shaman can increase his Threat Rating, it increases the Spirit Energy. Conversely, if he loses Threat Rating, then the Queen's Energy goes down.

The shaman does not have to summon the Queen Spirit, but his powers quickly reach a limit without her active presence on the physical plane.

Queen Spirit

B	Q	S	C	I	W	E	R	Attacks
F + 5	F + 6 x 5	F + 6	F	F	F	(F)A	F x 3*	(Str)S3 or Special

*In Astral Space, she receives a +10 initiative bonus, and a +5 when physically manifest.

Powers: Animal Control (Insects), Compulsion, Enhanced Senses (Smell), Fear, Immunity To Normal Weapons, Paralyzing Touch, Summoning, Venom

Weaknesses: Reduced Senses (Sight), Vulnerability (Insecticides)

SPECIAL POWERS

Some comments on the special powers of Insect Spirits are necessary. Any powers not described here operate per those in the basic **Shadowrun** rules.

Animal Control (Insects)

The Queen can send swarms of insects to gather information, attack en masse (deadly in the case of Wasp Spirits), and so on.

Compulsion

The Queen can exude a wide variety of pheromones that affect Humans with overriding compulsions. She can affect anyone smelling the essences, which are active to a distance of her Force in meters. She can also secrete the pheromones in a form that can be mixed into food, drink, used as a drug, and otherwise blended.

Skill

When summoned, a Worker can be given any non-magical Build/Repair or other similar skill the summoner wishes. It can use this skill with a rating equal to its Force.

Summoning

As per the rules above. If the host is a player character or important non-player character, make a Resisted Success Test using the Queen's Force versus the character's Willpower, each with a Target Number of 6. The Queen receives a Target Modifier of +1 for every point of Essence the character has lost under 6. If the Queen does not win, the character cannot be possessed by her Spirits.

If the Queen is destroyed or disrupted, all her Spirits, whether summoned by herself or the shaman, are destroyed. Possessed Humans also die.

Banishing or Dispelling may work, but if the Spirit, including the Queen, is in True Form, its Force is effectively doubled. Even if the Spirit is defeated, the host body will die. Once the initial incubation of the Spirit has begun, there is no saving the host.

INSECT THREAT

Insect shaman Threat Ratings are affected by tasks that make the nest stronger or weaker. Keep in mind that these tasks can be utterly absurd to Human "common sense." Possible examples:

- The shaman must get a series of articles distributed in the datanets, making allegations about a policlub or other group that threatens the nest. If the articles can be disproved, the task is foiled.
- A series of neolithic antiquities must be stolen from several collections (in museums and private hands). These are to be used as raw materials in preparing a unique enchantment with a rating equal to the shaman's present Threat Rating.
- The nest requires the use of a certain city block for a week, starting on a specific date. Residents will be cleared out by bribery, extortion, or else captured and possessed.
- The shaman must get 20 possessed Humans working on a given project.

"Trust me, chummer, it ain't ever over."
—PRH, a mage of some repute

RULES MODIFICATIONS

Some rules presented in the original **Shadowrun** rule book have been modified and/or revised since the book was first published. Later printings were updated, but this section presents all the additions and corrections as a convenient reference.

MAGICIANS AND TECH

When using the rules on p. 53 of **Shadowrun** to build an Archetype who uses magic, players have found odd loopholes when it came to the Tech Priority. Some folks discovered that a Tech Priority Level of 3 allowed them to buy up enough power focuses to choke a horse. It helps that a typo in the equipment section has the focuses going for 10,000 nuyen per Rating Point (it should have read 100,000 nuyen). The rules in this book introduce a kind of limited magician called an adept. A non-Metahuman adept can have a Tech Priority of 4!

In the interests of game balance, the gamemaster can use one of several possible options to prevent a magician or adept from loading up on magic items to the point his gaming starts to do a fair imitation of a tactical nuke.

Option 1

Focus prices are adjusted in the Magical Supplies Price Lists at the end of this Appendix. With these price adjustments, even a million nuyen wouldn't go far enough to unbalance play. All the character types in this **Grimoire** are built from this basis.

Option 2

This option allows a magician to automatically bond any focus he purchased with Tech nuyen. Alternatively, give magicians points for bonding equal to their Magic Attribute. The Magic Attribute is first reduced to account for any cyberware the magician has implanted, and that modified rating is used. One Magic Point will bond 1 Rating Point of a focus.

Option 3

Use the statistics below to replace the "Tech" column of the **Master Character Table**, p. 53, **Shadowrun**. Allow the magician to automatically bond anything he buys.

Priority	Tech/Force
0	100/5
1	1,000/10
2	20,000/20
3	150,000/50
4	300,000/50

An Adept Archetype with Tech 4 gets 50 spell points, just like a magician with Tech 3. Adept status should *never* give the adept an advantage over a full-blown magician. Some adepts do not get spell points at all; they can't cast spells and so do not use spell points.

SPELL DAMAGE

The **Shadowrun** rules contain a serious error on pages 81 and 92. Both places state that after the Combat Spell's damage has been calculated, the target resists the damage normally, using his Body Attribute against the damage as though it were from a physical weapon.

This is wrong.

The damage by Combat Spells is based solely on the Resisted Success Test between the caster and the target. If a magician casts a Staging 1 Spell and scores four successes more than his opponent, the spell has been raised to a Deadly effect, and the target is dead.

Note that this damage bypasses all external armor, as it is "circuited" directly into the target through Astral Space. Dermal armor *does* assist in defending against Physical Combat Spells. Having paid Essence to have the armor implanted, the wearer has made it part of his physical being. That is why the target of a Physical Combat Spell can add his Dermal Armor Rating to his Body Attribute when resisting the spell. Note that he does *not* get this advantage against Mana Combat Spells.

This clarification may unbalance some existing games or simply displease some gamers. In that case, we recommend also using the rules for **Damaging Manipulations** (p. 52) for all Combat Spells. This seriously underpowers Sorcery in the opinion of the game's designers, however.

RESISTANCE TESTS

The basic **Shadowrun** rules (p. 81) state that the Target Number for resisting a spell is the caster's Sorcery Skill Rating. That is correct.

The Gamemaster's Screen states that its Target Number is the Force of the spell. That is *incorrect.* Resisting a spell cast by a magician with Sorcery 7 takes a Target Number of 7, no matter how high or low the Spell Force may be.

NEW TOTEMS

The new Wilderness Totems are Gator, Owl, Shark, and Lion. The new Urban Totems are Cat, Gator, and Owl.

Cat

Characteristics: Cat is stealthy, vain, and sometimes cruel. She is cunning and learns many secrets, but does not like to share her knowledge with others. Cat is an Urban totem, for she is quite at home with mankind, either in their company or as a solitary huntress in the streets and alleyways. Cat shamans are solitary types, with no commitment to anything but themselves.

Environment: Urban

Advantages: +2 dice for Illusion Spells; +2 dice for Conjuring City Spirits.

Disadvantages: Cat may toy with an opponent in combat, even when the situation is desperate. She will threaten, sneer, and hiss, displaying her dominance. She will also use showy magic, flashy combat, or other irrelevancies in the process of the kill. An unwounded Cat shaman must make a Willpower Test with a Target Number 6 when she wants to cast a Combat Spell. If she fails the test, she will not use all her successes if the spell works, but will inflict only a Light wound. If the shaman is wounded, all this playing around stops. Cat is fastidiously clean, suffering a +1 on her tests due to distraction if she is dirty or unkempt.

Gator

Characteristics: Great fighter, big eater. Swift to act when action is called for, lethargic, even torpid the rest of the time. Gator is often ill-tempered, especially when prodded to action. But once he grips, he holds, and will not turn away from a path he has chosen.

Environment: Swamps or rivers in the Wilderness. Gator is also an Urban totem because myth, if not reality, has him in the sewers of great cities. In magic, myth is as good as reality, and so Gator thrives among Urban shamans.

Advantages: +2 dice for Combat and Detection Spells; +2 dice for Conjuring Spirits of Swamp, Lake, and River (if Wilderness totem chosen) or City Spirits (if Urban totem chosen).

Disadvantages: Gator is lazy and greedy. As an eater, he prefers to glut himself with food and then laze around. As a shadowrunner, he prefers a job with a big payoff that will let him take it easy until it is all gone. It can take some hefty argument to make Gator exert himself. His greed makes him loathe to share material goods and he will almost never make loans or pick up a check. Once on a job, he goes for a direct solution and is impatient of subtlety. It takes a Willpower Test with a Target Number of 6 for a Gator shaman to break off a fight, a chase, or other direct action. He also subtracts 1 die for Illusion Spells.

Lion

Characteristics: Lion is the brave and powerful warrior. His method is direct and pointed, for he is not a creature of subtlety. Lion prefers to work from surprise and ambush, allowing others to perform tasks for him while he holds his strength in reserve. He will take the offensive if necessary. Any threat to his kin or family is a threat to him.

Environment: Prairie

Advantages: +2 dice for Combat Spells; +2 dice for Prairie Spirits.

Disadvantages: −1 die for Health Spells. Lion is vain and demands the most from himself, especially when it comes to his physical condition and appearance. He must live well and demands respect and loyalty from those around him.

Owl
Characteristics: Owl is a wise and silent observer. She does not speak unless she has something important to say. Owl lives by night and shuns the sunlight, in which she is practically helpless. What she hunts, she finds. Owl is helpful to her friends and fearsome to her enemies.
Environment: Anywhere, Urban or Wilderness. Spell learning is conducted by night, however.
Advantages: +2 dice for all Sorcery and Conjuring by night.
Disadvantages: +1 to *all* Target Numbers (even non-magical ones!) when in direct sunlight; +1 to all magical Target Numbers, whether or not in daylight.

Shark
Characteristics: Shark is the cold, relentless hunter of the sea, utterly savage in battle. Shark calls no place home, but wanders the sea and knows all its secrets. Shark would be a likely totem for shamans of any seafaring or shore-dwelling culture: Hawaiian kahunas, Japanese miko, Haitian houngans, Eskimo angekok, as well as the NAN tribes of the Pacific Northwest and any surviving shamans among the few Australian aborigines still living in the Dreamtime.
Environment: On or by the sea.
Advantages: +2 dice for Combat and Detection Spells and Conjuring Sea Spirits.
Disadvantages: A Shark shaman will go berserk in combat if he is wounded or when he kills an opponent. When either happens, the shaman must make a Willpower Success Test with a Target Number 6. He goes berserk for three combat turns, minus one turn for every success he rolls. Three or more successes and he stays rational. A berserk Shark will attack the nearest living thing, fighting to kill with his best weapons or spells. He may, alternatively, continue to hurl magic or use weapons on the body of his last victim, savagely blasting or hacking it. Even if he isn't berserk, Shark believes that the best enemy is a dead enemy. He rarely uses non-lethal methods in combat. If challenged in any way, he does not stop to reason or threaten, but strikes. And if he strikes, it is to kill.

MAGICAL PRICES

One thing to keep in mind during play is that the figures given here are *list prices*. Most magical goods must be purchased from people who consider haggling a fine art. Thus, the gamemaster should feel free to call for Opposed Tests in Negotiation when someone goes shopping at the lore store. Target Number is 4. The winner gets a price break of 5 percent for every extra success he scores. The lowest a vendor will go is 50 percent off list, but the sky is the limit if he gets an advantage over a customer. Hey, its a free market, chummer!

This section briefly describes all the magical gear and goodies introduced in this book. The tables that follow give the prices for *all* the magical equipment available in **Shadowrun**, so it will not be necessary to flip back and forth between the two books.

ENCHANTING SUPPLIES

Alchemical Radicals

Alchemically processed materials. These weigh 1 percent as much as the raw materials and cost 4 times raw material cost.

Orichalchum

The potent magical metal is not cheap, but if a character needs it and does not have the facilities, time, or skill to make it, he can buy it. The cost is double the price of the radicals it takes to make it. A unit weighs 10 grams.

Raw Materials

These are guaranteed, genuine, pure materials gathered by ecologically sound talismongers in the unsullied wilderness. Suitable for use in enchanting, they will also serve to make virgin telesma. One unit of herbal raw materials weighs 5 kilograms. Mineral or metallic ores weigh 10 kilograms. Cost is based on relative rarity of the material.

Refined Materials

Magically refined raw materials can make handmade telesma, but not virgin ones (that requires the caster to do his own refining). One unit of refined material weighs half as much as the raw materials. Refined materials cost twice the raw material cost.

FOCUSES

All focuses have a cost per Rating Point equal to their First Bonding cost (see p. 47), not counting any modifiers, x 15,000 nuyen. For weapon focuses, add the weapon's (Reach +1) x 100,000 nuyen to cover the orichalcum used in the focus.

Fetish focuses are reduced in price by a factor of 10 because they are expendable, used up in a single spell.

This formula is a rule of thumb that factors in typical materials, time, Karma, and so on. When pricing a focus made by a player-character magician or one the gamemaster has designed in detail, figure the actual cost of the materials and add 25 percent. Then add 10,000 nuyen x the Base Karma Cost. The character should treat this as list price when haggling with prospective customers.

The weight of focuses varies wildly, depending on the form of the item.

SPELL FORMULAS

The cost of a legally purchased spell formula is calculated from its Base Drain (before applying any modifiers). Each Drain Category has a base value, shown on the following table. Multiply this by the Staging for the Drain Code. An L2 Spell costs 100 nuyen: Base cost 50 nuyen for an L x the Staging of 2.

MAGICAL SUPPLIES

Ally Conjuring Materials

These are the ritual supplies needed to summon an Ally. Units equal to the Spirit's Force are needed for Rituals of Summoning and Change.

Ward Casting Materials

These are the special ritual supplies needed to set wards. Units equal to the Force of the wards are necessary.

Watcher Conjuring Materials

These are the ritual materials used when conjuring Watchers with an extended lifespan (measured in days). The materials are not needed to summon Watchers for brief periods (measured in hours). One unit per day of the Spirit's lifespan is required.

MAGICAL SUPPLIES PRICE LIST

ENCHANTING SUPPLIES

GEAR	Weight	Price
Enchanting Kit	20	10,000¥
Enchanting Shop	300	100,000¥

Raw Material	Refined Form	Radical Form	Form
Herbals	50	100	200
Crystals	100	200	400
Semi-precious Gems	200	400	800
Precious Gems	500	1,000	2,000
Iron	50	100	200
Copper	100	200	400
Silver	300	600	1,200
Gold	10,000	20,000	40,000
Mercury	600	1,200	2,400
Tin	30	60	120
Lead	30	60	120

Orichalcum: 88,000 per unit.

FOCUSES	Price
Spell Lock	45,000
Fetish Focus	3,000 x Rating
Specific Spell Focus	45,000 x Rating
Spell Purpose Focus	75,000 x Rating
Spirit Focus	60,000 x Rating
Power Focus	105,000 x Rating
Weapon Focus	([Reach + 1] x 100,000) + (90,000 x Rating)

MAGICAL SUPPLIES

Material	Weight	Cost
Ally Conjuring Materials	—	1,000 per unit
Elemental Conjuring Materials	—	1,000 per unit
Ward Casting Materials	—	1,000 per unit
Watcher Conjuring Materials	—	1,000 per unit
Medicine Lodge Materials	2x Rating	500 x Rating
Expendable Fetishes		
Combat Spells	—	20
Detection Spells	—	05
Healing Spells	—	50
Illusion Spells	—	10
Manipulation Spells	—	30
Reusable Fetishes	.1	10 x Expendable
Ritual Sorcery Materials		
Detection Spells	—	100 per unit
Health Spells	—	500 per unit
Illusion Spells	—	100 per unit
Manipulation Spells	—	1,000 per unit

HERMETIC LIBRARY (ANY MAGICAL SKILL)

Computer Media	—	Mp x 100
Hardcopy Media	50 x Rating	500 x Rating

SPELL FORMULAS

Consult Base Drain code (before applying modifiers):

Drain Code	Price
L	50 x Staging
M	100 x Staging
S	500 x Staging
D	1,000 x Staging

"If you have to look it up, maybe you shouldn't be playing with it?"

—The late John Link, magical instructor

dept: A magician capable of using magic in only a limited way.

Alchemy: A concentration of the Enchanting Skill used to turn raw materials into powerful magical substances called radicals. Radicals are very useful in making focuses.

Arcanum (pl. arcana): A specialization of Alchemy. Each arcanum deals with the magical uses of either herbal, mineral, or metal materials in the Enchanting Skill.

Centering: A power of metamagic available to Initiates, Centering allows the use of a non-magical skill to reduce Drain or penalties associated with magical work.

Coven: A magical group, most often one committed to Wicca, also known as Witchcraft. Wicca is an Earth-oriented religion that worships the Goddess of Nature in Her many aspects. Most covens are matriarchal, placing authority in the hands of a female high priestess, though some sects differ in this regard.

Dispelling: A power of metamagic available to Initiates that allows them to negate sustained or permanent spells.

Enchanting: A Magic Skill used to construct magical items and equipment.

Etheric Plane: The astral plane closest to the physical world.

Focus: An enchanted item. Most common types are fetish focus, specific spell focus, spell purpose focus, spirit focus, weapon focus, and power focus. There are also "Unique Enchantments," which are custom items made for specific magical purposes.

GLOSSARY

Free Spirit: A Spirit that has escaped from a summoner's control and remains in our world. Free Spirits can be very powerful. Each appears to be a distinct individual, with its own unique characteristics and motivations.

Geas (pl. geasa): A restriction on the use of magic that is incurred by the loss of the Magic Attribute. If a magician does not fulfill his geasa, his magical abilities suffer penalties.

Grade: The level of Initiation that a magician has achieved. Grades begin at 0, meaning a Grade 0 Initiate has completed one Initiation.

Initiate: A magician who has achieved one or more grades of Initiation. Initiation requires the expenditure of Karma and may also require the candidate to complete an Ordeal.

Mage: A magician of the hermetic tradition.

Masking: A power of metamagic available to Initiates that allows them to disguise their auras so that they will look like mundanes. The power also allows Initiates to detect masked auras belonging to others.

Metamagic: An advanced form of magic available only to Initiates. See also **Centering, Quickening, Shielding, Masking,** and **Dispelling.**

Metaplane: A plane of Astral Space beyond the etheric plane. Under normal circumstances, only Initiates can visit the metaplanes, though certain Spirits can open gateways to the metaplanes that anyone can use. There are eight presently known metaplanes: the four hermetic metaplanes of Fire, Water, Air, and Earth, and the four shamanic metaplanes of Man, Waters, Sky, and Land.

Ordeal: A task, obligation, or challenge to which an Initiate must submit as part of the Initiation process.

Order: A magical group, most often under the hermetic influence.

Quickening: A power of metamagic available to Initiates that allows them to make sustained spells become permanent without the use of spell locks. Use of this power does cost Karma.

Shaman: A magician of the shamanic tradition.

Shielding: A power of metamagic available to Initiates, this is a stronger version of the spell defense that a non-Initiate can provide.

Spirit Energy: A reserve of energy developed by Free Spirits that gives them increased power in the physical world.

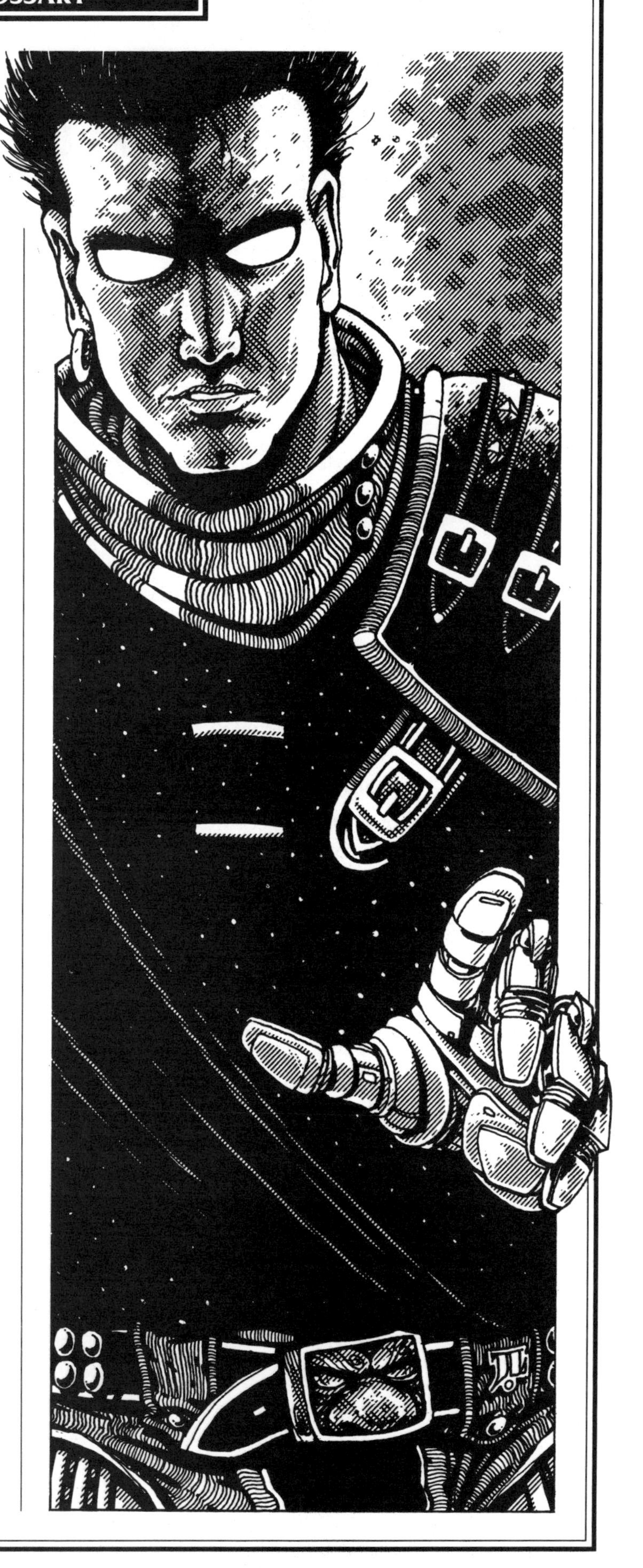

"In a bind? let your Magic Fingers do the walking."
—Street Saying

The *Manual of Thaumaturgy* is the handbook of the working magician, as indispensable to him as the *Physician's Desk Reference* is to a doctor or pharmacist, or the "rubber handbook" to an engineer. The reference section of the *Manual* is loaded with the complex formulas and theorems of magical theory, including Crowley's Postulates, The Enochian Projection, The Weisman-Arguelles Curve, and other yardsticks of modern magical practice.

The most widely used section of the *Manual* is the directory of registered spells, practical descriptions of hundreds of spells, both major and minor. Magicians can order the formulas directly from the copyright holders. Though unscrupulous magicians at times might attempt to "reverse-engineer" spell formulas from the descriptions given here, this practice defrauds the rightful owners of their royalties. It is also a less dependable method.

Subscriptions to the *Manual* are available only to licensed magicians with valid credentials. The editors take no responsibility for material obtained from pirate versions of the *Manual* that began to appear in hardcopy, chips, and underground datanets within a few weeks after initial release.

USING THE DIRECTORY

This section includes descriptions of new spells and revised spells, as well as listings of previously published spells. The spells are organized according to type: Combat, Detection, Health, Illusion, and Manipulation. Also included is a complete table listing all new, revised, and previously published spells for ease of reference.

For easy reference, all spells given in the **Shadowrun** rulebook are reprinted here. Spells that have not changed from the original **Shadowrun** rules are notated, "As in basic game." Some previously published spells have been revised. The gamemaster may decide whether or not magician-players who already have these spells must use these new statistics.

SPELL DIRECTORY

Each spell in the Directory contains information on the Drain Code, whether a spell is Mana (M) or Physical (P), and any Special Effects. Information on the spell's Duration uses the following codes:

I (Instantaneous)

S (Sustained)

P(x) (Permanent, with (x) the base number of turns the spell must be sustained for the effect to become permanent. To determine the actual time required, divide this number by the number of successes rolled for the spell).

COMBAT SPELLS

Following are a number of new Combat Spells, as well as revised versions of previously published spells.

Death Touch
Drain: M1 **Type:** Mana **Duration:** Instant
Special Effect: Touch required. Staging 1.

Fire Bolt
Drain: D3 **Type:** Physical **Duration:** Instant
Special Effect: Staging 1. Elemental Fire side effects.

***Fire Cloud**
Drain: S3 **Type:** Physical **Duration:** Instant
Special Effect: Staging 3. Elemental Fire side effects. Area Spell.

Fire Dart
Drain: M3 **Type:** Physical **Duration:** Instant
Special Effect: Staging 3. Elemental Fire side effects.

Fire Missile
Drain: S3 **Type:** Physical **Duration:** Instant
Special Effect: Staging 2. Elemental Fire side effects.

***Fireball (Revised)**
Drain: D3 **Type:** Physical **Duration:** Instant
Special Effect: Staging 2. Elemental Fire side effects. As in basic game. Area Spell.

***Mana Cloud**
Drain: M1 **Type:** Mana **Duration:** Instant
Special Effect: Staging 3. Area Spell.

Manablast
Drain: D1 **Type:** Mana **Duration:** Instant
Special Effect: Staging 1. A bolt of magical power that causes Physical Damage.

Power Cloud
Drain: M2 **Type:** Physical **Duration:** Instant
Special Effect: Staging 3. Area Spell.

Powerblast
Drain: D2 **Type:** Physical **Duration:** Instant
Special Effect: Staging 1. Area Spell.

Ram (Revised)
Drain: M2 **Type :** Physical **Duration:** Instant
Special Effect: Staging 1.

Ram Touch
Drain: L2 **Type:** Physical **Duration:** Instant
Special Effect: Staging 1. Touch required.

Slay (Race/Species)
Each version of this spell is different and has a specific formula. That is, Slay Ork, Slay Normal, Slay Dog, Slay Western Dragon, Slay Cockroach, Slay Feathered Serpent, and so forth are all separate spells.
Drain: M1 **Type:** Mana **Duration:** Instant
Special Effect: Staging 1. This spell affects only members of specified sentient race or non-sentient species.

Stun Bolt
Drain: M1 **Type:** Mana **Duration:** Instant
Special Effect: Staging 1. Stun Damage.

Stun Cloud
Drain: L1 **Type:** Mana **Duration:** Instant
Special Effect: Stun Damage. Area Spell.

Stun Missile
Drain: L1 **Type:** Mana **Duration:** Instant
Special Effect: Staging 2. Stun Damage.

Stun Touch
Drain: L1 **Type:** Mana **Duration:** Instant
Special Effect: Touch required. Staging 1. Stun Damage.

Stunball
Drain: M1 **Type:** Mana **Duration:** Instant
Special Effect: Staging 2. Stun Damage. Area Spell.

Stunblast
Drain: S1 **Type:** Mana **Duration:** Instant
Special Effect: Staging 1. Stun Damage. Area Spell (called "Sleep" in basic game).

Urban Renewal
Urban Renewal could, theoretically, lay waste to everything in the area. In practice, check only its effects against significant objects (the wall behind which the goons are hiding, the heavy weapons on the corp guards, the cycles the gangers are riding). Assume the spell does a showy amount of cosmetic damage to windows, innocent vehicles, and so on.).
Drain: M2 **Type:** Physical **Duration:** Instant
Special Effect: Staging 1. Area Spell.

Wrecker
Drain: L2 **Type:** Physical **Duration:** Instant
Special Effect: Staging 1. Only works against vehicles.

DETECTION SPELLS

Following are a number of new Detection Spells as well as revised versions of previously published spells.

Analyze Device (Revised)

This spell not only reveals the workings of the device, but also gives the magician extra skill dice for using the device while the spell is sustained. The bonus is equal to the magician's successes in casting the spell. This is a change from the basic game. This spell does *not* work in identifying or using magical items, focuses, and so on.

Drain: S2 **Type:** Physical **Duration:** Sustained

Special Effect: The spell is cast on the object to be analyzed, overcoming its resistance (see **Object Resistance Ratings**, **SR** p. 81).

Analyze Truth (Revised)

Drain: M1 **Type:** Mana **Duration:** Sustained

Special Effect: Hypersenses spell. The subject of the spell can tell if a statement made in his presence is true or false. A voluntary subject is required.

Mike Orkstaff, Goblin Detective, has Analyze Truth cast on him by a friendly shaman, then heads into Wacko's Bar to ask about a recent murder. The shaman has Sorcery 6 and rolls 6 dice to cast the spell, with results of 7, 5, 5, 4, 3, 1. The bartender says he didn't see anything. The barkeep has Willpower 3. Rolling 3 dice, he scores 4, 3, 3 (no successes). The spell has 5 dice scoring 3 or more, so Mike knows the bartender is lying because he is afraid of the killer. Sensitized by the spell, he sees the barkeep's eyes slide to the rear booth in the sleazy dive. Mike walks over and sees two enormous samurai nursing their drinks. He asks them if they know anything about the killing. The samurai have Willpower 5. One of them rolls 8, 7, 6, 6, 2. Mike can't tell if he's for real or not. The other guy rolls and Mike gets three successes against him. Not only is this samurai lying that he didn't see anything, but indications are strong that he participated in the killing. Of course, both samurai now stand up to rearrange Mike's anatomy.

Clairvoyance (Revised)

Drain: M1 **Type:** Mana **Duration:** Sustained

Special Effect: As in basic game. A voluntary subject is required. Note that this can be cast on anyone—either the magician or someone else.

Clairvoyance (Extended Range)

Drain: S1 **Type:** Mana **Duration:** Sustained

Special Effect: Range increase x 10 (Successes x Magic Attribute x 10 meters).

Combat Sense

Drain: M2 **Type:** Physical **Duration:** Sustained

Special Effect: As in basic game.

Detect Enemies (Revised)

Drain: M1 **Type:** Mana **Duration:** Sustained

Special Effect: As in basic game. Note that this can be cast on anyone—either the magician or someone else. A voluntary subject is required.

Detect Enemies (Extended Range)

Drain: S1 **Type:** Mana **Duration:** Sustained

Special Effect: Range increase x 10 (Magic Attribute x 10 meters radius).

Detect Individual (Revised)

Drain: L1 **Type:** Mana **Duration:** Sustained

Special Effect: As in basic game. Note that this can be cast on anyone—either the magician or someone else. A voluntary subject is required.

Detect Life (Revised)

Drain: L1 Type: Mana Duration: Sustained

Special Effect: As in basic game. Note that this can be cast on anyone—either the magician or someone else. A voluntary subject is required.

Detect (Life Form), (Revised)

Drain: L1 **Type:** Mana **Duration:** Sustained

Special Effect: As in basic game. Note that this can be cast on anyone—either the magician or someone else.

Detect (Object), (Revised)

Drain: L2 **Type:** Physical **Duration:** Sustained

Special Effect: Note that this can be cast on anyone—either the magician or someone else. A voluntary subject is required.

Identify Device

This spell tells the caster what the device does, how it is meant to be used, the location of any controls, and their basic functions. The spell does not confer any skill. If the magician has a skill that would make him familiar with the device, however, he subtracts his Skill Rating from his Target Number to cast the spell. This is closer to the Analyze Device Spell in the basic game, but the application of skills to the casting is different.

Drain: M2 **Type:** Physical **Duration:** Instant

Special Effect: The spell is cast on the object to be analyzed, overcoming its resistance (see **Object Resistance Ratings**, **SR** p. 81).

Personal Analyze Truth

Any statement made in the subject's hearing range can be evaluated if the subject pays attention to it. When a character tries to lie within hearing range of the subject, make a Willpower Resistance Test with a Target Number equal to the caster's Sorcery Skill. If he fails to resist the Analyze Truth spell, then the falsehood is detected. The more extra successes the spell achieves, the more insight the subject gets into the nature of the lie.

Drain: L1 **Type:** Mana **Duration:** Sustained

Special Effect: Only verbal statements can be analyzed. Each time a statement is made, the speaker can try to beat the spell.

Personal Clairvoyance
Drain: L1 **Type:** Mana **Duration:** Sustained
Special Effect: The magician can only cast Personal Clairvoyance on himself.

Personal Clairvoyance (Extended Range)
Drain: M1 **Type:** Mana **Duration:** Sustained
Special Effect: Range increase x 10 (Successes x Magic Attribute x 10 meters).

Personal Combat Sense
Drain: L2 **Type:** Physical **Duration:** Sustained
Special Effect: As in basic game.

Personal Detect Enemies
Drain: L1 **Type:** Mana **Duration:** Sustained
Special Effect: The magician can only cast Personal Detect Enemies on himself.

Personal Detect Enemies (Extended Range)
Drain: M1 **Type:** Mana **Duration:** Sustained
Special Effect: Range increase x 10 (Magic Attribute x 10 meters radius).

HEALTH SPELLS

Following are a number of new Health Spells, as well as revised versions of previously published spells.

Antidote (Wound Category) Toxin (Revised)

Note that while the spell is being sustained, drugs do *not* take further action against the subject. For example, the action of a poison doing damage every action does *not* proceed while the victim is being treated with this spell. The spell may be used whether the toxin has done damage or not. A version with the original requirement (must begin treatment before toxin takes effect) would get a –1 Drain Category and –1 Staging Modifier.

L Toxin
Drain: L2 **Type:** Mana **Duration:** Permanent (5)
M Toxin
Drain: M2 **Type:** Mana **Duration:** Permanent (10)
S Toxin
Drain: S2 **Type:** Mana **Duration:** Permanent (15)
D Toxin
Drain: D2 **Type:** Mana **Duration:** Permanent (20)
Special Effect: As in basic game. But note that spell is now Mana Spell (working via the body's immune system). The Drain Code, however, is still Staging 2 because the spell can be applied outside the "Golden Hour."

Decrease (Attribute), (Revised)

The Drain Code for the Attribute Decrease Spell has increased. The modifier of Ranged Health Spell increased the Drain Category. The Mana Form of the spell cannot affect attributes modified due to cyberware. The Physical version can affect any attribute, cybermodified or not.

As in the basic **Shadowrun** game, the subject of the spell resists using the affected attribute, not necessarily Body or Willpower. The *full* score in the attribute is used to resist the spell, even if the attribute is already reduced by it. For example, a character with Body 5 who suffers –2 points to his Body due to this spell would still resist the spell again with a rating of 5, not 3.

The various forms of the spell can affect any Physical or Mental Attribute and the Reaction attribute, as described in the basic game. Each form of the spell is different, so, for example, a magician would have to learn Minor Strength Decrease, Minor Cybered Strength Decrease, Medium Strength Decrease, and so on, as separate spells.

Minor
Drain: M2 **Type:** Mana **Duration:** Sustained
Special Effect: Staging 3 for decrease.
Medium
Drain: S2 **Type:** Mana **Duration:** Sustained
Special Effect: Staging 2 for decrease.
Massive
Drain: D2 **Type:** Mana **Duration:** Sustained
Special Effect: Staging 2 for decrease.

Decrease (Cybered Attribute)
Minor
Drain: M3 **Type:** Physical **Duration:** Sustained
Special Effect: Staging 3 for decrease.
Medium
Drain: S3 **Type:** Physical **Duration:** Sustained
Special Effect: Staging 2 for decrease.
Massive
Drain: D3 **Type:** Physical **Duration:** Sustained
Special Effect: Staging 1 for decrease

Detox (Wound Category) Toxin (Revised)
M Toxin
Drain: L1 **Type:** Mana **Duration:** Permanent (10)
S Toxin
Drain: M1 **Type:** Mana **Duration:** Permanent (15)
D Toxin
Drain: S1 **Type:** Mana **Duration:** Permanent (20)
Special Effect: As in basic game, but Staging of Drain has been reduced to 1. Better living through Sorcery.

Healthy Glow
Drain: L1 **Type:** Mana **Duration:** Permanent (5)
Special Effect: Brightens eyes, hair, sloughs dead skin cells, improves circulation, promotes general well-being. A cosmetic spell, favored by the rich as a status symbol and pick-me-up. The spell is "permanent" in that it does not require magical sustenance, but will wear off in time, based on subject's lifestyle, diet, vices, and so on.

Increase (Cybered Attribute)
Increase Cybered Attribute +1
Drain: L3 **Type:** Physical **Duration:** Sustained
Increase Cybered Attribute +2
Drain: M3 **Type:** Physical **Duration:** Sustained
Increase Cybered Attribute +3
Drain: S3 **Type:** Physical **Duration:** Sustained
Increase Cybered Attribute +4
Drain: D3 **Type:** Physical **Duration:** Sustained
Special Effect: As in basic game, but can be cast on any Physical Attribute, whether it is cyber-modified or not.

Oxygenate
Drain: L2 **Type:** Mana **Duration:** Sustained
Special Effect: Oxygenates blood of the subject, giving extra Body dice to resist suffocation, strangulation, or effects of gas inhalation. Also lets subject breathe water. A voluntary subject is required.

Prophylaxis
L Pathogen
Drain: L2 **Type:** Mana **Duration:** Sustained
M Pathogen
Drain: M2 **Type:** Mana **Duration:** Sustained
S Pathogen
Drain: S2 **Type:** Mana **Duration:** Sustained
D Pathogen
Drain: D2 **Type:** Mana **Duration:** Sustained
Special Effect: Enhances the immune system, giving extra Body dice to resist suffocation, strangulation, or effects of gas inhalation. Also lets subject breathe water. A voluntary subject is required.

Resist Pain
Moderate
Drain: L2 **Type:** Mana **Duration:** Permanent (10)
Severe
Drain: M2 **Type:** Mana **Duration:** Permanent (15)
Special Effect: Overcomes the penalties due to Physical Damage (*not* Mental Damage). This spell does not heal damage, but cancels effects of wounds. For example, if a character with Light or Moderate Wounds is treated with Resist Moderate Pain, he does not suffer from the +2 Target Number and –2 Initiative due to his damage. If his wounds do not rise above Moderate, he suffers no additional penalties.

The spell is "permanent," modifying the endorphin levels of the patient. If the subject's damage rises above the specified level, or his wounds are actually healed, then the spell is over.

Stabilize
Drain: M1 **Type:** Mana **Duration:** Permanent (20)
Special Effect: Applied to a subject with Deadly Wounds, stabilizes him, so that he does not die. Add the number of minutes since Deadly Wound was taken to magician's Target Number.

ILLUSION SPELLS

Following are a number of new Illusion Spells, as well as revised versions of perviously published spells.

Chaos (Revised)
Drain: S2 **Type:** Physical **Duration:** Sustained
Special Effect: As in basic game. Note, however, that this is a Physical Spell, not a Mana Spell. Only a Physical Spell could affect nonliving sensors, as Chaos does.

Chaotic World (Revised)
Drain: D2 **Type:** Physical **Duration:** Sustained
Special Effect: As in basic game. However, note that this is a Physical Spell, not a Mana Spell.

Entertainment (Revised)
Drain: L1 **Type:** Mana **Duration:** Sustained
Special Effect: As in basic game. Note that this spell can only create visual illusions and that these are not visible via video or trideo.

Invisibility (Revised)
Drain: L2 **Type:** Physical **Duration:** Sustained
Special Effect: As in basic game, but note that the type is Physical Spell, not Mana Spell, in order to deceive cameras.

Mask (Revised)
Drain: L1 **Type:** Mana **Duration:** Sustained
Special Effect: As in basic game. Will not deceive cameras.

Overstimulation
Drain: S1 **Type:** Mana **Duration:** Sustained
Special Effect: Induces a powerful stimulation of the sensory centers in the brain. While spell is sustained, subject suffers penalties as if a number of boxes equal to spell's successes were filled in on Mental Condition monitors. Ten or more successes leave the victim incapable of action. This spell can also be used as an interrogation technique.

Physical Mask
Drain: L2 **Type:** Physical **Duration:** Sustained
Special Effect: A version of mask effective against cameras, voice analyzers, and so on.

Spectacle
Drain: M1 **Type:** Physical **Duration:** Sustained
Special Effect: Multi-sensory version of Entertainment.

Trid Entertainment
Drain: L2 **Type:** Physical **Duration:** Sustained
Special Effect: Same as Entertainment, but this version of the spell can be "seen" by electronic cameras.

Trid Spectacle
Drain: M2 **Type:** Physical **Duration:** Sustained
Special Effect: Multi-sensory version of Trid Entertainment.

MANIPULATION SPELLS

Following are a number of new Manipulation Spells, as well as revised versions of previously published spells.

Clout
Drain: L1 **Type:** Mana **Duration:** Instant
Special Effect: A telekinetic punch. Target is hit by (Willpower)M1 Stun Damage (use caster's Willpower). The caster makes Unresisted Success Test with Target Number 4. Fire Combat Modifiers apply to this Target Number. Caster's extra successes increase damage and reduce effects of target armor as in normal physical combat. Target resists damage as in normal physical combat.

The suit who got his pocket picked spots his wallet floating into Neddy's hands and starts to yell. Neddy casts Clout, rolling four extra successes. Two of the successes raise the spell to 6D1 Stun Damage, because Neddy has Willpower 6 and the remaining two points reduce the exec's impact armor to 1 point. The target rolls his Body dice to resist 6D1 damage, scoring one success. That, plus the point of armor, reduce the Clout to Moderate Damage.

Influence
Drain: L3 **Type:** Mana **Duration:** Permanent (10)
Special Effect: Similar to Control Thoughts, but a single suggestion or order is permanently implanted in the victim's mind. He will carry out this order or act under the suggestion as though it were his own idea. The spell can be overcome if the falseness of the idea can be proved to the victim, or the caster can be forced to withdraw it. The threshold is the victim's Willpower.

Levitate Item (Revised)
Drain: L2 **Type:** Physical **Duration:** Sustained
Special Effect: As in basic game. Also note that the Levitate Item Spell cannot affect something firmly attached to a living being. If the item is held by a living being, the being is allowed to make an Unresisted Strength Test, with the caster's Sorcery Skill plus Force of Spell as the Target Number to hold onto the item. Reduce the caster's extra successes by the number of successes made on this test. If the caster's successes are reduced to 0 or less, the spell fails to work.

Rikki Ratboy tries to levitate the Iron Killer's Uzi out of his hands. Rikki has Sorcery 7 and casts Levitate Item at Force 2. First, he rolls to overcome the Uzi's resistance (Manufactured, High-Tech item: 7) and achieves two extra successes. The gun jerks in Killer's grasp, almost escaping. Killer clamps down. He rolls 8 Strength dice with a Target Number equal to Rikki's Sorcery (7) plus the Force of the Spell (2). A result of 9 is needed.

Killer rolls one success. Rikki is left with one success, which lets him levitate the weapon to a height of his Magic Attribute in meters. The Uzi zips out of Killer's grasp and hovers six meters in the air.

Mob Mind

In using the Mob Spells to influence large crowds of non-player characters, assume that "innocent bystanders" will have Willpower 3. Make one test to see whether the spell affects them, treating the crowd as a single character. Major characters (player or non-player) will defend against the spell individually.

Drain: S1 **Type:** Mana **Duration:** Sustained
Special Effect: Area Spell. Allows the caster to control the thoughts of all who are within range.

Mob Mood
Drain: M1 **Type:** Mana **Duration:** Sustained
Special Effect: Area spell. Allows the caster to affect the emotions of all who are within range. This is not an overwhelming control but rather a mood alteration spell.

Use (Skill)
Drain: L2 **Type:** Physical **Duration:** Sustained
Special Effect: A limited form of Magic Fingers. The spell can use a skill telekinetically, with gamemaster's discretion on which skills are allowed. Typical examples are Armed and Unarmed Combat, B/R Electronics, Demolitions, Driving, and so on. Knowledge Skills would not be suitable. As with Magic Fingers, Use (Skill) is cast with an Unresisted Success Test and a Target Number 6. The extra successes are the Strength and Quickness of the "magic fingers." The magician uses his own Skill Rating with the spell. If you have Unarmed Combat 2 and cast Use Unarmed Combat to telekinetically punch someone in the teeth, the attack still uses a Skill of 2.

Neddy has Stealth 4 and a Use Stealth Spell. He casts the spell and gets 5 extra successes. He telekinetically picks the pocket of a corp exec down the street (a Stealth activity). Any tests based on Quickness in this case would use a rating of 5 instead of Neddy's own Quickness.

Transformation Manipulations

Acid
Drain: S3 **Type:** Physical **Duration:** Instant
Special Effect: Staging 2. Damaging Manipulation. Elemental Acid Effects.

Acid Bomb
Drain: D4 **Type:** Physical **Duration:** Instant
Special Effect: Staging 1. Area spell. Damaging Manipulation. Elemental Acid Effects. Formerly known as Toxic Wave.

Acid Volt
Drain: D3 **Type:** Physical **Duration:** Instant
Special Effect: Staging 1. Damaging Manipulation. Elemental Acid Effects.

Anti-bullet Barrier (Revised)
Drain: S2 **Type:** Physical **Duration:** Sustained
Special Effect: Same as Physical Barrier, but only provides hard cover against bullets and other ballistic weapons. Add its rating, (the extra successes rolled by the caster) as additional ballistic

armor against Fire Combat hits. This applies when an attacker shoots at a target through the barrier.

Anti-spell Barrier (Revised)
Drain: S1 **Type:** Mana **Duration:** Sustained
Special Effect: Same as Mana Barrier, but acts only to protect against spells. When a magician casts a spell across the barrier, all those that it protects receive automatic successes equal to its rating in resisting the spell.

(Critter) Form
Drain: L3 **Type:** Mana **Duration:** Sustained
Special Effect: This is similar to Shapechange, but the spell only allows a change into the form of a specific Critter.

Fashion
Drain: L2 **Type:** Physical **Duration:** Permanent (5)
Special Effect: The spell instantly tailors clothing, transforming whatever the subject is wearing into any fashion the caster wishes. A voluntary subject is required. The caster's extra successes measure the degree of style in the tailoring. The spell does not affect the protective value of clothing, but changes the cut, color, and fit.

Flame
Drain: S3 **Type:** Physical **Duration:** Instant
Special Effect: Staging 2. Damaging Manipulation. Elemental Fire Effects.

Flame Bomb
Drain: D4 **Type:** Physical **Duration:** Instant
Special Effect: Staging 1. Area spell. Damaging Manipulation. Elemental Fire Effects.

Flame Volt
Drain: D3 **Type:** Physical **Duration:** Instant
Special Effect: Staging 1. Damaging Manipulation. Elemental Fire Effects.

Ignite (Revised)
Drain: S4 **Type:** Physical **Duration:** Permanent (10)
Special Effect: As in basic game. Elemental fire affects on items he is carrying/wearing.

Makeover
Makeover and Fashion are two spells much in vogue among the well-to-do as status symbols, but shadowrunners can see more practical applications in using the spells for quick changes in appearance.
Drain: L1 **Type:** Mana **Duration:** Permanent (5)
Special Effect: The spell creates a complete makeover: cosmetics, hair, clothes, and so on. It even polishes teeth and eliminates plaque. Its changes are as permanent as those made in a real beauty salon. A voluntary subject is required. The caster's extra successes measure the degree of style in the makeover.

Personal Anti-Spell Barrier
Drain: L1 **Type:** Mana **Duration:** Sustained
Special Effect: A personal form of Mana Barrier that only acts against spells. This would affect spells cast at the person inside the barrier, *or* spells cast by that person.

Personal Physical Barrier
Drain: M2 **Type:** Physical **Duration:** Sustained
Special Effect: Acts as a barrier but protects only one person. It is mobile. If the subject of the spell moves, the protective barrier moves with him.

Shapechange
Drain: M3 **Type:** Mana **Duration:** Sustained
Special Effect: A voluntary subject is required. Transforms subject into a normal Critter, though it retains Human consciousness. Physical Attributes are taken from table on p.190 of **Shadowrun**, with caster's extra successes added to base ratings. Increase the Critter's Reaction Rating by the subject's Intelligence, to adjust for the Human mind using its animal energy. Mental Attributes are the subject's own. Clothing and equipment are not transformed. Magicians under this spell can cast spells, but cannot fulfill geasa or use Centering Skills that require activities their animal forms cannot perform (e.g., speech).

Neddy dodges a burst of gunfire and dives through the nearest door. Drek! A broom closet! He hears the pounding feet of his pursuers in the corridor outside. Grimacing at the thought of taking them all on, he casts Shapechange upon himself. Because it is a voluntary spell, he still uses his Willpower as a Target Number (Mana Spell), but makes no Resistance Test. He achieves 5 extra successes. A Wild Cat with Strength 7 can easily claw open a ventilation grate and escape the closet before the corp goons break down the door. The stupefied goons are left staring at the well-tailored suit lying in a heap on the floor.

Neddy's Physical Attributes in this shape are: Body 7, Quickness 9 x 4, Strength 7. These scores add 5 (his extra successes) to the normal stats for a Wild Cat. Reaction is increased by Neddy's Intelligence, so it becomes 5 plus Neddy's Intelligence.

If he has to fight, Neddy's claws do 4M2 damage, with –1 Reach.

Transform
Drain: S3 **Type:** Mana **Duration:** Sustained
Special Effect: Transforms subject into a normal Critter. Transformed being has no awareness of its former state. It has only animal consciousness. Threshold is target's Willpower. Clothing and equipment are not transformed.

Turn Beings to Goo (Mana)
Drain: S3 **Type:** Mana **Duration:** Sustained
Turn Beings to Goo (Physical)
Drain: M4 **Type:** Physical **Duration:** Sustained
Special Effect: Like Turn to Goo but only works on living things. Note that there are two ways to get this effect: by making it either a Mana Spell (reducing Staging) or a limited Physical Spell (reducing Drain Code).

Turn to Tree
Drain: M2 **Type:** Mana **Duration:** Sustained
Special Effect: Transforms living being into a tree. Threshold is the victim's Body Attribute.

TABLE OF SPELLS

NOTE: An asterisk before a spell name indicates that further game mechanics are given with the spell's complete description.

COMBAT SPELLS

Name	Drain	Type	Duration
Death Touch	M1	M	I
Special **Effect:** Touch required. Staging 1.			
Fire Bolt	D3	P	I
Special Effect: Staging 1. Elemental Fire side effects.			
***Fire Cloud**	S3	P	I
Special Effect: Staging 3. Elemental Fire side effects. Area Spell.			
Fire Dart	M3	P	I
Special Effect: Staging 3. Elemental Fire side effects.			
Fire Missile	S3	P	I
Special Effect: Staging 2. Elemental Fire side effects.			
***Fireball**	D3	P	I
Special Effect: Staging 2. Elemental Fire side effects. As in basic game. Area Spell.			
***Fireblast**	D4	P	I
Special Effect: Staging 1. Elemental Fire side effects (also called "Hellblast" in basic game). Area Spell.			
Mana Bolt	S1	M	I
Special Effect: Staging 1. As in basic game.			
***Mana Cloud**	M1	M	I
Special Effect: Staging 3. Area Spell.			
Mana Dart	L1	M	I
Special Effect: Staging 3. As in basic game.			
Mana Missile	M1	M	I
Special Effect: Staging 2. As in basic game.			
***Manaball**	S1	M	I
Special Effect: Staging 2. As in basic game. Area Spell.			
***Manablast**	D1	M	I
Special Effect: Staging 1. As in basic game. Area Spell.			
Power Bolt	S2	P	I
Special Effect: Staging 1. As in basic game.			
Power Cloud	M2	P	I
Special Effect: Staging 3. Area Spell.			
Power Dart	L2	P	I
Special Effect: Staging 3. As in basic game.			
Power Missile	M2	P	I
Special Effect: Staging 2. As in basic game.			
Powerball	S2	P	I
Special Effect: Staging 2. Area Spell. As in basic game.			
Powerblast	D2	P	I
Special Effect: Staging 1. Area Spell.			
Ram	M2	P	I
Special Effect: Staging 1.			
Ram Touch	L2	P	I
Special Effect: Staging 1. Touch required.			
Slay (Race/Species)	M1	M	I
Special Effect: Staging 1. Affects only members of specified sentient race or non-sentient species.			
Stun Bolt	M1	M	I
Special Effect: Staging 1. Stun Damage.			
Stun Cloud	L1	M	I
Special Effect: Staging 3. Stun Damage. Area Spell.			
Stun Missile	L1	M	I
Special Effect: Staging 2. Stun Damage.			
Stun Touch	L1	M	I
Special Effect: Touch required. Staging 1. Stun Damage.			
Stunball	M1	M	I
Special Effect: Staging 2. Stun Damage. Area Spell.			
Stunblast	S1	M	I
Special Effect: Staging 1. Stun Damage. Area Spell (also called "Sleep" in basic rules).			
Urban Renewal	M2	P	I
Special Effect: Staging 1. Area Spell. Check only effects against significant objects.			
Wrecker	L2	P	I
Special Effect: Staging 1. Only works against vehicles.			

DETECTION SPELLS

Name	Drain	Type	Duration
Analyze Device	S2	P	S
Special Effect: The spell is cast on the object to be analyzed, overcoming its resistance. **Note:** The spell gives the magician extra skill dice for using the device while the spell is sustained.			
Analyze Truth	M1	M	S
Special Effect: Hypersenses spell. The subject of the spell can tell if a statement made in hispresence is true or false. A voluntary subject is required.			
Combat Sense	M2	P	S
Special Effect: As in basic game.			
Clairvoyance	M1	M	S
Special Effect: As in basic game. A voluntary subject is required. Can be cast on the magician or anyone else.			
Clairvoyance (extended)	S1	M	S
Special Effect: Range increase x 10 (Successes x Magic Attribute x 10 meters).			
Detect (Life Form)	L1	M	S
Special Effect: As in basic game. Can be cast on the magician or anyone else.			
Detect (Object)	L2	P	S
Special Effect: As in basic game. Can be cast on the magician or anyone else. A voluntary subject is required.			
Detect Enemies	M1	M	S
Special Effect: As in basic game. Can be cast on the magician or anyone else. A voluntary subject is required.			

Detect Enemies (extended) S1 M S
Special Effect: Range increase x 10 (Magic Attribute x 10 meters radius).

Detect Individual L1 M S
Special Effect: As in basic game. Can be cast on the magician or anyone else. A voluntary subject is required.

Detect Life L1 M S
Special Effect: As in basic game. Can be cast on the magician or anyone else. A voluntary subject is required.

Identify Device M2 P I
Special Effect: The spell is cast on the object to be analyzed, overcoming its resistance.
Note: The spell does not confer any skill upon being cast.

Mind Probe M1 M S
Special Effect: As in basic game.

Personal Analyze Truth L1 M S
Special Effect: Only verbal statements can be analyzed. Each time a statement is made, thespeaker can try to beat the spell.

Personal Clairvoyance L1 M S
Special Effect: The magician can only cast this spell on himself.

Personal Clairvoyance (extended) M1 M S
Special Effect: Range increase x 10 (Successes x Magic Attribute x 10 meters).

Personal Combat Sense L2 P S
Special Effect: As in basic game.

Personal Detect Enemies L1 M S
Special Effect: The magician can only cast this spell on himself.

Personal Detect Enemies (extended) M1 M S
Special Effect: Range increase x 10 (Magic Attribute x 10 meters radius).

HEALTH SPELLS

Name	Drain	Type	Duration
Antidote L Toxin	L2	M	P(5)

Special Effect: As in basic game. Spell is Mana, with Staging 2 because the spell can be appliedoutside the "Golden Hour."

Antidote M Toxin M2 M P(10)
Special Effect: As in basic game. Spell is Mana, with Staging 2 because the spell can be appliedoutside the "Golden Hour."

Antidote S Toxin S2 M P(15)
Special Effect: As in basic game. Spell is Mana, with Staging 2 because the spell can be applied outside the "Golden Hour."

Antidote D Toxin D2 M P(20)
Special Effect: As in basic game. Spell is Mana, with Staging 2 because the spell can be applied outside the "Golden Hour."

Cure L Disease L2 M P(5)
Special Effect: As in basic game.

Cure M Disease M2 M P(10)
Special Effect: As in basic game.

Cure S Disease S2 M P(15)
Special Effect: As in basic game.

Cure D Disease D2 M P(20)
Special Effect: As in basic game.

Decrease Minor Attribute M2 M S
Special Effect: Staging 3 for decrease.

Decrease Medium Attribute S2 M S
Special Effect: Staging 2 for decrease.

Decrease Massive Attribute D2 M S
Special Effect: Staging 2 for decrease.

Decrease Minor Cybered Attribute M3 P S
Special Effect: Staging 3 for decrease.

Decrease Medium Cybered Attribute S3 P S
Special Effect: Staging 2 for decrease.

Decrease Massive Cybered Attribute D3 P S
Special Effect: Staging 1 for decrease.

Detox M Toxin L1 M P(10)
Special Effect: As in basic game, but Staging of Drain is reduced to 1. Better living through Sorcery.

Detox S Toxin M1 M P(15)
Special Effect: As in basic game, but Staging of Drain is reduced to 1. Better living through Sorcery.

Detox D Toxin S1 M P(20)
Special Effect: As in basic game, but Staging of Drain is reduced to 1. Better living through Sorcery.

Heal L Wounds L2 M P(5)
Special Effect: As in basic game.

Heal M Wounds M2 M P(10)
Special Effect: As in basic game.

Heal S Wounds S2 M P(15)
Special Effect: As in basic game.

Heal D Wounds D2 M P(20)
Special Effect: As in basic game.

Healthy Glow L1 M P(5)
Special Effect: Improves cosmetic appearance of subject. The spell requires no magical sustenance, but wears off in time.

Increase Attribute +1 L2 M S
Special Effect: As in basic game. The spell will not affect any attribute that is enhanced by cyberware.

Increase Attribute +2 M2 M S
Special Effect: As in basic game. The spell will not affect any attribute that is enhanced by cyberware.

Increase Attribute +3 S2 M S
Special Effect: As in basic game. The spell will not affect any attribute that is enhanced by cyberware.

Increase Attribute +4 D2 M S
Special Effect: As in basic game. The spell will not affect any attribute that is enhanced by cyberware.

Increase Cybered Attribute +1 L3 P S
Special Effect: As in basic game. Can be cast on any Physical Attribute, whether it is cyber-modified or not.

Increase Cybered Attribute +2 M3 P S
Special Effect: As in basic game. Can be cast on any Physical Attribute, whether it is cyber-modified or not.

Increase Cybered Attribute +3 S3 P S
Special Effect: As in basic game. Can be cast on any Physical Attribute, whether it is cyber-modified or not.

Increase Cybered Attribute +4 D3 P S
Special Effect: As in basic game. Can be cast on any Physical Attribute, whether it is cyber-modified or not.

Oxygenate L2 M S

Special Effect: Oxygenates blood of the subject, giving extra Body dice to resist suffocation, starngulation, or gas inhalation. Also allows for breathing of water. A voluntary subject is required.

Prophylaxis L Pathogen L2 M S

Special Effect: This spell gives extra Body dice to resist *any* infection, drug, or toxin. Subject resists beneficial and harmful medicines as well.

Prophylaxis M pathogen M2 M S

Special Effect: This spell gives extra Body dice to resist *any* infection, drug, or toxin. Subject resists beneficial and harmful medicines as well.

Prophylaxis S Pathogen S2 M S

Special Effect: This spell gives extra Body dice to resist *any* infection, drug, or toxin. Subject resists beneficial and harmful medicines as well.

Prophylaxis D Pathogen D2 M S

Special Effect: This spell gives extra Body dice to resist *any* infection, drug, or toxin. Subject resists beneficial and harmful medicines as well.

Resist Moderate Pain L2 M P(10)

Special Effect: Overcomes the penalties due to Physical Damage. This spell does not heal damage,but cancels effects of wounds.

Resist Severe Damage M2 M P(15)

Special Effect: Overcomes the penalties due to Physical Damage. This spell does not heal damage,but cancels effects of wounds.

Stabilize M1 M P(20)

Special Effect: Applied to a subject with Deadly Wounds, stabilizes him, so that he does not die. Add the number of minutes since Deadly Wound was taken to magician's Target Number.

Treat L Wounds L1 M P(5)

Special Effect: As in basic game.

Treat M Wounds M1 M P(10)

Special Effect: As in basic game.

Treat S Wounds S1 M P(15)

Special Effect: As in basic game.

Treat D Wounds D1 M P(20)

Special Effect: As in basic game.

ILLUSION SPELLS

Name **Drain** **Type** **Duration**

Chaos S2 P S

Special Effect: As in basic game, but this is a Mana Spell.

Chaotic World D2 P S

Special Effect: As in basic game.

Confusion S1 M S

Special Effect: As in basic game.

Entertainment L1 M S

Special Effect: As in basic game. This spell creates only visual illusions that are not visible via trideo.

Invisibility L2 P S

Special Effect: As in basic game. This is a Physical Spell that can deceive cameras.

Mask L1 M S

Special Effect: As in basic game. Will not deceive cameras.

Overstimulation S1 M S

Special Effect: Subject suffers Mental Condition penalties equal to the spell's successes. Can be used as an interrogation technique.

Physical Mask L2 P S

Special Effect: A version of mask effective against cameras, voice analyzers, and so on.

Spectacle M1 P S

Special Effect: Multi-sensory version of Entertainment.

Stimulation M1 M S

Special Effect: As in basic game. A voluntary subject is required. Number of Successes measures intensity of experience.

Trid Entertainment L2 P S

Special Effect: This spell creates visual illusions that can be viewed by trideo.

Trid Spectacle M2 P S

Special Effect: Multi-sensory version of Trid Entertainment.

MANIPULATION SPELLS

Name	Drain	Type	Duration
***Clout**	L1	M	I
Special Effect: A telekinetic punch.			
Control Actions	M2	M	S
Special Effect: As in basic game.			
Control Emotions	L1	M	S
Special Effect: As in basic game.			
Control Thoughts	L2	M	S
Special Effect: As in basic game.			
Hibernate	L2	P	S
Special Effect: As in basic game.			
***Influence**	L3	M	P(10)
Special Effect: A single suggestion or order is permanently implanted in subject's mind.			
***Levitate Item**	L2	P	S
Special Effect: This spell cannot affect something attached to a living being.			
Levitate Person	M2	P	S
Special Effect: As in basic game.			
Mob Mind	S1	M	S
Special Effect: Area Spell. Allows the caster to control the thoughts of all who are within range.			
***Mob Mood**	M1	M	S
Special Effect: Area Spell. Allows the caster to affect the emotions of all who are within range.			
Magic Fingers	M2	P	S
Special Effect: As in basic game.			
Poltergeist	S2	P	S
Special Effect: As in basic game.			
***Use (Skill)**	L2	P	S
Special Effect: This spell can use a skill telekinetically.			

Transformation Manipulations

Name	Drain	Type	Duration
Acid	S3	P	I
Special Effect: Staging 2. Damaging Manipulation. Elemental Acid effects.			
Acid Volt	D3	P	I
Special Effect: Staging 1. Damaging Manipulation. Elemental Acid effects.			
Acid Bomb	D4	P	I
Special Effect: Staging 1. Area Spell. Damaging Manipulation. Elemental Acid effects. Formerly known as Toxic Wave.			
Armor	L3	P	S
Special Effect: As in basic game. A voluntary subject is required.			
***Anti-bullet Barrier**	S2	P	S
Special Effect: Only provides cover against bullets and ballistic weapons.			
***Anti-spell Barrier**	S1	M	S
Special Effect: Only protects against spells.			
(Critter) Form	L3	M	S
Special Effect: Similar to Shapechange, but only allows a change to a specific Critter.			
***Fashion**	L2	P	P(5)
Special Effect: This spell instantly tailors the subject's clothing.			
Flame	S3	P	I
Special Effect: Staging 2. Damaging Manipulation. Elemental Fire effects.			
Flame Bomb	D4	P	I
Special Effect: Staging 1. Area Spell. Damaging Manipulation. Elemental Fire effects.			
Flame Volt	D3	P	I
Special Effect: Staging 1. Damaging Manipulation. Elemental Fire effects.			
Ignite	S4	P	P(10)
Special Effect: As in basic game. Elemental Fire effects items he is carrying/wearing.			
***Makeover**	L1	M	P(5)
Special Effect: This spell creates a complete makeover: cosmetics, hair, clothes, and so on.			
Mana Barrier	D1	M	S
Special Effect: As in basic game.			
***Personal Anti-spell Barrier**	L1	M	S
Special Effect: Only protects against spells.			
Personal Physical Barrier	M2	P	S
Special Effect: Acts as a Barrier but protects only one person. The spell moves with the subject.			
Petrify	M3	P	S
Special Effect: As in basic game.			
Physical Barrier	D2	P	S
Special Effect: As in basic game.			
***Shapechange**	M3	M	S
Special Effect: Transforms subject into a normal Critter, but with a Human consciousness.			
***Transform**	S3	M	S
Special Effect: Transforms subject into a normal Critter.			
Turn Beings to Goo (Mana)	S3	M	S
Special Effect: Only works on living beings.			
Turn Beings to Goo (Physical)	M4	P	S
Special Effect: Only works on living beings.			
Turn to Goo	S4	P	S
Special Effect: As in basic game.			
Turn to Tree	M2	M	S
Special Effect: Transforms living beings into a tree. Threshold is the victim's Body Attribute.			

INDEX

INDEX

BAR
Rick Harris '90